Ethics, Distance, and Accountability

The Political Thought and Intellectual Context of Rammohun Roy (c.1772–1833)

Shomik Dasgupta

OXFORD
UNIVERSITY PRESS

OXFORD
UNIVERSITY PRESS

Oxford University Press is a department of the University of Oxford.
It furthers the University's objective of excellence in research, scholarship,
and education by publishing worldwide. Oxford is a registered trademark of
Oxford University Press in the UK and in certain other countries.

Published in India by
Oxford University Press
22 Workspace, 2nd Floor, 1/22 Asaf Ali Road, New Delhi 110002, India

© Oxford University Press 2021

ISBN-13 (print edition): 978-0-19-012912-5
ISBN-10 (print edition): 0-19-012912-3

ISBN-13 (eBook): 978-0-19-099301-6
ISBN-10 (eBook): 0-19-099301-4

Typeset in Adobe Jenson Pro 10.7/13.3
by Tranistics Data Technologies, Kolkata 700 091
Printed in India by Rakmo Press Pvt. Ltd.

For
my parents
and in memory of
Gauri Das Gupta and Mihir Prakash Gupta

Contents

Preface

Rammohun Roy (1772/4(?)–1833) lived during a period of momentous historical change. During his lifetime, the East India Company (EIC) established itself as a sovereign power in South Asia; the Permanent Settlement transformed the economy, agriculture, and trade of Bengal; and the influence of Western political philosophies, religious discourses, and the English language launched a social and cultural revolution of ideas in Calcutta.

Rammohun responded to this fast-changing historical climate in numerous tracts, texts, newspaper editorials, journal articles, and petitions. He was a keen political observer and an indefatigable writer. The body of work that he produced amounted to an all-encompassing political thought with which he hoped to transform the EIC's political relations with the people of Bengal. He advocated the complete restructuring of the EIC's administration in eastern India. In his opinion, the Company had instituted a flawed system of government—for it was not accountable to the people it governed in India but to a distant and invisible House of Commons in London.

Rammohun conceptualized political power as visible, localized, and domiciled. By that logic, the EIC was uncomfortably different; and he hoped to restructure its modes of governance entirely, from the ground up. In 1829, when the Mughal Emperor Akbar II appointed him as his ambassador to the court of George IV, Rammohun seized the opportunity to articulate his ideas in London. In fact, he produced a full-length book on his conception of good government while residing in that city. His ideas were also influenced by an 11-year stint with the EIC's district administration in formal as well as informal capacities. As a former native employee, he now made a persuasive case for the Company to be accountable to local centres of power, manned and operated by an ethical Bengali public.

Rammohun was not simply evoking the *idea* of an ethical public. He was actively invested in contributing towards the creation of a politically self-aware and ethical Bengali public sphere. His views on the subject consistently appeared in numerous tracts on Hindu religion and scripture. Here, he forcefully argued that everyday ethical practice was the most appropriate form of religious worship. His interpretation of religion was bold and illiberal, for he violently disagreed with any other interpretation but his. Unsurprisingly, this stance brought him into sharp conflict with the religious orthodoxy and social conservatives of Bengal.

Although it may appear from this narrative that Rammohun addressed Bengali society and the EIC in separate works, this was not always the case. Occasionally, both groups were addressed together. His writings against the practice of sati (1818–30), for instance, addressed Bengali society as well as the EIC. He implored with the former to be ethical and with the latter to be accountable. Aghast at the strong conservative opposition to sati, he even authored a petition against the practice and tabled it in the Privy Council in England. In 1832, when the Privy Council affirmed the passage of anti-sati legislation, Rammohun was delighted. To him, this judicial decision also represented a vindication of his political thought and set a precedent that he intended to follow up on. Unfortunately, he died soon afterwards, in 1833, before he was able to pursue any further plans.

After Rammohun's death, his contemporaries struggled to make sense of his thought and initially made no attempt at an overall assessment of his political project. It took until 1845 to produce the first known biography of the man. Kishorichand Mitter, his biographer, considered Rammohun to be a classical liberal, but confused and contradictory in his thought. Assessments such as these persisted through the 19th century, alongside a tendency by influential biographers such as Sophia Collet, Nagendranath Chattopadhyay, and Mary Carpenter to perceive Rammohun as a representative of whichever political and religious view they happened to subscribe to—be it Christianity, Hinduism, Vedantism, Brahmoism, or social reform. The 20th century added a new political context. Rammohun was refashioned as a nationalist and the 'Father of Modern India' by Ramananda Chatterjee in 1906. In 1933, on the 100th anniversary of his death, Brajendranath Seal argued that his thought was not just 'national' but also 'universal' in its appeal and scope. Seal also sorted his writings into hermetically sealed 'religious' and 'political' categories respectively.

Brajendranath Seal's arguments were taken up by scholars through the 1940s, as Rammohun was credited with founding (or at least serving as the key inspiration behind) several social, political, and cultural movements in Bengal. This argument was paraphrased by Susobhan Sarkar by the term 'Renaissance'. Sarkar's arguments developed into an influential school of historiography in the 1950s and 1960s. However, not all historians agreed with its views. R.C. Majumdar, for instance, was very disapproving of what he perceived to be overtly celebratory assessments of the man, while David Kopf argued that Rammohun's contribution to the 'Renaissance' had been negligible. Instead, Kopf was of the opinion that the 'Renaissance' owed its origins to modern education, new institutions of learning (such as the Fort William College), and the introduction of the printing press in Bengal.

In 1975, Sumit Sarkar, Barun De, Ashok Sen, and Rajat Ray successfully demonstrated that Rammohun's historical importance had been over-emphasized, and that he could not have possibly inaugurated a 'Renaissance' in a country that was economically ravaged by colonial policy. Their critique set the discursive stage for a more historically contextualized view of Rammohun. In the 1980s and 1990s, historians attempted to place his political thought in new interpretative frames. He was either seen as a quintessential Vedantic or a political thinker who dwelt on the themes of liberalism and modernity. He, however, continued to be perceived as a man of intellectual compromise and paradox. And occasionally, he would still be referred to as the 'Father of Modern India'.

Rammohun's liberalism and Vedantic influences have also been the subject of much scholarly scrutiny in this century. In 2012, C.A. Bayly brilliantly argued that Rammohun may have been inspired by Western liberalism and referred to him as 'the first Indian liberal'. Two years later, Brian Hatcher made a strong case for Rammohun's Vedantic interpretations to be seen as a forerunner to contemporary middle-class Hinduism. Recently, Hatcher has reframed his ideas in a new book, *Hinduism Before Reform (2020)*. Both Bayly and Hatcher have been very influential in scholarly as well as popular assessments of Rammohun's thought. Their works also implicitly accept Brajendranath Seal's, sorting of Rammohun's thought into 'religious' and 'political' categories (but with the caveat that they are not as airtight as had been previously thought). Interestingly, it is only recently that another important observation of Seal's has been commanding attention: the need to pay a closer attention to the role of early modern thought in Rammohun's writings. Partha Chatterjee's *The Black Hole of the Empire: History of a Global Practice of Power* (2012) is perhaps the most important representative of this trend. Chatterjee breaks new interpretative ground by arguing that Rammohun was influenced by 'anti-absolutist' strands of early modern Indo-Persian thought in his critique of the EIC's government, and that he was not a contradictory thinker.

My book draws on Chatterjee's valuable insights but also moves beyond their hermeneutic scope. I argue that Rammohun's written works in English, Bangla, Arabic, and Persian provide theoretical accounts of themselves when placed in dialogue with each other as well as with other lesser-known works of the time. I also trace the specific early Indian, early medieval, as well as early modern Indo-Persian texts that he referred to in order to produce his own ideas of good governance and ethics. I show that his ideas were also a response to a prevailing institutional context for he was deeply influenced by his 11-year-long association with the EIC's district administration and often drew on his experiences to formulate and conceptualize his ideas. In the final analysis, I argue that his political thought was a bold and ambitious attempt to make the EIC accountable to the people of Bengal.

Acknowledgements

I began work on this book after completing my PhD thesis from King's College London, University of London. My supervisor, Jon Wilson, provided me with critical academic guidance and support. I am very grateful to Dr Wilson for his kind help.

Katherine Schofield and Sujit Sivasundaram introduced me to new fields of historical scholarship, which in turn led to new fields of enquiry and avenues to explore the work of Rammohun Roy. I owe an enormous intellectual debt to them for explaining various aspects of medieval Persian philosophy, material culture, history of the book, circulation, and the early modern public sphere to me. Sanjukta Gupta introduced me to several new critical editions and rare translations of early Indian and early modern Sanskrit works. She also generously allowed me to borrow rare and out-of-print books from her personal library on Indological literature and shared her views on Rammohun Roy. Richard Gombrich corrected my writing, offered advice, and patiently listened to my ideas. Arthur Burns commented on my writing and his ideas changed the way I look at my work. Siddharth Dasgupta prompted me to rethink my work by citing new texts and contexts for research. Feriel Kissoon alerted me to the nuances of method, theory, and historical time. Thomas Newbold read through multiple drafts and shared his expertise in early modern Bengali history.

I learnt a great deal from a correspondence with Brian Hatcher. His comments, encouragement, clarifications, and thoughts on various matters helped me conceptualize my own. I am very grateful to Thomas Ertl for his comments on an earlier draft of my work and for giving me an opportunity to present my work at the Department of History, University of Vienna. Swarupa Gupta's intellectual generosity, detailed critique of various arguments, and kind invitation to Presidency College, Calcutta, to present a paper helped me write a better book. I have had the unique privilege of being taught by historians of medieval and modern India during my undergraduate and university education. Particularly, Yogesh Sharma, Pius Malekandathil, the late Nandini Sahay Prasad, Dilbagh Singh, Najaf Haider, Rohit Wanchoo, Tasneem Suhrawardy, Sangeeta Luthra Sharma, Amrita Tulika, and Mahesh Gopalan influenced and shaped my historical thinking through their lectures, comments, and ideas. Govind Menon, G. Sarath Chandra, Prem Kumar, and Robin Tayal were very generous with their time and gave perspective to things which I would never have otherwise had. Prasanta Das was a friend, mentor, and guide. He is sorely missed.

I have been fortunate to be able to consult the India Office Records as well as the Rare Books, Music and Manuscripts Collections at the British Library. The School of Oriental and African Studies' Library and Archives provided unfettered access to detailed ground-level research on the EIC's administrative history. The Maughan Library allowed me to borrow critically important secondary source material on Bengali cultural history for weeks at a time. The National Library and the West Bengal State Archives have a formidable collection of rare books, manuscripts, and government gazettes, which they kindly allowed me to consult.

The editors of the Oxford University Press (OUP) have been very flexible with deadlines and schedules. I am particularly indebted to Nandini Ganguli, Prakriti Roy, and Marianne Paul for their time and patience.

The criticism and encouragement of OUP's anonymous referees have immensely contributed to this book. I am deeply grateful to them. Mahesh Rangarajan's encouragement and guidance has shaped this book in myriad ways. I will always be indebted to Dr. Rangarajan for the interest that he took in my work.

I thank Ananya Ghoshal for helping me with the Bangla primary and secondary sources on Rammohun Roy. Ananya read and commented on the final draft of this work. Her linguistic expertise and literary skills have shaped the deep structure of this book.

Any errors of interpretation, translation, or language in this book are entirely mine.

Introduction

Rammohun Roy (1772/4(?)–1833) is frequently counted amongst the most influential intellectuals of modern India.[1] In life, he achieved international fame and notoriety for his views on religion, social reform, law, and governance.[2] Since his death, his writings have been quoted, critiqued, condemned, and celebrated by writers, poets, artists, lawyers, theologians, and journalists in South Asia, Europe, and North America.[3] Rammohun is, by all accounts, modern India's first major global intellectual.

Rammohun wrote in five languages, authored texts on administration and grammar, and founded newspapers, schools, and new religious organizations. He composed Bangla songs, translated Hindu scriptures, wrote detailed commentaries on Christian theology, and was deeply committed to social reform. His diverse intellectual pursuits and posthumous influence have often overawed and confused scholars. To some, he is the harbinger of a modern era, the founder of various intellectual movements from modernist thought to vernacular journalism and

Bangla prose; [4] to others, he was a naive liberal intellectual whose views were whimsical at best.[5]

In this book, I will argue that the most important context of Rammohun's writings was making the political power of the East India Company's (EIC's) government accountable to an ethical Bengali public. Rammohun argued that from 1765 onwards, a distant and invisible government in London had contributed to the misgovernance of Bengal by investing in an administrative system which lacked political accountability. Instead, he proposed a new system of accountable government with local centres of power. The most detailed account of this argument can be found in *Exposition of the Practical Operation of the Revenue and Judicial Systems of India and of the General Character and Conditions of its inhabitants as submitted in evidence to the authorities in England*, published in 1832 in London (hereafter, *Exposition*).

Exposition was Rammohun's last major work. It developed his ideas from earlier writings in Calcutta and explained them by using references which his readership in London would have been familiar with. For instance, he attempted to explain Bengal district administration to his British readers by referring to William Blackstone's four-volume *Commentaries on the Laws of England* (1765–1770).[6] Blackstone's works were well-known during this time as a host of British scholars, judges, and philosophers commented on their impact on legal administration in the UK.[7]

Historians have, however, failed to account for the methods by which Rammohun's ideas were articulated to his audience and readers. Ultimately, this has led to long-standing uncertainties regarding his political thought and intellectual context. Indeed, one can detect a persistent scholarly discomfort with his writings from the 19th to the 20th century, and until the present day. The overall trend has been to present him as a man of paradox and intellectual compromise.[8] As Amiya Sen, his biographer, opines: 'Scholars are still undecided on whether he visualized a free India or remained a captive of the development chronology of the [British] Empire.'[9]

Methodologically, historians have attempted to resolve the paradox posed by Rammohun's writings by selectively placing his work under a range of thematic and analytic categories. However, as Andrew Sartori has so thoughtfully remarked, this approach has led to 'a long tradition of finding in Rammohun whatever one happens to be looking for—cosmopolitanism, Anglophilia or proto-nationalism; neo Hinduism, ecumenism or proto-secularism; democratic values, class ideology or native corruption'.[10] Indeed, the historians and biographers who argue otherwise only hint that Rammohun had managed to reconcile the contradictions in his thought before hastily changing the subject.[11]

This book is an attempt to resolve the paradox of Rammohun Roy. I situate his works in their historical context through a focused archival and textual approach to the authorial intention, circulation, and popular reception of his writings. The aim is to present a new critical reappraisal of his intellectual and institutional context(s). Through a careful study of his works on the administration of the EIC, property and inheritance law (Dayabhaga), the freedom of the press, the jury system, Hindu scripture, sati, and the Bible, I will unravel the deep structure of a clearly articulated and consistent political project.

The book begins with a reappraisal of *Exposition*. Although mostly ignored in historical scholarship, *Exposition* is an important work since it can be read as a statement of Rammohun's political thought. A considerable portion of the text was devoted to showing how accountability in the EIC's revenue and judicial administration could be achieved by shifting administrative responsibility from European officials to the native employees of the EIC in Bengal. This viewpoint was backed by the unequivocal assertion that European collectors in district administration would be quite helpless without native employees to aid them.[12]

Rammohun's argument was a strong rebuttal of the view held by Company officials at Calcutta and London that native employees were inefficient, devious, and corrupt.[13] His emphasis on native employees has, however, been the subject of very limited scholarly engagement. The everyday working lives and administrative responsibilities of native employees in Bengal are also an understudied area of historical research.[14] One is therefore tempted to ask if Rammohun was exaggerating the role of native employees and if it is at all possible to trace their historical and institutional context.

I argue (in Chapter 2) that Rammohun's assessment of native employees has to be seen from the perspective of his own association with EIC administration (1804–14). During this period, he worked as *munshi* (language teacher), *faujdar* (court official), and dewan (revenue assistant to the district collector), in official as well as unofficial capacities, in different administrative divisions such as provincial capitals (Murshidabad), districts in the 'interior' of Bengal (Decca–Jelalpur, Ramghur, and Bhagalpur), and frontier districts (Rangpur). This contributed to a broad experience of Company administration. Although official records on his association with the Company are very sparse, an examination of the district revenue and judicial records of the Company enables us to gain a perspective of the everyday administrative responsibilities of native employees during the same period as Rammohun's association and in the same districts that he worked. The discussion is also motivated by the necessity of accounting for a gap in his writings. As Figure I.1 shows, we have no evidence of any writings during the period 1804–14. And till date, historians have not been concerned with this gap in his work. I argue, however, that an ignorance of this context has led to the mistaken assumption that he was *not* concerned with Company governance while accounting for the gap points to another conclusion: that his writings were *influenced* by his association with the Company.

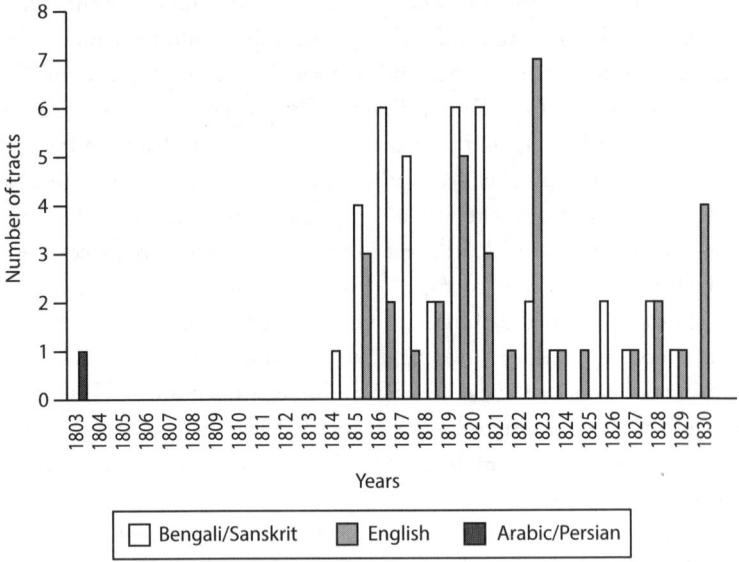

Figure I.1 Mind the Gap: Rammohun's Arabic, Persian, Bangla, Sanskrit, and English works, 1803–30

Source: Created by the author from information contained in Tables A.1 and A.2.

A detailed discussion of Rammohun's association with the EIC reveals that *Exposition* had not presented an exaggerated assessment of the importance of the native employees. Further, his ideas of distance and governmental accountability in *Exposition* were almost certainly informed by his experiences as a native employee. He consistently referred to his experiences with the Company as a source by which he could conceptualize his ideas for institutional reform. The focus on the historical and institutional context of *Exposition* does not, however, articulate or even refer to Rammohun's intellectual context—a lacunae which is addressed in Chapter 3. I show that he was deeply influenced by the *akhlaq* tradition, particularly its principal text, *Akhlaq-i Nasiri* by Nasir ud-Din Tusi. *Akhlaq-i Nasiri* (Nasirean Ethics) was a familiar work in early colonial Bengal, studied by a Persian-educated native elite as well as EIC scholar–officials.

The influence of *Akhlaq-i Nasiri* comes out clearly in *Tuhfat-ul-Muwahidin* (*A Gift to the Believers of One God*, c.1803), Rammohun's earliest known work. *Tuhfat* was addressed to a readership of native elite. *Tuhfat* is also the only Perso-Arabic tract that he ever authored. Soon after writing it, he became associated with the EIC and did not appear to publish much for the next 10 years. His publications picked up pace after 1815, when he left the Company and moved to Calcutta. For the next 14 years, he regularly published essays, tracts, interpretations, and translations of Hindu scripture from Sanskrit.

For Rammohun, Sanskrit was the linguistic repository of scriptural knowledge on a singular divinity, a Supreme Being (alternatively referred to as 'God' and 'Almighty power'). He never doubted the existence of a 'sole regulator of the universe' and argued that a belief in the Supreme Being also contained within it the epistemic justification for the will to act ethically.[15] This argument became an important feature in all his tracts on Hindu scripture, appearing in some as a simple and straightforward assertion;[16] or, in others, as a lengthy, repetitive argument.[17] Since most of his intended audience could not read Sanskrit, his interpretations of Hindu scripture appeared in Bangla and English. As Rammohun explained:

> [...] there is no translation of the Vedas into any of the modern languages of Hindustan with which I am acquainted and it is for that reason that I have translated into Bengali the Vedanta, the Cena Upanishad of the Sama Veda, the Isho Upanishad of the Yajur Vedas.[18]

Rammohun opined that the chief purpose of life was to worship an invisible god. He had very definite views on worship. Controversially, he opposed the performance of rituals and the legitimacy of the Brahmin caste to decree what constitutes right or wrong modes of worship.[19] Instead, he asserted that a commitment to social ethics was the only legitimate form of worship.[20]

Rammohun's arguments concerning religion and scripture featured prominently in his bi-lingual tract *Second defence of the Monotheistic system of the Vedas* (1816), published the same year in Bangla as *Bhattacharyer sahit vichar* (*Reply to a Bhattacharya*). As the Bangla title suggests, his writings were not produced in isolation but in debate. In this case, it was as a response to the criticism of one of the most well-known Sanskrit pandits of the time, Mrityunjay Vidyalankar. Vidyalankar publicly disagreed with Rammohun and consistently argued that he was misquoting scripture.[21]

Vidyalankar was not an isolated critic. In fact, Rammohun's ideas concerning religion were not acceptable to many conservative upper-caste Hindus who were furious, perplexed, and confused that a fellow Brahmin should articulate and print such views.[22] Influential and angry rebuttals were authored, commissioned, printed, and published in English and Bangla in Calcutta and Madras, only to be answered with (mostly) polite but firm rejoinders from Rammohun which stressed that his opinions were widely shared.[23]

Rammohun consistently claimed that his writings were in the pursuit of the public good. These claims did not sit comfortably with his critics and matters came to a head in 1822 when Kashinath Tarkapanchanan, a Sanskrit pandit based at Fort William College, Calcutta, sensationally argued that Rammohun was only aggressively asserting his own ambition to emerge as an important authority on scripture and religion in Bengal.[24] True to form, Rammohun promptly responded by writing, 'I don't want victory for myself. I want the truth to win.'[25] His response, however, was not just one line but the conclusion of a lengthy tract, *Pathyapradan* (*Medicine for the Sick Offered by One Who Laments His Inability to Perform Righteousness*).[26] *Pathyapradan* had been preceded by the shorter *Chari proshner uttar* (*Reply to Four Questions*). Both tracts were written in Bangla and appeared between 1822 and 1823.

Tarkapanchanan's disagreement does, however, lead to an uncomfortable question: who was Rammohun writing for? Admittedly, an unresolved tension runs through the body of his work. While Rammohun claimed to write for an ethical public, the matter was not quite as straightforward. Some writings appealed to an already *existing* public who were interested in questions of ethics; while others evoked the *idea* of an engaged and ethical public.

Tentatively, I suggest that this tension probably arose because his writings were not only meant for a wider public but also his close friends, allies, and associates. At Calcutta, he had an influential group of friends but not everyone was interested in discussing religion with him.[27] Many knew him in the capacity of a businessman.[28] A small minority were interested in his ideas on religion, society, and ethics, and organized themselves into the Atmiya Sabha.[29]

The Atmiya Sabha met every Saturday.[30] Discussions were held on Hindu scripture. Music was an important aspect of these meetings. Hymns were composed by members, and Ghulam Abbas, a prominent Calcutta musician, was invited to sing them.[31] Rammohun presided over the Atmiya Sabha's meetings and his writings may have been influenced by this context. Rather revealingly, his translations of the Isho Upanishad, Kena Upanishad, Katha Upanishad, Mundaka Upanishad, and Mandukya Upanishad coincide with the period in which the Atmiya Sabha was active (1816–20). In other words, his allies, friends, and associates may have well been his first readers and his ethical public.[32]

Rammohun's activities in Calcutta had a defining impact on his intellectual life and career. In this context, *Tuhfat*, written almost a decade earlier, when he was based in the city of Murshidabad, is oft considered by historians to be the product of an earlier age.[33]

Rammohun did not however forget *Tuhfat*. In fact, a close examination of the conceptual similarities between *Tuhfat* and later writings at Calcutta reveals the extent to which his works reiterated a consistent argument, articulated in many languages, to different readerships. The degree to which he intended to communicate his ideas to a wide readership can be ascertained by sifting through the available publication data on his works. This data reveals his intellectual priorities. For instance, in sharp contrast to his contemporaries, he published sparingly in 'elite' printing presses, rather preferring 'low-print' popular presses, indicating that he had a wider audience in mind. Indeed, his works appeared so often that many in Calcutta firmly believed that he was not one man but

a committee of writers.[34] Even in contemporary times, scholars have sometimes been confounded by the question of whether or not Rammohun
actually authored all the works which have been traditionally ascribed to
him. As Dermot Killingley explains, 'Rammohun did not put his name
to any of his Bengali and Sanskrit works. However, external and internal
evidence suggest that these works were composed by Rammohun; his
authorship seems to have been an open secret in his time.'[35] After his
death, the authorship of many works was disputed and new writings
have been ascribed to him as recently as 1963.[36]

For Rammohun, the act of writing out his ideas, printing them out, and
circulating them in the form of tracts, pamphlets, and texts was an important aspect of his political project.[37] Consider the case of Subrahmanya
Shastri, a writer from Madras, who objected to Rammohun's ideas
regarding idol worship. While Shastri published his objections in *Madras
Courier*, an English-language newspaper, Rammohun opted to print and
circulate multiple copies of his response, *Subrahmanya Shastri'r sahit
vichar* (*Reply to Subrahmanya Shastri*, 1820) in Bangla, Hindi, Sanskrit,
and English. The English-language tract alone had a print run of 500
copies while the Bangla tract was acknowledged as 'popular' work in
Calcutta.[38] Circulation was clearly an important concern.

However, at this juncture, we are confronted with a problem. During
Rammohun's lifetime, the print literacy of adult males and females in
Bengal was less than 9 per cent.[39] Since this statistic raises the distinct
possibility of a very limited circulation of his writings, I refer to new
research on the history of the book by Francesca Orsini, Sheldon
Pollock, Anindita Ghosh, and Stuart Black to show that this is not the
case. Their research has shown that early modern writers and intellectuals appealed to written as well as oral traditions (such as reading aloud
and performance narratives) to promote a wider circulation of their
ideas. The phenomenon was so widespread that V. Narayan Rao has
even coined the term 'oral literacy' to refer to it. Thus, the question before
us is not regarding the print literacy of Bengali society but whether
Rammohun himself was 'oral literate'.[40]

Rammohun's writings contain some important evidence of his 'oral
literacy'. First, a clear majority of his works were humorous, informal,
dramatic, ironical, sarcastic, and short (this would have made them
easy to narrate and read aloud). Second, he progressively introduced

linguistic innovations (shorter sentences, smaller words, and greater clarity of prose) in his writings to aid the process. Third, the free availability of his writings in the popular press meant that they could also be easily circulated. His strategies yielded some success since his writings were reprinted in the popular press during his lifetime and by private publishers after his death.

Rammohun's intended readership was not, however, restricted to his Bengali readers. Rather, he attempted to make his ideas accessible to EIC officials as well. I argue (in Chapter 4) that this was especially the case in tracts on property law—*Brief Remarks Regarding Modern Encroachments on the Ancient Rights of Females According to the Hindu Law of Inheritance* (1822) and *Essay on the Rights of Hindus over Ancestral Property According to the Law of Bengal* (1830). These tracts referred to concepts such as liberalism, parliamentary government, constitutions, the division of executive and legislature, and familiar late-18th-century texts to articulate and explain his political project to an intended readership of the Company's officials. Rammohun also cited Orientalist scholars such as William Jones and H.T. Colebrooke who would have been familiar figures to Company officials.

Rammohun's tracts on property included detailed interpretations of the Dharmashastras (hereafter, DhS). The DhS were early Indian texts on governance, religion, society, and statecraft. Rammohun frequently referred to the DhS to develop his own ideas of governmental accountability. My argument follows from B.D. Chattopadhyay's work on DhS. Chattopadhyay argues that the DhS advocated a policy of progressive allocation of political power by state administrations to local communities. This policy aimed to enable local polities to become self-reliant on matters relating to everyday governance (or 'autonomous spaces', as Chattopadhyay refers to it). Even large state administrations were accountable to local communities for the successful creation and maintenance of 'autonomous spaces'.

The similarities between a DhS policy of 'autonomous spaces' and Rammohun's ideas of governmental accountability can be seen in his writings. For example, *Exposition* conceptualized EIC's administration as an inordinately complex, inefficient 'arbitrary authority' which was not accountable to either parliamentary overseers in London (the Board of Control) or its subjects in Bengal, and proposed a detailed plan whereby the Bengali public could hold the Company accountable in matters relating to everyday governance far more effectively than any institution or committee in London. An implication of this plan was that the British Parliament would force the Company to grant greater financial, political, and bureaucratic autonomy to the natives of Bengal and thereby restructure the administration by introducing greater flexibility and accountability. So, Rammohun advocated a policy of radical devolution of centralized political power and the creation of local 'autonomous spaces' in Bengal.

Rammohun published, printed, and distributed *Exposition* in London. His publication choices would, however, have created problems of accessibility for his audience/readership in Bengal. In this context, *Expositions'* ideas of distance, government, and accountability also featured as key arguments in his Bangla and English writings in Calcutta (on property law and freedom of the press). For Bengali readers, he referred to popular Puranic motifs (such as the mythical hero Parasurama) to explain his ideas; for English-language readers (his intended audience being Company officials), the argument was made with references to liberal philosophy, parliamentary democracy, and British history.

Rammohun's reference to the DhS was not unusual. As Brian Hatcher has shown, the DhS were texts of debate amongst contemporary Bengali intellectuals, particularly Sanskrit pandits. Hatcher argues that the DhS were employed by Bengali intellectuals to articulate their views on 'the existing norms of textual authority, social order, debate and argumentation to engage with an emerging set of colonial policies, institutions, material tools and professional opportunities' for much of the 19th century.[41] In this context he opines that Bengali intellectuals who referred to the DhS were not reinterpreting these texts based on a classical liberal or conservative ideology, but rather attempting to 'explore' new social contexts, practices, and colonial technologies using pre-modern forms of thought.[42] He refers to this argument by the term 'shastric imaginary'.[43] Hatcher also refers to Rammohun's writings on sati but does not develop this argument further. Neither does he consider that Rammohun's interpretations of the DhS may have also been a part of his political thought.

Hatcher's ideas of the 'shastric imaginary' and his suggestions on Rammohun's writings on sati are considered in greater detail in Chapter 5. Rammohun consistently wrote against the practice of sati; he cited the lack of governmental accountability on the issue and argued that the Company administration was guilty of wilfully neglecting the welfare of the victims. Rammohun's argument for Company accountability was also related to ethics in contemporary Bengali society. His method of appealing to Bengali society and Company officials by using different categories, concepts, terms, and ideas can also be seen in these writings. To Bengali society, he cited the DhS to argue that sati was an unethical practice; and to Company officials, he referred to liberal constitutionalism to argue that the government was responsible for the welfare of its subjects and could be held accountable for any failure to do so.

I argue that the most ambitious of Rammohun's efforts to reach out to a European readership was his interpretation of the Gospels of the New Testament in the Bible. Chapter 6 examines the ways in which Rammohun selectively and deliberately misinterpreted the Gospels to make it appear as if they were in line with his political thought on societal ethics and governmental accountability. Controversially, he asserted that the Gospels and Hindu scripture had 'a common basis' and that his ideas of ethics and law in Hindu scripture were not different from his interpretation of the Gospels' idea of the same. His writings on the Gospels were not sparse. As R. Sugirtharajah noted, Rammohun wrote more on the Gospels than he did on the Vedanta.[44] But Sugirtharajah was at a loss to explain his intense focus on the Gospels. So, in fact, were Rammohun's contemporaries.[45] To his friends in the Atmiya Sabha, it would have appeared rather odd that the man who had only published translations and interpretations of Hindu scripture until 1820 henceforth began to publish voluminous interpretations of Christian theology as well.

Rammohun's interpretation of the Gospels was shorn of any Biblical background but were a general argument for everyday ethical practice in contemporary Bengali society. He was particularly interested in Unitarianism and argued that it had a common message with the Vedas—that there is one invisible divinity and the only proper way to worship is through ethical practice. He even founded a Unitarian Mission in support of these ideas. Unfortunately, Calcutta society did not take to the Mission and it failed. Soon afterwards, he founded the Brahmo Sabha where its members, drawn from his own Atmiya Sabha associates, engaged in a participatory form of worship.

The Brahmo Sabha conceptualized ethical conduct as a form of worship. Good behaviour was held to be epistemically indispensable to the worship of the *parameshwar* or the Supreme Being.[46] The Supreme Being, Rammohun opined, had created all human beings; and one must always respect the divine by being good to all.[47] He implored to the Brahmos to treat others as they themselves would prefer to be treated.[48] Just four years later, in 1832, he wrote an argument detailing the ways in which an ethical public in India could hold the EIC accountable for its government far more effectively than political authorities in London, and published it as *Exposition*. Its publication signalled an important development: that Rammohun's ideas concerning government and accountability were implicitly influenced by his conception of ethics and religious practice. A unity of thought can therefore be identified in his writings.

This book will conclude that Rammohun's political thought was the product of a theory which underpinned his works—a theory of ethics, distance, and accountability. My conclusion sharply differs from current scholarly perspectives which perceive Rammohun as a liberal scholar who was little-read during his lifetime. A prominent representative of this view is C.A. Bayly's *Recovering Liberties: Indian Thought in the Age of Liberalism and Empire*.[49]

Bayly argued that the intellectual context which framed and ordered Rammohun's writings and thought was that of a brief period of optimism amongst Bengali intellectuals in Calcutta on the possibilities of an indigenous liberal response to British rule. Bayly paraphrased this argument as 'the moment'. In his view, 'the moment' was a response to two historical developments: first, the gradual decline of pre-colonial ('Mughal') institutional and political influences in Bengal; and second, the presence of new commercial opportunities in Calcutta brought about by the EIC (such as access to new markets, joint stock entrepreneurial ventures, and capital). In this view, Rammohun was the most important Indian liberal thinker of 'the moment', a 'canonical' writer whose ideas on government, property, press, and jury contributed to a trans-national debate on liberal constitutionalism. While the argument of *Recovering Liberties* is tightly woven, we note that over half of Rammohun's writings (such as works on Hindu scripture, Biblical interpretation, and sati) do not fall within its scope. Thus, Bayly's interpretation of Rammohun's liberalism is not applicable to a clear majority of his work.

Andrew Sartori's *Bengal in Global Concept History: Culturism in the Age of Capital* broadens out Bayly's argument by suggesting that the *entire* corpus of Rammohun's writings can be placed within the 'epistemic framework' of classical liberalism.[50] He asserts that in the early 19th century, the EIC's investment in capital and new forms of business organization in Bengal linked the region to a vast global network of ideas and commerce. Economically, this resulted in a brief period of prosperity in Calcutta; and intellectually, liberalism emerged as 'the dominant ideological paradigm' in the city.[51] This argument is also presented as the historical context of Rammohun's writings and thought. In much the same vein as *Recovering Liberties*, Sartori also argues that Rammohun was the 'founder' of modernist thought in India and the most prominent liberal thinker of the early 19th century.[52]

Methodologically, Bayly and Sartori advocate global and transnational approaches to the study of modern Indian intellectual history. Both stress that the history of ideas in the 19th century must be contextualized with worldwide intellectual trends, political discourses, and economic developments. Specifically, they show that Rammohun was a global intellectual figure in the early 19th century and provide new evidence of the ways in which his writings influenced liberal discourse in Europe and the United States of America. Further, they argue that Rammohun did not mimic intellectual trends in Europe but articulated a distinctly "Indian" *form* of liberal thought. These arguments present Rammohun in a new light and have been widely accepted by scholars of Indian intellectual history, world history, and the history of political thought.[53] This book, however, situates his writings in their own 'local' historical context of Company administration and early modern political philosophy in Bengal. The discursive focus is on the principal themes and concerns of his writings rather than a macro-historical project which covers a large part of 19th-century political thought. This method does not imply a rejection of Bayly and Sartori. Rather, it calls for a more nuanced and contextualized engagement of Rammohun's engagement with liberalism and intervention in global intellectual/political discourse.

Discursively, Bayly and Sartori are of the view that liberalism is the most important influence on Rammohun's thought and they opine that indigenous intellectual contexts and institutional influences had but a liminal impact on his thought. Rather, both stress that the main feature of Rammohun's thought is that he made 'an astonishing leap from the intellectual status of a late-Mughal state intellectual to that of the first Indian liberal'.[54] We note, however, that neither historian interrogates the conceptual category of 'late-Mughal state intellectual'.[55] Their views prevent us from perceiving Rammohun in any other meaningful interpretative frame than liberalism and present him as an isolated, misunderstood liberal.

This book, however, shows that Rammohun was a popular writer in his lifetime and his works were intended for, and successfully appealed to, a wide audience in Bengal. Regarding his intellectual context, we learn that his writings and thought were influenced by the political philosophy of *akhlaq* and the DhS; and this continued to be the case after his intellectual engagement with liberalism. His engagement with liberalism thus did not lead to a complete rejection of earlier intellectual influences. The current perception of Rammohun as an isolated, elite, exclusively liberal thinker can hence be qualified. I will argue that liberalism in the early 19th century did not have as important an influence as is currently perceived and the resilience of older Indian political traditions continued to have a far greater influence on native intellectuals than is currently known.

Notes

1. Ramchandra Guha (ed.), *Makers of Modern India* (Delhi: Penguin India, 2010).
2. Lynn Zastoupil, *Rammohun Roy and the Making of Victorian Britain* (New York: Palgrave Macmillan, 2010), 1–8.
3. David Kopf, 'Rammohun Roy and the Bengal Renaissance: A Historiographical Essay', in *Rammohun Roy and the Process of Modernisation in India*, ed. V.C. Joshi (Delhi: Vikas Publishing House, 1975), 21–45; Adrienne Moore, *Rammohun Roy and America* (Calcutta: Satis Chandra Chakravarty, 1942), 125–50.
4. Brajendranath Banerji, *Rammohun Roy* (Calcutta: Bangiya Sahitya Parisad, 1943), 70.
5. R.C. Majumdar, *On Rammohan Roy* (Calcutta: Asiatic Society, 1972), 20.
6. Michael Lobban, 'Blackstone and the Science of the Law', *The Historical Journal*, 30, no. 2 (January 1987): 311–17.

7. Lobban, 'Blackstone and the Science of the Law', 311–17.
8. The following is but a representative list:

   A.R. Desai, *Social Background of Indian Nationalism* (Calcutta: Popular Prakashan, 1948), 85; Rajani P. Dutt, *India Today* (London: Victor Gollancz, 1940), 270–85; Iqbal Singh, *Rammohun Roy: A Biographical Inquiry into the Making of Modern India*, vol. 1 (Bombay: Asia Publishing House, 1958), 4; Nemai Sadhan Bose, *Awakening in Bengal* (Calcutta: Firma K.L. Mukhopadhyay, 1960), 27–55; Arabinda Poddar, *Renaissance in Bengal: Search for Identity* (Simla: Indian Institute for Advanced Study, 1977), 1; Wilhelm Halbfass, *India and Europe: An Essay in Philosophical Understanding* (Delhi: Motilal Banarsidass, 1990), 203; Zastoupil, *Rammohun Roy*, 1–8.
9. Amiya Sen, *Rammohun Roy: A Critical Biography* (Delhi: Penguin Viking, 2012), 26.
10. Andrew Sartori, *Bengal in Global Concept History: Culturism in the Age of Capital* (London: Chicago University Press, 2008), 77.
11. Nagendranath Chattopadhyay, *Mahatma Raja Rammohun Roy Jibancharit* (Life Story of Raja Rammohun Roy) (Calcutta, 1912); Sophia Dobson Collet, *Life and Letters of Rammohun Roy*, ed. Dilip Biswas and Prabhat Ganguli (Calcutta: Sadharan Brahmo Samaj, 1963); Susobhan Sarkar, *Notes on the Bengal Renaissance* (Calcutta: People's Publishing House, 1946); and David Kopf, *British Orientalism and the Bengal Renaissance, the dynamics of Indian Modernisation, 1773–1835* (Berkeley: University of California Press, 1969).
12. Rammohun Roy, *Exposition of the Practical Operation of the Revenue and Judicial Systems of India and of the General Character and Conditions of its inhabitants as submitted in evidence to the authorities in England* (London: Smith, Elder and Co., 1832), 97.
13. F.J. Shore, *Life of Lord Teignmouth*, 2 vols (London: Hatchard and Son, 1843), 62.
14. An argument which is developed in greater detail in Chapter 2.
15. Kalidas Nag and Debajyoti Burman (eds), *The English Works of Rammohun Roy* (Calcutta: Sadharan Brahmo Samaj, 1950), 2:42 (henceforth, Nag and Burman (eds), *EW*).
16. Dermot Killingley, *The Only True God: Bengali and Sanskrit Works on Religion by Rammohun Roy, Selected and Translated* (Newcastle upon Tyne: Grevatt & Grevatt, 1982), 17. In *Utsavanander sahit vichar*, Rammohun simply noted, 'The knower of God continues to do good.'
17. Nag and Burman (eds), *EW*, 2:53. For example, in Isho Upanishad (1816): He who perceives the whole universe in the Supreme Being is he who does not feel contempt towards any creature whatsoever. When a person

possessed of true knowledge conceives that God extends over the whole universe, that is, God furnishes every particle of the universe with the light of his existence how can he as an observer of the real unity of the pervading Supreme existence be affected with infatuation or grievance?

18. Nag and Burman (eds), *EW*, 2:85.

19. Nagendranath Chattopadhyay, *Mahatma Raja Rammohun Roy Jibancharit* [Life Story of Mahatma Rammohun Roy] (Calcutta: Sadharan Brahmo Samaj, 1912 [1881]) (henceforth, *JB*), 61.

20. Nag and Burman (eds), *EW*, 2:117.

21. Kopf, *British Orientalism and the Bengal Renaissance*, 113. See also: Partha Chatterjee, *The Black Hole of Empire: A History of a Global Practice of Power* (Princeton: Princeton University Press, 2012), 139.

22. Chattopadhyay, *JB*, 59.

23. Chattopadhyay, *JB*, 69.

24. For Kasinath Tarkapanchanan's career, see: Brian A. Hatcher, 'Pandits at Work: The Modern Shastric Imaginary in Early-Colonial Bengal', in *Trans-Colonial Modernities in South Asia*, ed. Michael S. Dodson and Brian A. Hatcher (London: Routledge, 2012), 57. Bruce Robertson has doubts about Tarkapanchanan's authorship (Bruce Robertson, *Raja Rammohan Ray: The Father of Modern India* [New Delhi: Oxford University Press, 1995], 37). Nevertheless, historians are divided over the issue. See, for instance: Amiya Sen, *Explorations in Modern Bengal, c. 1800–1900: Essays on Religion, History and Culture* (New Delhi: Primus Books, 2010). In 2012, Sen's biography of Rammohun cited Robertson's doubts but did not offer an opinion on them. I address the question of authorship in Chapter 3.

25. As quoted in Chattopadhyay, *JB*, 70.

26. Chattopadhyay, *JB*, 75.

27. Manmathanath Ghosh, 'Friends and Followers of Rammohun Roy', in *Rammohun Roy: The Man and His Work*, ed. Amal Home (Calcutta: Rammohun Centenary Committee, 1933), 124–34.

28. Ramaprasad Chanda and Jatindra Kumar Majumdar (eds), *Selections from Official Letters and Documents Relating to the Life of Raja Rammohun Roy* (Calcutta: Calcutta Oriental Book Agency, 1938), 97–8 and 263–4 (henceforth, *LD*).

29. Pandit Sivanath Sastri, 'Rammohun Roy: The story of his life' in *Rammohun Roy: The Man and His Work*, ed. Amal Home (Calcutta: Art Press, 1933), 12.

30. Sastri, 'The Story of Rammohun's Life', 12.

31. Sastri, 'The Story of Rammohun's Life', 12.

32. Chattopadhyay, *JB*, 47–8.

33. Bruce Robertson, *Raja Rammohan Ray: The Father of Modern India* (New Delhi: Oxford University Press, 1995), 97–109.
34. Killingley, *Only True God*, 23.
35. Killingley, *Only True God*, 2.
36. Rammohun Roy, *Dialogue between a Theist and an Idolater: An 1820 Tract*, trans. Stephen Hay (Calcutta: Firma K.L. Mukhopadhyay, 1963).
37. Chattopadhyay, *JB*, 59.
38. See Tables A.1 and A.3.
39. P.J. Marshall, *Bengal: The British Bridgehead: Eastern India 1740–1828* (Cambridge: Cambridge University Press, 1987), 30.
40. Francesca Orsini, 'Introduction', in *The History of the Book in South Asia*, ed. Francesca Orsini (London: Ashgate, 2013), xiv.
41. Hatcher, 'Pandits at Work', 45–6.
42. Hatcher, 'Pandits at Work', 51–4.
43. Hatcher, 'Pandits at Work', 45–6.
44. R.S. Sugirtharajah, *The Bible and Asia: From the Pre-Christian Era to the Postcolonial Age* (Cambridge, MA: Harvard University Press, 2013), 87.
45. Sastri, 'Rammohun Roy: The Story of His Life', 14.
46. Rammohun Rachanabali. Edited by Ajitkumar Ghosh. Calcutta: Haraf Prakashani, 1973. Henceforth, BW.
47. *BW*, 342.
48. *BW*, 342.
49. Christopher Bayly, *Recovering Liberties* (Cambridge: Cambridge University Press, 2011). The basic argument of *Recovering Liberties* can be found in two earlier works: *The Birth of the Modern World, 1780-1914* (Oxford: Wiley-Blackwell, 2004), 293; and 'Rammohun Roy and the Advent of Constitutional Liberalism in India, 1800-30', *Modern Intellectual History*, 4, no. 1 (April 2007): 25–41. Here we have taken *Recovering Liberties* as our text since it is the most developed form of Bayly's ideas of Rammohun Roy.
50. Sartori, *Bengal in Global Concept History*, 79.
51. Sartori, *Bengal in Global Concept History*, 79.
52. Sartori, *Bengal in Global Concept History*, 71.
53. Christopher Bayly's arguments on liberalism have been widely recognized and accepted: Amartya Sen, *The Argumentative Indian: Writings on Indian History Culture and Identity* (Delhi: Allen Lane, 2005), 32; Robert Travers, *Ideology and Empire in Eighteenth Century India* (Cambridge: Cambridge University Press 2007), 20–3; Sartori, *Bengal in Global Concept History*, 87–92; Chatterjee, *The Black Hole of Empire*, 155; Javed Majeed, 'Introduction', in *The Reconstruction of Religious thought in Islam by*

Muhammad Iqbal, ed. Saed Sheikh (Stanford: Stanford University Press 2012), xi; David Armitage, *Foundations of Modern International Thought* (Cambridge: Cambridge University Press, 2013), 30; Barnita Bagchi, 'Connected and Entangled Histories: Writing Histories in the Indian Context', *International Journal of the History of Education*, 50, no. 6 (August 2014): 30; Ramchandra Guha, *Rammohan Roy: The First Indian Liberal* (Delhi: Penguin Random House India, 2018).

54. Sartori, *Bengal in Global Concept History*, 77.
55. Sartori, *Bengal in Global Concept History*, 77.

1 *Reading* Exposition

R ammohun published *Exposition* in 1832 in London while he was an official envoy of the Mughal Emperor.[1] If one were to examine the historical circumstances in which this came to be, three distinct but intertwined narratives would come into play—first, the story of the EIC's rapid rise to political power in India in the late 18th century; second, the Mughal Emperors and their struggle for survival against an increasingly hostile EIC on the one hand and rising regional powers in North India on the other; and third, the Great Reform Act of 1832, a parliamentary measure which generated widespread debate and controversy in Britain.

We begin with the EIC and the Mughals. In 1765, the Mughal Emperor Shah Alam II granted the Diwani of Bengal, Bihar, and Orissa in eastern India to the EIC. In theory, the Diwani granted the right to collect revenue on behalf of Shah Alam II. In practice, the EIC was effectively the sovereign and began an aggressive conquest for more territories from this point onwards. By 1805, the EIC had emerged as the most formidable political power in South Asia, captured Delhi, and reduced the Emperor (and his eldest son and heir apparent, Prince Mirza Akbar Shah) to monthly pensioners.[2]

Shah Alam II watched over these political developments melancholically and accepted his status as a figurehead of Mughal rule.[3] Upon his death, EIC officials in Calcutta responded with a 'public testimony of respect'.[4] Minute guns were directed to be fired from the ramparts of Fort William in Calcutta and all the stations of the army under the Presidencies of Bengal, Madras, and Bombay.[5] Consequently, Mirza Akbar Shah was crowned Emperor Akbar II in 1806.

If the death of Shah Alam II represented an era in which Mughal Emperors had (as Michael Fisher so eloquently put it), 'virtually lost all economic, political and military power',[6] the EIC was about to make matters worse, as Akbar II's heir apparent was henceforth denied a monthly personal allowance (as well as the right to confer titles, a point which will become significant later on).[7] Unhappy with this state of affairs, Akbar II sent written appeals to the Governor General's Council in Calcutta.[8] Unfortunately, his efforts were in vain. By 1808 the Court of Directors had even approved of an official policy to 'very properly discourage' any further appeals.[9] This did not however stop Akbar II, as he now began sending emissaries directly to Calcutta. In 1809, he asked for permission to send his emissary Shah Haji on an apparently harmless mission to gift a ceremonial robe to Governor General Lord Minto. However, Shah Haji's real mission was to present Akbar II's grievances to Minto in person and demand 'a public acknowledgement of the vassalage and submission of the British Government to Delhi'.[10] A furious Minto rejected the ceremonial robe and complained against Akbar II's 'extremely disingenuous' methods to the Court of Directors.[11]

Akbar II's methods may, in fact, have had some effect since the Court of Directors approved of a reduced monthly stipend for the heir apparent soon afterwards.[12] And so Akbar II's efforts to convince the EIC for a full stipend continued. In 1812, he even fell victim to a scam organized by a Murshidabad resident, Pran Kishan, and invested him with the title of Rajah, so that the latter could represent him in London.[13] The EIC was not amused and their relations with Akbar II had decidedly cooled by 1815 when Governor General Lord Hastings visited the Mughal court and was not given a chair to sit on when he met the Emperor.[14]

Hastings was upset but secured his revenge in 1819 by organizing the coronation of the ruler of Awadh 'to represent a challenge to the very identity of the Mughal Emperor'.[15] From the 1820s onwards, successive Governors General distanced themselves from Akbar II and ignored his court in Delhi.[16] Instead, they concentrated on military conquest and the acquisition of more territories, and fashioned a political economy based on militarization and war.[17]

In 1829, an aging, embattled, and progressively sidelined Akbar II appointed Rammohun as his emissary to the court of the British Monarch.[18] Rammohun had a Mughal connection—his grandfather had been associated with Shah Alam II.[19] Now he was to represent Akbar II's claims in Britain because the EIC had consistently refused to entertain his requests in India.

Rammohun's appointment marked the end point of over two decades of petitions, letters, and representations made by the Mughal Emperor. Much to the irritation of officials in Calcutta and Delhi, Akbar II bestowed Rammohun with a title, Rajah, and engaged him to draft a petition for the British monarch.[20] As matters stood, he would now have to represent the interests of Akbar II in the language of the British monarch and perform a delicate balancing act of diplomacy in a country that he had never been to. To make matters worse, the Governor General's Council attempted to withhold official papers which Rammohun required, and refused to recognize his appointment as envoy or the title Rajah.[21] Rammohun was left with little choice but to undertake the voyage as a private individual.

Independently of the Mughal background, Rammohun had been wanting to visit Britain since he also had an objective of his own: to table an *anti-sati petition* in the House of Commons from the 'inhabitants of Calcutta'.[22] He duly headed out on a four-month-long sea voyage to Britain and disembarked at Liverpool. Upon arrival, he immediately declared his status as the envoy of the Mughal Emperor and was accepted as such.[23] (Indeed, the British government even invited him for an audience with King William IV.)[24]

In 1831, Rammohun found himself in a charged political atmosphere of economic distress, rising food prices, and agrarian unemployment with increasingly aggressive calls for a reassessment of the 'place of the Houses of Parliament in national life'.[25] Britain was a country that was alive to the possibility of radical political change and that year marked the political climax of more than half a century of protests and petitions.[26] Riots had erupted across its counties as arrests and court martials were made by a government that was fearful of a violent overthrow of power.[27] At stake was the future of a political system that had continued, unchanged, for nearly 200 years and disenfranchised vast sections of British society in favour of protecting the interests of the hereditary landed aristocracy.[28] Unable to contain the chaos, Prime Minister Arthur Wellesley—the first Duke of Wellington, the man who had defeated Napoleon—resigned. His successor, Sir Robert Peel, was more conciliatory but resigned soon afterwards amidst more political protests and unrest.[29]

Rammohun took up lodgings in London, a city whose newspapers frequently reported the possibility of a local agrarian and industrial revolt.[30] He had not forgotten his mission for Akbar II and immediately set about meeting as many political representatives as possible. He also argued Akbar II's case with the chairman and deputy chairman of the EIC and the secretary of the Board of Control.[31] His efforts yielded a degree of success. Rammohun quickly emerged as 'the lion of the season' as Members of Parliament (MPs), cabinet ministers, Privy Court councillors, and EIC directors officially met, informally conversed, dined, and had luncheon with him.[32] These meetings yielded results as he was also able to place Akbar II's petition before the Board of Control and the Court of Directors and achieve a partial increase in the Emperor's monthly pension.[33]

A large part of Rammohun's success lay in his unique cultural identity. British newspapers referred to him as 'the great Brahmin Philosopher' with a mystical appeal.[34] Contemporaries who met him were not quite sure about their assessment of the man. Take, for instance, the views of the writer, biographer, and politician John Bowring. Bowring had earlier met Rammohun in Calcutta and corresponded with him for nearly a decade. But as he later wrote to his friend, the philosopher Jeremy Bentham, he was still quite taken aback by the effect that Rammohun had had on British society:

> I am sure that it is impossible to give expression to those sentiments
> of interest and anticipation with which his [Rammohun's] advent here
> is associated in all our minds, I recollect those writers have indulged

themselves with enquiring what they should feel if any of those time honoured men whose names have lived through the ages, and should appear among them. They have endeavoured to imagine what would be their sensations of a Plato or a Socrates or a Milton or a Newton would unexpectedly honour them with their presence. ... In my mind, the effect of distance is very much like the effect of time; and he who come among us from a country thousands of miles off, must be looked upon with the same interest as those illustrious men who lived thousands of years ago.[35]

Rammohun came from a country so far away that geographical distance and historical time appeared to have merged into one. To his British contemporaries, meeting him was as disconcertingly strange as meeting an ancient Greek philosopher or an early modern thinker.

Rammohun's mystical image, however, did not dissuade him from more immediate and worldly concerns. He diligently read English newspapers, attended parliamentary debates on electoral reform, and also wrote about the EIC's government in India. His ideas were presented to the Select Committee hearing on the Charter Renewal Act in 1831 (at around the same time as the Great Reform Bill discussions were taking place in the Commons) and published by the Parliament. The published Select Committee proceedings were then carefully read by British lawmakers to frame a new East India Bill.[36] However, the East India Bill ignored Rammohun's suggestions.[37] Disappointed, he decided to publish a large selection of his ideas as a new printed book, *Exposition*.[38]

Exposition was the work of a man inspired by the radical political atmosphere around him in Britain but from the perspective of his experience with the EIC's government in India.

Rammohun argued that the EIC had alienated itself from the people it governed and boldly attempted to alter this state of affairs by basing his argument on a Mughal conception of political power, emphasizing that power must be visible, localized, decentralized, and domiciled.[39] His argument had three main strands to it: first, that the EIC derived its legitimacy and political authority from the British Crown and Houses of Parliament; second, that the Company had introduced a new system of government in India, but without the sanction of the sovereign Mughal rulers; and third, that the EIC could be made accountable to local centres of power (such as Panchayats) and the Bengali public instead of a distant and invisible Board of Control and Court of Directors in London.

At its core, *Exposition* was a well-argued case for administrative and governmental accountability. It was the discursive end point of a concern that can be traced to a period that was well before the 1830s. In fact, Rammohun had been interested in the subject as early as 1821. That year, he even wrote to John Bowring on his plans to author a memorial on the revenue administration of the EIC (which unfortunately kept getting delayed in spite of a fairly rigorous publication schedule).[40] Unfortunately, he never published his memorial.

In the 1960s, Dilip Kumar Biswas tracked down and published Rammohun's original handwritten manuscript.[41] We now know that Rammohun's 'first production in political affairs' was a six-page note on the critical necessity for official documentation on the land rights of peasants (*ryots*) in Bengal.[42] He opined that while peasants had historically been invested with land rights, the situation had changed with the institution of the Permanent Settlement of 1793 since from that time onwards, the government exclusively focused on collecting copious data on revenue collection rates of the zamindars rather than documenting the land rights of the peasants.[43] The lack of documentation had led to large-scale extortion of the peasants by the zamindars.[44] Such forms of extra-economic coercion could, however, be effectively checked if district collectors and magistrates, the two branches of rural government, were to maintain detailed land records of their own.[45] According to Rammohun, the magistrate and the collector were a check on each other's administrative power. So, as long as both offices worked in tandem, neither could emerge as more important than the other. In this schema, the peasant's economic rights would be documented by collectors and shared with the district magistrate's office. The peasant could then cite official data to refuse the exorbitant demands of the zamindars as well as seek legal redress by filing a suit at the magistrate's office.[46]

Rammohun was putting forward a very definite political view: that the EIC had a responsibility to protect the vulnerable and could be held accountable if their subjects were being harassed and exploited. Further, he was of the opinion that a sound governmental system was that which was structured as a system of checks and balances (which, as Chapter 4 will reveal, was an influence of his reading of the Dharmashastras).

Here, we focus on his view that the Permanent Settlement was also such a system. And, indeed, he was right. Lord Cornwallis's chief justification for the Permanent Settlement in Bengal was the critical need to introduce a separation of powers between the executive and the legislature. More than a decade later, Rammohun had developed his views on governance and the Permanent Settlement to a point that he could publish a full-length book on the subject, *Exposition*.

I interpret *Exposition* as a source of Rammohun's political thought. Since historical works on his writings have not considered *Exposition* from this perspective, this is an original interpretation of the text.[47] This chapter is divided into four sections. The first examines *Exposition*'s context, readership, and reception. The second focuses on its interpretation of Indian history. The third explores its critique of the Permanent Settlement. The fourth is concerned with Rammohun's critique of a new regulation (passed in 1828) by which collectors could henceforth seize private property in their districts without the sanction of other governmental authority since they were now also invested with judicial powers.

Context, Readership, and Reception

Exposition retained the format of Rammohun's assessment of the EIC to the Select Committee of the House of Commons. The body of the text was organized in a series of brisk questions and answers, as is typical of the Select Committee hearings of the time. However, it was not a mere reproduction of ideas presented to the Commons but also included new material such as an introduction, an index, and an appendix to provide a familiar context for readers. Popular books such as Blackstone's *Commentaries* were referred to and included as well. A discursive similarity also helped: Blackstone's 'attempt to reconcile local laws within an empirical framework' fell in neatly with Rammohun's emphasis on the critical importance of local laws in Bengal within the larger context of EIC administration.[48]

Rammohun's references to Blackstone also signal his familiarity with current political debates in London. He was also personally acquainted with the MPs at the House of Commons and Lords. In March 1830, Secretary of War Charles Wynn presented a petition to the House of

Commons which cited Rammohun's ideas.[49] Wynn knew Rammohun personally, having met him at a dinner organized by the Royal Asiatic Society (and would be presented with a copy of the *Exposition* soon after it was printed).[50] He had previously been the president of the Board of Control, the EIC's parliamentary overseer. Wynn's petition would have found at least one influential reader—the radical MP, Joseph Hume.

Hume was familiar with Rammohun's work. His personal papers include contemporary writings on Rammohun's assessment of the salt tax; Rammohun's private secretary, Sandfort Arnot's ideas of a free press in India; and the Stamp Act (to which Rammohun was a signatory).[51] While there is no evidence that Hume responded to Rammohun's works, the presence of these writings indicates an intellectual interest in his political project. There was also an institutional context. Like Rammohun, Hume had also been associated with the EIC.[52]

While not ideologically oriented towards any particular political discourse in India, Hume developed a radical political programme for institutional reform in Britain. The scope of his arguments extended to the EIC's administration in India. Hume argued that long delays in courts and 'poor policing' had led to an expensive administrative system. Rammohun's ideas of Company reform were similar to Hume's. Rammohun also criticized delays in courts and poor policing and argued that the current system of administration had led to unnecessary and wasteful expenditure.

Rammohun's views would have also been in agreement with some EIC officials who appeared before the Select Committee. Consider, for instance, the views of the EIC official, William Chaplin. Chaplin was summoned to appear before the Select Committee on 30 March 1830. In his deposition, he recommended that native employees must be allocated 'a larger share' in the EIC's administration, with higher salaries and better promotions.[53] When asked whether he believed that such recommendations were viable, he unequivocally responded in the affirmative, opining:

> I think they [the natives] are adapted to all offices. In point of natural ability, I do not conceive them at all inferior to Europeans. Their intimate knowl-edge of the languages is also a consideration which must give them efficiency in the administration of all offices; a knowledge which Europeans, even after twenty five years' residence, can never acquire in so perfect a degree.[54]

However, it would be a mistake to imagine that Rammohun's contemporaries would have all agreed with him. A case in point here is the
depositions of Joseph Hume's close friend James Mill, the Utilitarian
philosopher employed in the EIC's Examiners Office at Leadenhall
Street.[55] As Head Examiner, Mill had a direct impact on EIC policy
since it was he who made the final call on which official dispatches from
India would be placed before the Court of Directors for their consideration.[56] In 1831, he deposed to the Select Committee on the Charter
Renewal Act as the 'star witness' of the EIC on eight separate occasions.[57]

Mill's depositions were often concerned with the broad impact of
EIC policies on the Indian population. His answers were generally well
argued and precise. In a deposition concerned with land revenue, he
admitted to the Select Committee that the Permanent Settlement had
had an adverse impact on the livelihood of peasants; in another deposition on the role of the judiciary in India, he unequivocally declared
that the inhabitants of Calcutta, Bombay, and Madras were able to hold
Supreme Courts accountable because they were 'an intelligent public'.[58]
Unfortunately, Mill was biased towards the EIC's native employees. All
native employees, he believed, were corrupt, untrustworthy, and inca-
pable of running an administration. Mill's bias fundamentally challenged
Rammohun's proposal to substantially increase the administrative roles
of the native employees with more posts, better salaries, and greater
monetary incentives.[59] Had the two men discussed their ideas with each
other, such opposing views could have led to an engaging and important
debate on governance, but we have no evidence of any such occurrence.

Although *Exposition* was published in 1832, the text found an audience and readership after this period as well. In 1839, William Howitt
(the Quaker poet and author of a 'popular history' of native populations
under colonial governments) argued that Rammohun's conception of
the absolute necessity of a free press was correct.[60] Howitt's intervention was not an isolated example. The same year, an anonymous tract on
EIC governance (authored by an untraceable A.B. but found amongst
Hume's personal papers) cited *Exposition* and agreed with Rammohun
that the Company needed to introduce more administrative positions
for Indians.[61] A.B. and Rammohun also shared similar ideas on governance. In an earlier tract, A.B. had argued that local judicial bodies in
London should be given greater power since they were more effective

in dispensing justice.[62] This was similar to Rammohun's stress on local centres of judicial power in Bengal in *Exposition*.

The arguments of *Exposition* continued to be debated in the next decade after publication. In 1840, George Thompson (then secretary to the British India Association and later the envoy of the Maharaja of Sattara in England) delivered a speech on 'The Present State of British India' at the music hall in Leeds and subsequently published it in *The Leeds Times*. Subtitled 'In reply to the *Edinburgh Review*', Thompson argued that the *Review* had misunderstood Rammohun's assessment of EIC administration.[63] To make his case, Thompson compared Rammohun's ideas to that of John Shore's (Governor General of Bengal, 1793–97, and close collaborator of Lord Cornwallis) and noted that their respective opinions of Company administration in Bengal were the same. Thompson concluded that Rammohun's conception of the Company's government was correct.

Thompson's article shows that the readership of *Exposition* was not confined to London. Perhaps the most remarkable case of the geographical reach (and longevity) of *Exposition* was Francis Horsley Robinson's tract on the India Bill in 1853. Robinson agreed with Rammohun that there was a severe shortage in posts in the EIC's administration. He also argued that more posts ought to be allocated to native employees.[64] Robinson had previously been a member of the Board of Revenue in the Northwest Provinces in India.[65]

We can infer that *Exposition* was a subject of debate and discussion by a wide readership of reformers, public intellectuals, and former EIC officials.

The question that arises here is: why was *Exposition* so widely read? A possible reason could be that Rammohun's methods of explaining his argument were spectacularly successful. Nowhere is this more apparent than in the introduction. The introduction's lucid and accessible narrative on Indian history familiarized readers with the subject matter of the text.[66]

On Indian History

Exposition's introduction familiarized readers with a distant and invisible India. India referred to two concepts—first, a supra-regional territory and second, an administrative system comprised of a union of states.

Rammohun explained the boundaries of India with familiar references such as latitudinal and longitudinal coordinates; contemporary geographical references to China, Tibet, and Persia; and substantiated it with a map.[67] Although readers in Britain would have found these references familiar, he was anxious to stress that the EIC did not create these boundaries. Rather their origins could be traced to Early India, a period 'India was anciently called Bharat Varsha' after 'a humane and powerful prince'.[68] Rammohun opined that the concept of Bharat Varsha was fairly well known in early Indian literature—for example, in the works of the Sanskrit playwright and poet Kalidasa.

From a discussion of external boundaries, Rammohun's narrative neatly shifted to internal territories and cited the Manava Dharmashastra (MDhS) as the main source on understanding territoriality in India.[69] The territories of Bharat Varsha were divided into Aryavarta ('land of the civilized people') and Brahmavarta ('land of the gods' or 'land of sacred and civilized people').[70] Rammohun cartographically located these territories with reference to contemporary rivers, latitudes, and longitudes to avoid alienating his readers.[71]

Rammohun was, however, anxious to highlight the originality of his interpretation for his readers and even engaged in a short critique of William Jones's translation of MDhS to argue that his method of combining myth, geography, and history was an original reading of source material.[72] He now proceeded to introduce his concept of Empire, arguing that it was a supra region which comprised of Aryavarta and Brahmavarta.[73] His idea of Empire was a conceptual innovation. As John Derret showed, Sanskrit, the language in which the MDhS and Kalidasa's works were written, has no definitional equivalent of the concept of Empire.[74]

For Rammohun, 'Empire' did not refer to a single political unit but a cultural territory with common rites, rituals, and ceremonies—practices which served to legitimize political power in early India.[75] He bitterly noted that the presence of a cultural territory did not lead to a common administrative system. Instead, early India was prone to warring principalities and 'multiplied divisions and subdivisions of the land into separate and independent kingdoms under the authority of numerous princes hostile to each other'.[76] In consequence, 'the country was at different periods invaded and brought under temporary subjection to foreign princes celebrated for power and ambition'.[77] This political situation, however, changed in medieval India. He opined that where early Indian polities had failed to create a large administrative network and a strong political union, later medieval governments would succeed. The process would, however, be preceded by centuries of conflict until the Mughal Emperor Babur oversaw the establishment of a politico-administrative system of Empire.[78] In *Exposition*, the Mughals are the only political dynasty to be conceptualized as the sovereign rulers of India.[79]

Rammohun's assessment of the Mughals was not, however, celebratory. He argued that the Mughal system of government was disproportionately affected by its Emperors. This led to political instability. He astutely observed that 'the star of Mughal ascendency inclined towards descent' from 1712. After this period, the political sovereignty of the Mughals was increasingly 'assumed' by 'nobles' as a politically opportunistic response to declining Mughal power than an attempt to introduce new ideas of welfare, administration, and governance. Consequently, post-1712, governments were administrations of misrule and political instability, and eventually paved the way for EIC's rule in India—'a country in which patriotism has never made its way'.[80]

Rammohun did not explain his use of the term 'patriotism'. But its presence would not have gone unnoticed by his British readers. Jonathan Parry has drawn our attention to the word and shown that patriotism was a familiar political term in London in the 1830s and referred to British attitudes towards political developments in Europe such as the Franco-Prussian War.[81] Parry notes that 'patriotism' also gained currency in debates on 'national identity' in newspapers, weekly journals, and popular literature.[82] The term was primarily used to address the public sphere in Britain.

So, was Rammohun referring to a lack of patriotism in India or the public sphere? As far as patriotism is concerned, C.A. Bayly showed that ideas of patriotism were articulated in works on ethics, morality, good government, and political debates in pre-colonial India and 'well into the 19th century'.[83] Going by this argument, it would be safe to assume that Rammohun was probably criticizing the lack of a public sphere in India.[84]

Rammohun's criticism took shape in his discussion of Ranjit Singh, the king of Punjab, in the early 19th century. Rammohun was very impressed with his style of governance. Ranjit Singh, he opined, was 'highly gifted with prudence and moderation'.[85] To him, these were not mere social attributes but established Singh as a local ruler who was not dependent on his administration to inform him of the conditions of his inhabitants and the political and economic implications of his policies. The accessibility and visibility of Singh was indicated by his 'affability in private intercourse' and a 'judicious discharge of public duties.'[86] The references to local and visible forms of political power would feature as important points of criticism of the Company's government in the main text of *Exposition*. His assessment of Singh's government was an assessment of Mughal systems of rule. He pointed to the absence of a politically informed public sphere ('arbitrary rule'), a system of government based on an active, visible, and accessible rulers ('conciliatory system of government').[87]

The final section of the introduction comprised of an outline of the political history of the EIC in the mid-18th century. During this period, the Company's main concern had been to 'manage territorial possessions in India' and maintain commercial privileges.[88] Rammohun blithely noted that this led to a narrow interpretation of administration and its eventual misgovernance of Indian territories. He was right. The EIC's politics during this period was, in fact, marked by the Court of Directors refusing to abandon its identity as a board of commercial merchants; and, as Jacob Thiessen has pointed out, being generally averse to 'making its internal organization more governmental.'[89] Consequently, Company officials in India had a rather paradoxical identity—they were bureaucrats as well as merchants.[90]

At this point, however, *Exposition* introduced a dramatic political factor in the narrative. Alarmed by the frequent intimations of 'misrule' in India, the EIC had been officially chided by the British government for 'bringing reproach to the national character.'[91] The significance of our earlier discussion of Rammohun's use of the term 'patriotism' becomes apparent here. Also, by emphasizing the contribution of a distant and invisible London in the misgovernance of Bengal, Rammohun directed attention to the importance of local centres of power within Bengal itself.

Rammohun asserted that the EIC misgovernance led to the parliamentary supervision of its administration. Under the Regulating Act of 1773, its internal administration was now divided into three large administrative units (Presidencies) in Bombay, Calcutta, and Madras.

The process by which London intervened from 1765 to 1773 represented but the first phase of Company governance.

The second phase began in 1784 with the formation of the Board of Commissioners in London. In contrast to the 'commercial' Company, the Board was a political body.[92] He argued that the Board instituted a new system of governance in which 'the established usages of the country were adopted for the most part as a model of their conduct in the discharge of political, revenue and judicial functions with modifications at the discretion of local authority.'[93] The Board thus continued with Indian political traditions. This period also oversaw Charles Cornwallis's first appointment as Governor General in Bengal.[94]

Rammohun perceived the introduction of Cornwallis's Permanent Settlement in 1793 as the third (and final) phase. He opined that the Permanent Settlement completely restructured the internal administration of the Company in Bengal through 'changes in every department, particularly the revenue and the judicial systems.'[95] At a macro-level, the Permanent Settlement broke away from earlier systems of governance and introduced a new system of administration 'approximating to institutions in England' than earlier systems of administration in India.[96]

The question of the legitimacy of the Permanent Settlement to introduce such sweeping changes is important in this context. Since the EIC did not possess any political sovereignty in India and had introduced settlements without consulting the Mughal Emperor Akbar II, its actions were open to criticism.[97] By contrast, the system of government which had preceded the Permanent Settlement and continued Indian political traditions was assessed more favourably. The introduction to *Exposition* ended here.

Rammohun's narrative of Indian history set the context for his ideas on EIC governance and outlined his conception of Indian political traditions. His argument that the Permanent Settlement of 1793 represented a sharp break from earlier systems of rule in India will be explored further in the next section.

A Critique of the Permanent Settlement

The Permanent Settlement was the most important topic of discussion in *Exposition*. Rammohun opined that its success depended on the successful implementation of the judicial institutions in Bengal which 'approximated to institutions in England'.[98] Consequently, the failure to implement such 'institutions' in India figured heavily in his criticism.

Rammohun argued that the Company followed contradictory policies in judicial administration. Although the Permanent Settlement had bypassed Indian systems of governance in theory, in practice, the Company continued to adopt Mughal judicial procedure in everyday administration. For example, the official language of the court was Persian—an impractical and problematic imitation of Mughal court traditions since few judges and natives understood Persian.[99] He opined that practices such as these had led to corruption, perjury, forgery of court documents, and excessive delays in the judiciary.[100] By 'judiciary' he meant the entire judicial hierarchy in Bengal from the Sudder (Supreme civil court) and Nizamat (Supreme criminal court) at Calcutta, to the provincial courts of appeal at Dhaka, Murshidabad, Rajshahi, Patna, and Bareilly, and, finally, the district courts. The districts were, however, the focus of his assessment of the judicial system of Bengal.

Exposition identified three basic problems in the judicial system—an insufficient number of courts, a defective system of organization of court documents ('dispatch'), and an excessive dependence on underpaid and unregulated native employees.[101]

Rammohun argued that an insufficient number of courts in the districts ('interior') of Bengal led to problems in accessibility for the 'poorer classes' and disadvantaged their position to 'wealthier neighbours'.[102] He instead outlined a new system of localization of judicial power which would involve a restructuring of the ways in which the judicial system was currently organized with a sharp increase in the number of courts located near the 'populous parts of town' where cases could be decided without being hampered by geographical distance.[103]

The lack of courts in the districts also led to organizational problems in the investigation of judicial suits. Rammohun noted that the Sudder courts' investigation of judicial cases 'at a distance of more than fifty miles' led to long delays and a glut of cases. He opined that this could be avoided if circuit court judges were 'directed and relied on' to conduct judicial investigations and thereby 'save useless expense'.[104]

Rammohun asserted that the reorganization of the judiciary with greater administrative responsibilities delegated to the interior and greater powers of the Sudder courts would not create problems of accessibility. In this context, he argued that Sudder courts, though organized on the system of 'English Courts', were not accorded the powers of the judiciary in England. For example, the 'highly desirable' writ of habeas corpus had not been introduced in the Sudder. The significance of this observation would not have been lost to his readership in Britain.[105]

From a discussion of the organization of the judiciary, the argument shifted to the problems faced by officials and judges in their everyday tasks. The chief problem of Company courts was that judges and natives had 'no common language'. Since judges could rarely interpret the 'real nature of grievances', it led to 'decisions founded on conjecture and liable to error'.[106] In *Exposition*, he also explained this problem by referring to the judiciary in England. Quoting William Blackstone, he noted that judges in England were required to be conversant in the language of the petitioners to the court since unfamiliarity in this regard led to defective judicial decisions. He added that according to Blackstone, 'subordinate courts' in England were particularly vulnerable to this problem.[107]

Rammohun argued that the judicial administration in Bengal also depended 'greatly' on native employees throughout the judicial administration from the Sudder to the district courts.[108] Native employees read and wrote bills, depositions, abstracts of cases, and undertook clerical work for the judges.[109] In civil courts, native employees could even try cases on land and 'moveable property' worth up to 500 rupees. In criminal courts (Nizamat Adalat), their 'knowledge of criminal law' was indispensable to judges.[110]

Rammohun's critique of Company administration was directed at a specific policy of the Permanent Settlement—namely, that the judicial system in Bengal had *created* an ambiguous and unregulated native judicial service. He argued that the Company's judicial policy was defective since it had led to a general lack of 'control and discipline' and compelled inhabitants to cultivate 'friendly relations' with native employees to get their work done. From routine clerical tasks to issuing summons and subpoenas to cases of serious fraud, native employees' demand for 'pre-requisites' was the main cause of obstruction of the judicial businesses.[111] This problem was serious enough to 'defeat' the purpose of the judicial system itself.[112] His assessment was not that native employees were unsuitable for judicial tasks. Rather, he was sympathetic to native employees since they were 'meanly situated' in the judicial hierarchy 'in point of rank and pay'.[113]

Rammohun's discussion of native corruption pointed to a larger concern: a re-evaluation of the role of British officials in the districts. He drily reported that civil and criminal cases took up to four years to resolve in the district courts and up to five years in Sudder courts.[114] Further, appeals of cases worth more than 50,000 rupees were sent to the King's Court of Appeal in London. Often, judgements were pronounced on translations which turned out to be defective.[115] This led to more delays. As a solution, he suggested a number of changes to Company policy.[116] A system of checks and balances was structured into his proposed system. At the core of his suggestions was a better paid native employee who was monitored and supervised by three Company officials—the judicial secretary, the judge, and the head writer.[117]

The head writer was particularly important. Rammohun proposed that the head writer be made personally responsible for regulating native corruption (and suggested that his salary be increased). The head writer was not immune from accountability. Indeed, he proposed that this position ought to be made accountable to a native clerk ('superintendent of the papers') who would maintain a separate register to record the time taken for cases to be resolved (so that 'no delay takes place').[118] The register would also serve as an attendance sheet for judges and record their reasons for absence. Misconduct by judges was to be reported by the clerk to the immediate higher court. A failure to report misconduct could result in the clerk being dismissed from his post.[119]

Rammohun's proposals were a response to a specific context. He argued that the judges of Bengal were not accountable for their tasks in the current system. This led to delays. The situation was particularly dire in the district courts where native employees were not selected 'carefully' and 'held in a state of much dependence by judges which incapacitated them from standing up firmly'.[120] Taking the example of the native pleaders, he argued that

> the native pleaders are so unfortunately situated from their being such a great distance between them and the judges who belong to the rulers of the country ... and having no prospect of promotion as English barristers have, that they are treated as an inferior *caste* of persons [emphasis in original].[121]

Rammohun's use of the term 'inferior caste' was a reference to a dysfunctional judicial hierarchy presided over by EIC officials ('rulers of the country'). The term also highlighted the Permanent Settlement's failure to introduce reforms for native employees to have similar roles as their judicial counterparts in Britain: barristers.[122] Moreover, the judicial system did not lack capable native employees. 'There are natives empowered to decide cases of any description,' he noted.[123] The problem therefore lay with the inability of judges in the lower court to appoint experienced and capable native employees. The discussion of the abilities of judges marked an important turning point in *Exposition*. So far, the discussion had been limited to the judicial administration of Bengal. Now, Rammohun shifted to a broader context: the impact of EIC policy on the administration of its territories in India. This context, he argued, 'merits the deepest consideration of the legislature' (House of Commons).[124]

Rammohun opined that the EIC's policy of sending judges to India at a young age was a faulty one. Rejecting the official line that civil servants acquired a knowledge of new languages more easily at a very young age, he compared the EIC's recruitment policy with that of Christian missionaries and observed that the latter were sent out to India 'at a mature age of 25–35 years' but nevertheless gained linguistic skills in 'two or three years' owing to their 'free communication with people'.[125] In this context, he suggested that 'no civil servant should be sent to India under 24 or at least 22 years of age'.[126] Further, the Company's decision to send very young men to India also led to other problems such as an 'indiscreet choice of native officers' which ultimately proved to be 'very injurious to the [native] community'.[127]

With characteristic boldness, Rammohun made the point that prior to sailing for India, prospective judges ought to qualify as lawyers and produce 'a certificate from an English professor of law' to prove their competence.[128] This would lead to a greater number of 'accurate decisions' and thus 'little need of appeals to revise decisions'.[129] In this context, *Exposition* quoted Blackstone's assertion that a judicial system which did not have qualified judges would only but bring 'contempt on itself'.[130]

Rammohun now turned his attention to the Privy Court of Appeals in London. From experience, he knew that translations from an 'oriental tongue and provincial language' to 'a European language' were more likely to be inaccurate. Consequently, judicial decisions based on them would be faulty. After sketching out this context in some detail, he proceeded to argue that the Court of Appeals at London ought to be relocated to Calcutta. He opined that a local Court of Appeals would take less time (a maximum of one year) and have access to better translations of key court documents. The creation of new posts for native employees to assist in translations could further streamline the process. The salaries for these posts would be paid from a fee by interested parties as a part of the appeals process (the non-payment of the fee would result in the appeal being quashed).[131]

Rammohun's final suggestion was regarding the lack of judicial accountability to the Bengali public. He suggested that court proceedings should be accessible to the public and that 'anyone should have the right to make notes and publish the same'.[132] This meant that court decisions could be debated and critiqued in newspapers and journals. He added that to prevent misuse, 'intentional errors' that could be judicially proved should be subject to prosecution.[133]

Rammohun's suggestions were a response to the problems of *the original system of the Permanent Settlement*. However, in 1830, the Company introduced radical changes.[134] His assessment of these new changes is the subject of the next section.

The Problems of Distance

Rammohun's response to the Company's changes to the Permanent Settlement in 1830 is best represented in his critique of the role of the judges in Bengal's provincial courts. Under the Permanent Settlement, provincial court judges had been important intermediaries between Sudder and district courts. This is because they held an additional position—judges on circuit. While on circuit, provincial court judges presided over cases involving the death penalty, life imprisonment, as well as general 'law and order'.[135] Their duties in circuit did not, however, cause any delays in the daily proceedings of provincial courts since there was always one judge 'in station' for every two on circuit.[136] However, in 1830, the EIC disbanded this system (henceforth referred as the '1830 measures').[137]

Provincial judges were not the only casualty of the 1830 measures. The entire administrative system in Bengal was overhauled with the creation of a new administrative position: revenue commissioner. Revenue commissioners took over the role of the judge and revenue collector respectively and combined them in a single post. Further, revenue commissioners were now answerable to the Board of Revenue (Sudder court) instead of the Provincial Court of Appeal (Sudder Diwani Adalat) at Calcutta.

The post of revenue commissioner led to major administrative problems. While at Calcutta, the lack of experience of the Board of Revenue (Sudder court) in judicial matters led to frequent delays and instances of 'appeals going twice over', in the districts, the 1830 measures created problems for Company officials because they had trained for careers in either the revenue service or the judiciary, but not both.[138] As Rammohun put it, '[Company officials] may now be appointed to discharge the highest judicial duties who never before tried the most trivial cause and another to superintend the collectors of revenue to whose duties he is a stranger.'[139] He pointed out that the chief consequence of revenue collectors going on circuit was that it not only hampered court affairs but revenue collection as well.[140]

There was, however, one significant aspect of the 1830 measures that Rammohun wholeheartedly agreed with—its policy on native employees. Post-1830, native employees were appointed to higher administrative posts such as Sudder Aumeen (chief judge of the district court).[141] This policy was a sharp departure from Cornwallis' regulations of 1793 which excluded all native employees from higher administrative posts.[142] In this context, he suggested changes to the post of Sudder Aumeen.

Administrative posts such as that of the Sudder Aumeen were crucial to Rammohun's argument about the suitability of native employees in higher bureaucracy. His discussion on the administrative responsibilities of this post also reveal his ideas on judicial accountability and accessibility. Under the current system, Sudder Aumeens were native employees who tried civil cases of up to 500 rupees.[143]

In *Exposition*, Rammohun attempted to expand the scope of responsibilities of Sudder Aumeen by insisting that they ought not be stationed at the same court as the judge but away from the district court, 'at proportionate distances', opining that this would render the judiciary more accessible to the natives.[144] However, this suggestion also led to a problem of accountability for Sudder Aumeens as there was no one to oversee their judicial work.[145] As a solution, he suggested that a new position of assistant judge be instituted as overseers.[146]

Rammohun conceptualized the assistant judge's post from the ground up. He stressed that their salaries would not lead to any extra expenditure since they would be paid from the proceeds of duties performed on land registration (in which all land deeds would now require to be presented to the court and registered for a fee). This was an inspired interpretation of the Permanent Settlement's Act of 1793 in which land registration had been optional. He suggested that it could now be made compulsory.[147] The assistant judge's role was also similar to that of the provincial judge under the Permanent Settlement. Under his proposed system, two assistant judges would be appointed for every district. While one would remain 'in station' at the district court, the other would be in charge of presiding over the work of the Sudder Aumeens in the districts.

The assistant judge's responsibilities extended beyond the court. They could receive complaints against police officers and forward the same to the magistrates since 'poor peasants' were unable to travel large distances to the district courts to seek redress.[148] This new role meant that the judiciary would have a greater engagement with the public than had been the case previously. Cases would only be forwarded to the district court judge if the assistant judge and Sudder Aumeen differed. This would reduce delays in court.

Apart from the Sudder Aumeen and the assistant judge, Rammohun proposed that district judges could be assisted by native 'assessors' to check documents and verify their contents.[149] Native assessors were to be appointed 'for life' and paid high salaries (300–400 rupees per month).[150] The native assessor was a powerful post as there was no official within the judiciary to act as a check on his power. In this context, he suggested that jurors drawn from Bengali society could be an important check on the native assessor.

Rammohun suggested that jurors may be selected from 'retired pleaders, retired native officers and agents employed by private individuals (*mukhtars*)' since they were familiar with judicial regulations and procedure.[151] A general list could be drawn up by judges from which 'thrice' the required number of jurors would be summoned. A lottery would then decide the final jury. Jurors who had any stake in the suit would be excluded from the final list of jury members.[152] Trial by jury was also his solution to the generic problem of an excessive dependence on native employees for judicial administration.

Bengali society would also have an important judicial role in a newly restructured Panchayat. Rammohun noted that unlike 'former times' the current system of Panchayat was ineffective and susceptible to 'private influence'.[153] As a solution, he suggested that a native judge and a European judge should be jointly appointed to direct its proceedings, and argued that the problem of 'private influence' could be resolved if Panchayat members were nominated by district judges. Panchayat members would also be jury members who advised the judge on all civil cases.

However, civil cases were held in Persian, a language which few natives understood. To render court proceedings more accessible, Rammohun suggested that court proceedings could be held in Bangla. He also opined that natives could familiarize themselves with the judicial process by having access to Bangla translations of the Company's current system of laws (regulations) which could be kept at all 'populous parts' of the town.[154] He predicted that the chief improvement brought about by the implementation of his suggestions would be less delays in the courts.[155]

In this context, Rammohun identified a problem. Even with Bangla translations, the Company's regulations were too dense and complicated for a jury. This applied to civil as well as criminal laws. Further, Company laws were organized on religious lines and this could be confusing for jurors.[156] As a solution, he suggested that the Company should employ 'persons thoroughly acquainted with Hindu and Muhammadan law' as well as 'principles of British law' to form a new code of civil and criminal laws.[157] This process of codification was conceptualized as a long-term process which would take 'many years'. The code of civil and criminal laws would be 'clear, precise and written in current language', a 'standard of justice' by itself which did not require any additional explanation from any particular text.[158] He did not, however, specify the details of what the code would contain. Instead, his focus was the process in which it could be formulated.

Rammohun opined that the current process of law-making adopted by the EIC was faulty. Laws originated as regulations drawn up by officials in the districts and approved by the Governor General.[159] The process of law-making was characterized by 'want of local knowledge' at the stage of framing the regulation itself. Consequently, most laws were found 'not to answer in practice'.[160] He suggested a new system in which laws would be enacted in the same way as an Act of Parliament in Britain where laws were discussed by 'the King, Lords and Commons' before being enacted.[161] This did not mean that he was proposing an identical system in India. Rather, by introducing his suggestions in terms that his readers would be familiar with, he was setting the context for *his argument* for making the Company's administration accountable to Bengali society.

Rammohun argued that in the case of India, Company regulations 'should be debated and discussed amongst persons who will be affected by them'. These included head native officers of the Board of Revenue (Sudder Dewani Adalat) as well as 'highly respectable' merchants and 'principal zamindars' of Bengal. A copy of these communications would be sent by the Company to the Court of Directors and a 'standing committee of the House of Commons' for 'confirmation and amendment'. Only after this process would a proposed regulation become law.[162]

Rammohun's suggestions identified potential local centres of power in Bengal (such as zamindars, merchants, and head native officers in revenue and judicial service) and underscored the critical importance of parliamentary intervention in framing law.[163] His suggestions for the Panchayat as an independent jury was an attempt to create local forms of accountable governance. In time, however, he hoped that his suggestions would lead to a new form of government in Bengal which did not require the Company to 'stand isolated in the midst of its subjects supporting itself merely by the exertion of superior force'.[164] The importance of participation and role of natives and native employees in Bengal was thus explained to readers in the distant but important city of London.

***

Conclusion

Exposition argued that the Company could be made accountable to the natives of India by creating new local centres of power manned by native employees and called for a policy in which the Company could govern Bengal effectively with help from its Bengali subjects and native employees. A marked emphasis on geographical distance and governmental accountability formed the core of this argument. 'I have kept in view the interests of the governors and the governed,' Rammohun wrote, 'without losing sight of a just regard to economy. I have been actuated by a desire to see the administration of justice in India placed on a solid and permanent foundation.'[165]

Rammohun's suggestions on Company governance articulated a basic point: that natives have a role in their own governance in Bengal. This does not mean that he was against *any* intervention from London. He argued that intervention from London was an important preventive measure against Company officials in India ('local government'). He noted that Company bosses in London should be aware of 'any regulations or orders in judicial or revenue matters' framed by the 'local government' in Bengal.[166] His critique of the 1830 measures is a case in point. By arguing that the measures constituted bad governance, he strongly implied that the Company bosses in London repeal them.[167]

Rammohun also presented an economical argument. To this extent, the appendix to *Exposition* cited records of financial accounts of the Company and showed that the new system of restructured administration would not involve any additional expenditure but rather save greater amounts of money.[168] This was a realistic project.

Exposition championed the role of the native employee in the Company and reinterpreted their roles as new centres of power, critical to his project of securing governmental accountability. Native employees were seen as potential jurors, members of the Panchayat, and members of the public who could critique Company policy in Bengal. Rammohun argued that native employees should be in 'places of authority and trust in government' (as he reminded his readers, administrators were in Britain).[169]

Rammohun's argument about the centrality of native employees in the EIC was also influenced by his own association with the Bengal revenue administration from 1802 to 1814. For the most part, his association was based on a personal acquaintance with collectors rather than bureaucratic eligibility requirements. This was not unusual. As the next chapter will show, the late 18th and early 19th century was a period of fluid networks of communication between native employees and collectors, of an excessive dependence on native employees for everyday administrative tasks, and an unwillingness by Company officials at Calcutta to engage or regulate native employees in the districts. Rammohun's ideas of the native employees in *Exposition* were based on a historical context.

Notes

1. Zastoupil, *Rammohun Roy*, 144. Reformers as well as Conservatives were oft surprised by Rammohun's understanding of British politics.
2. Amar Farooqui, 'Governance, Corporate Interest and Colonialism: The Case of the East India Company', *Social Scientist* 35, no. 9/10 (September 2007): 48.
3. Muzaffar Alam and Sanjay Subrahmanyam, *Writing in the Mughal World* (New York: Columbia University Press, 2011), 436.
4. Secretary to Government to Resident of Delhi, 5 December 1806, Rajah Rammohun Roy and the Last Moghuls: A Selection of Documents, ed. J.K. Majumdar (Calcutta: Art Press, 1939), 52. Henceforth, RRLM.
5. Secretary to Government to Resident of Delhi, 5 December 1806, *RRLM*, 52.
6. Michael H. Fisher, 'The Imperial Coronation of 1819: Awadh, the British and the Mughals', *Modern Asian Studies* 19, no. 2 (1985): 239.
7. Secretary to Government to Resident at Delhi, 5 December 1806, *RRLM*, 51.
8. Resident at Delhi to Secretary to Government, 19 February 1807, *RRLM*, 62.
9. Persian Secretary to Government to Resident at Delhi, 8 March 1809, *RRLM*, 85.
10. Persian Secretary to Government to Resident at Delhi, 8 March 1809, *RRLM*, 86.
11. Governor-General in Council to the Court of Directors, 1 August 1809, *RRLM*, 121.
12. Secretary to Government to Resident at Delhi, 3 September 1813, *RRLM*, 142.
13. Secretary to Government to Resident at Delhi, 3 September 1813, *RRLM*, 142–45.
14. Fisher, 'The Imperial Coronation of 1819', 251.
15. Fisher, 'The Imperial Coronation of 1819', 241.
16. Persian Secretary to Government to the King of Delhi, 27 July 1827, *RRLM*, 171.
17. Douglas M. Peers, 'Between Mars and Mammon: The East India Company and Efforts to Reform Its Army, 1796–1832', *The Historical Journal* 33, no. 2 (1990): 389.
18. King of Delhi to Rammohun Roy, 26 March 1830, *RRLM*, 331.
19. Sophia Dobson Collet, *The Life and Letters of Raja Rammohan Roy*. ed. Dilip Kumar Biswas and Prabhat Chandra Ganguli (Calcutta: Sadharan Brahmo Samaj, 1962 [1900]).
20. Officiating Secretary to the Lieutenant Governor of the North-western Provinces to the Political Secretary to the Government [Enclosure 5: Dwarkanath Tagore's Memorandum on the distribution of the Allowance to the King of Delhi], 8 April 1837, *RRLM*, 248.

21. Governor-General in Council to the Court of Directors, 14 October 1830, *RRLM*, 210–11. See also Brajendranath Banerji, *Rammohun Roy's Mission to England: Based on Unpublished Records* (Calcutta: N.M. Raychowdhury and Co., 1926), 11.

22. Banerji, *Rammohun Roy's Mission to England*, 1–23.

23. Zastoupil, *Rammohun Roy*, 144.

24. Amal Home, 'Rammohun Roy: The story of his life: Supplementary Notes' in *Rammohun Roy: The Man and His Work*, ed. Amal Home (Calcutta: Art Press, 1933).

25. Julian Hoppit, 'Introduction', in *Parliaments, Nations and Identities in Britain and Ireland, 1660–1850* (Manchester: Manchester University Press, 2003), 5.

26. Eric J. Evans, *Parliamentary Reform in Britain c.1770–1918* (London: Routledge, 2014), 18.

27. Aidt and Franck, 'Democratization under the Threat of Revolution: Evidence from the Great Reform Act of 1832', *Econometrica* 83, no. 2 (April 2015): 515.

28. Evans, *Parliamentary Reform in Britain*, 7.

29. Ellis Wasson, 'The Spirit of Reform', *Albion: A Quarterly Journal Concerned with British Studies* 12, no. 2 (Summer 1980): 165.

30. Aidt and Franck, 'Democratization under the Threat of Revolution', 517.

31. Nag and Burman (eds), *EW*, 4: 118–22.

32. Zastoupil, *Rammohun Roy*, 2–5.

33. J.K. Majumdar, 'Introduction', *RRLM*, lviii. Rammohun was not, however, happy with only a partial increase. He would have challenged it in Parliament, had it not been for his untimely death.

34. Home, 'Supplementary Notes', 58.

35. Home, 'Supplementary Notes', 58.

36. Home, 'Supplementary Notes', 63.

37. Home, 'Supplementary Notes', 63.

38. Home, 'Supplementary Notes', 63.

39. Jon Wilson, *The Domination of Strangers: Modern Governance in Eastern India, 1780–1835* (London: Palgrave Macmillan, 2008), 12.

40. Nag and Burman (eds), *EW*, 4: 113–14.

41. Dilip Kumar Biswas, *Rammohun Samikha* [A Survey of Rammohun's Writings] (Calcutta: Saraswat Library, 1960), 451–6.

42. Nag and Burman (eds), *EW*, 4: 113–14.

43. Biswas, *Rammohan Samikha*, 451.

44. Biswas, *Rammohan Samikha*, 452.

45. Biswas, *Rammohun Samikha*, 453–4.

46. Biswas, *Rammohun Samikha*, 454.

47. Collet, *Rammohun Roy*, 206; Singh, *Rammohun Roy*, 4; Sen, *Rammohun Roy*, i.

48. Lobban, 'Blackstone and the Science of the Law', 311–17.

49. Petition presented by Charles Wynn in the House of Commons, 4 May 1830, Joseph Hume Papers, University College London Library [hereafter, UCL].

50. Nag and Burman (eds), *EW*, 4: 105.

51. Unknown Author, Remarks on the Salt Monopoly of Bengal and reports from the Board of Customs, 1832, Joseph Hume Papers, UCL.

52. Miles Taylor, 'Joseph Hume and the Reformation of India, 1819–33', in *English Radicalism 1550–1850*, eds. Glenn Burgess and Matthew Festenstein (Cambridge: Cambridge University Press, 2007), 288. Hume had been employed as interpreter of Indian languages in the Company's army in Madras and Bengal.

53. 'Admission of Natives of India to Offices, Evidence of William Chaplin, commissioner of the Deccan before the Lord's Committee on East India Affairs, 30th March, 1830', in *The Asiatic Journal and Monthly Register for British and Foreign India, China and Australasia* 9, New Series (September– December 1832): 103.

54. 'Admission of Natives', 103.

55. William Foster, 'James Mill in Leadenhall Street, 1819–1836', *Scottish Historical Review* 10, no. 38 (January 1913): 162–73. For the friendship between Hume and Mill, see Leslie Stephen, *The English Utilitarians*, 3 vols (London, 1900).

56. Huw Bowen, *The Business of Empire: The East India Company and Imperial Britain, 1756–1833* (Cambridge: Cambridge University Press, 2006), 193.

57. James Mill, *Selected Economic Writings*, ed. Donald Winch (Chicago: Chicago University Press, 1966), 383–96.

58. *Minutes of Evidence taken before the Select Committee of the House of Commons on the Affairs of the East India Company, Feb. 28th to July 9th, Part IV, Judicial* (London, 1833), 163.

59. *Minutes of Evidence Taken before the Select Committee of the House of Commons on the Affairs of the East India Company in the Last Session of Parliament and also the Accounts and Papers Laid Before the Said Committee* (London, 1831), 725.

60. William, Howitt, 'The English in India' [c.1839], Wilson Anti-Slavery Collection, The John Rylands University Library Manchester [hereafter, JRL].

61. A.B., 'On the consequences of the probable changes of the renewal of the Charter of the East India Company' [c.1833], Joseph Hume Papers, UCL.

62. A.B., 'Letters demonstrating the benefits and conveniences of local courts for probate of wills in preference to concentration in London' [c.1834], Joseph Hume Papers, UCL.

63. George Thompson, 'Present state of British India: Report of a Lecture' [c.1840], Wilson Anti-Slavery Collection, JRL. In 1844, George Thompson

would be employed by Dwarkanath Tagore and Akbar II to represent the latter's claims for a higher pension in London.

64. Francis Horsley Robinson, 'What good may come out of the India bill: or, notes of what has been, is, and may be, the Government of India' [c.1853], Knowsley Pamphlet Collection, University of Liverpool [henceforth, UL].

65. *The East India Registry and Directory for 1823* (London, 1823), xliv.

66. Roy, *Exposition*, xvi.

67. Roy, *Exposition*, v–vii.

68. Roy, *Exposition*, v.

69. Roy, *Exposition*, vii–viii.

70. Roy, *Exposition*, vii–viii.

71. Roy, *Exposition*, vii–viii.

72. Roy, *Exposition*, vii.

73. Chapter 4 discusses the relationship between Rammohun's concept of empire and MDhS references to large territories and administrations knit by diverse cultural practices in greater detail.

74. John D. Derrett, *Essays in Classical and Modern Hindu Law*, vol. 1 (Leiden: EJ Brill, 1976), 1–2.

75. Roy, *Exposition*, vi.

76. Roy, *Exposition*, vi.

77. Roy, *Exposition*, viii.

78. Roy, *Exposition*, ix.

79. Roy, *Exposition*, ix.

80. Roy, *Exposition*, ix.

81. Jonathan Parry, *The Politics of Patriotism: English Liberalism, National Identity and Europe, 1830–1886* (Cambridge: Cambridge University Press, 2006), 49–50.

82. Parry, *The Politics of Patriotism*, 49–50.

83. Christopher Bayly, *Origins of Nationality in South Asia: Patriotism and the Making of Modern India* (Delhi: Oxford University Press, 1998), 14.

84. The concept of the 'public' and the 'public sphere' in recent historiography is referred to in detail in the third chapter.

85. Roy, *Exposition*, x.

86. Roy, *Exposition*, x.

87. Roy, *Exposition*, x.

88. Roy, *Exposition*, xi.

89. Jacob Thiessen, 'Anglo Indian Vested Interests and Civil Service Education, 1800–1858: Indications of an East India Company Line', *Journal of World History* 5, no. 1 (1994): 29.

90. Thiessen, 'Anglo Indian Vested Interests', 29.

91. Roy, *Exposition*, xii.

92. Roy, *Exposition*, xii.
93. Roy, *Exposition*, xiii.
94. Roy, *Exposition*, xiii.
95. Roy, *Exposition*, xiii.
96. Roy, *Exposition*, xiv.
97. Roy, *Exposition*, xiii.
98. Roy, *Exposition*, xiii.
99. Roy, *Exposition*, 7.
100. Roy, *Exposition*, 6.
101. Roy, *Exposition*, 3.
102. Roy, *Exposition*, 2.
103. Roy, *Exposition*, 6.
104. Roy, *Exposition*, 26.
105. Roy, *Exposition*, 26.
106. Roy, *Exposition*, 3.
107. Roy, *Exposition*, 114.
108. Roy, *Exposition*, 39.
109. Roy, *Exposition*, 9.
110. Roy, *Exposition*, 39.
111. Roy, *Exposition*, 31.
112. Roy, *Exposition*, 31.
113. Roy, *Exposition*, 3.
114. Roy, *Exposition*, 30.
115. Roy, *Exposition*, 30.
116. Roy, *Exposition*, 34.
117. Roy, *Exposition*, 34.
118. Roy, *Exposition*, 34.
119. Roy, *Exposition*, 34.
120. Roy, *Exposition*, 11.
121. Roy, *Exposition*, 8.
122. Roy, *Exposition*, 8.
123. Roy, *Exposition*, 10.
124. Roy, *Exposition*, 45.
125. Roy, *Exposition*, 46.
126. Roy, *Exposition*, 45.
127. Roy, *Exposition*, 47.
128. Roy, *Exposition*, 48
129. Roy, *Exposition*, 48.
130. Roy, *Exposition*, 114.
131. Roy, *Exposition*, 37.
132. Roy, *Exposition*, 35.

133. Roy, *Exposition*, 35.
134. Roy, *Exposition*, 29.
135. Roy, *Exposition*, 27.
136. Roy, *Exposition*, 27.
137. Roy, *Exposition*, 29.
138. Roy, *Exposition*, 38.
139. Roy, *Exposition*, 29.
140. Roy, *Exposition*, 28
141. John Rosselli, *Lord William Bentinck: The Making of a Liberal Imperialist 1774–1839* (London: Sussex University Press, 1974), 265. For a broader view of this policy on the history of 19th-century India, see Hugh Tinker, *South Asia: A Short History* (London: University of Hawaii Press, 1966), 153.
142. Rosselli, *Lord William Bentinck*, 266.
143. Roy, *Exposition*, 17.
144. Roy, *Exposition*, 17.
145. Section two of this chapter is based on this subject.
146. Roy, *Exposition*, 18.
147. Roy, *Exposition*, 19.
148. Roy, *Exposition*, 20.
149. Roy, *Exposition*, 18.
150. Roy, *Exposition*, 15.
151. Roy, *Exposition*, 22–4.
152. Roy, *Exposition*, 23.
153. Roy, *Exposition*, 24.
154. Roy, *Exposition*, 16.
155. Roy, *Exposition*, 23.
156. Roy, *Exposition*, 49.
157. Roy, *Exposition*, 43.
158. Roy, *Exposition*, 43.
159. Roy, *Exposition*, 49.
160. Roy, *Exposition*, 49.
161. Roy, *Exposition*, 49.
162. Roy, *Exposition*, 50.
163. Roy, *Exposition*, 51.
164. Roy, *Exposition*, 51.
165. Roy, *Exposition*, 153.
166. Roy, *Exposition*, 28.
167. Roy, *Exposition*, 28.
168. Roy, *Exposition*, 55.
169. Roy, *Exposition*, 54.

2   The East India Company and Its Native Employees

*E*xposition made a strong case for a new form of governance in Bengal in which the native employee would have a key role.[1] This chapter argues that the historical context of this argument is Rammohun's association with the EIC's district administration from 1804 to 1814. The argument is organized in two sections. The first section teases out and elaborates upon the discursive connections between his early association with the EIC and later ideas in *Exposition*; while the second section places his arguments concerning native employees within a larger framework of the EIC's administration in the late 18th and early 19th century.

Rammohun's Association with the EIC

Rammohun opined that native employees were critical to the functioning of the EIC's administration.[2] *Exposition* even asserted that the Company had inherited an administrative service from pre-colonial governments than created an official cadre on its own, thus implying that more natives (who were trained in such forms of governance) ought to be employed.[3] The argument emerges more clearly by reading his 'autobiographical sketch' (published in 1832):

> My ancestors were Brahmins of a high order [who] about a hundred and forty years ago gave up spiritual exercises for worldly pursuit ... and according to the usual fate of couriers with various success sometimes rising to honour and sometimes falling; sometimes rich and sometimes poor; sometimes excelling in success and sometimes miserable in disappointment.[4]

Rammohun's references to the changing fortunes of his family not only highlight the uncertainty, dynamism, and rapid changes involved in a career in early modern courts but also underline the historicity of his claim.[5] In fact, the earliest evidence of his family's association with courtly administration is that of his great-grandfather, Parasuram Bannerjee. Parasuram had been employed by the Nawabs of Bengal as the Roy Rayan (chief revenue accountant). He was even given the title 'Roy' in recognition of his scribal work.[6] As Kumkum Chatterjee has shown, such titles were only given after a prior familial association in high bureaucracy.[7] Following Chatterjee, we conclude that his family had been involved with the Nawabi court even before Parasuram.

Parasuram's son, Krishnachandra, succeeded him as Roy Rayan and adopted 'Roy' as the family's surname. Krishnachandra's son (and Rammohun's grandfather), Brojobinode Roy, was not only a Roy Rayan but also associated with the court of Mughal Emperor Shah Alam II.[8] As Roy Rayans, Rammohun's great-grandfather and grandfather earned enough to invest in real estate in Radhanagar (then a small village on the banks of the river Kana-Darakeshwar in the district of Burdwan) and settle down in the area.[9] Rammohun was born in the Roy ancestral home at Radhanagar.[10]

The Roy's intergenerational association with Nawabi bureaucracy was not uncommon in early modern Bengal. Rather, they can be seen as representative examples of elite scribal Hindu families whose professional lives centred on Perso-Arabic intellectual culture.[11] Rammohun's autobiographical sketch also provides some critical evidence to support this hypothesis by referring to 'an education in the Arabic and Persian languages—these being indispensable to those who attached themselves to the courts of Mohameddan princes'.[12]

I argue that Rammohun's education also reveals his affiliation with the Hindu scribal community of Bengal. My argument is based on Kumkum Chatterjee's research on the subject of scribal communities. According to Chatterjee, Hindu scribal communities had been employed by early modern courts in Bengal since the 13th century. Its members included 'Baidyas, Kayasthas and also Brahmins who played extremely important roles in manning middle and lower level bureaucratic offices'.[13] By the late 18th century, after nearly 500 years of intergenerational employment, these scribal communities had even developed into a caste by themselves.[14]

However, it would be a mistake to assume that all of Rammohun's family was involved in the courts of Murshidabad. A notable exception was his father, Ramakanta Roy. Ramakanta's main interests were in real estate and revenue farming.[15] He left the Roy ancestral home in Radhanagar in 1791, settled down in the nearby village of Langarpura, and lived there until 1800.[16] During this period, he trained Rammohun and his elder brother, Jagmohun, in revenue administration and collection.[17] Though we are not entirely sure of Rammohun's whereabouts between 1792 and 1795, it is very likely that he was learning about property-related matters from his father.[18]

Ramakanta's tutelage yielded managerial dividends. From 1796 to 1798, Rammohun himself managed Ramakanta's zamindari properties in the Bhursut *pargana* (district) and also travelled to Burdwan, Calcutta, and Langarpura to deal with property matters on his father's behalf.[19]

Ramakanta also drew up a will in 1796. Unusually for the time, he even gave away most of his assets to his heirs while he was still alive.[20] Although some scholars believe that Rammohun and his father did not get along and that he was disinherited, historical evidence does not support this view at all.[21] Indeed, Rammohun inherited his father's estates in Langarpura, Krishnanagar, Calcutta, and Gopinathpura on the condition that he make monetary contributions for the upkeep of the family idol in the Roy ancestral home.[22] His letters to his father reveal that he not only agreed to pay towards the maintenance of the idol but also kept in touch with him afterwards.[23] In 1799, he transitioned from a manager of his father's properties to a businessman in his own right. That year, he bought two valuable properties in Burdwan which yielded an annual income of 5,000 rupees.[24]

Ramakanta began to face grave financial difficulties just as Rammohun's business was taking off.[25] Around c.1797, Ramakanta had become the manager (*mukhtar*) of the lands of Rani Vishnu Devi of Burdwan.[26] A *mukhtar* was a position of power, status, and privilege. However, Ramakanta lost his influence after Vishnu Devi died and her son, Maharaja Tejchand, took over her estates. In 1800, Tejchand demanded almost 80,000 rupees in pending taxes from him.[27] Things went from bad to worse from this point on as Ramakanta defaulted on the amount and was sentenced to the Hooghly jail. He was able to secure his release only after signing a written undertaking that the amount would be paid back within 11 years.[28]

Rammohun was away on business in Patna and Benares when Ramakanta's incarceration took place, but he was back in Calcutta in c.1801 to invest in the city's burgeoning paper and moneylending business.[29] Both investments were spectacularly successful. Curiously enough, for reasons which are not entirely clear, he refused to monetarily support his father and was estranged from his family soon afterwards. Upon Ramakanta's death in 1803, he even performed his funerary rites (*sraddho*) separately from his family.[30] He, however, continued to refuse to get involved in the repayment of his father's debts. That responsibility was taken up by his brother, Jagmohun, in 1804.[31] Unfortunately, Jagmohun too went bankrupt and was sentenced to the Midnapore jail.[32] His situation in jail was so dire that Tarini Devi, his mother, had to grant him 10 rupees a month for his sustenance.[33]

Rammohun's attitude towards Jagmohun was rather strange. In 1805, he loaned him a 1000 rupees and demanded that the total amount be paid back with interest, knowing fully well that his brother was bankrupt and in jail.[34] Jagmohun never could pay back the loan and died in 1812.[35] After 1812, Rammohun became the eldest male member of the family.[36] From this point on, Ramakanta's chief creditor, Maharaja Tejchand, attempted to recover the money due by filing an (unsuccessful) judicial suit against Rammohun at the Trial Court of Calcutta. The case, however, dragged on till 1831 as Tejchand also filed an (unsuccessful) suit at the Provincial Court of Appeal.[37]

Rammohun relocated to Murshidabad in late 1803 in pursuit of gainful employment in the Nawabi courts.[38] He would have hoped to secure the lucrative position of Roy Rayan, like Brojobinode and Krishnachandra before him. His managerial experiences with Ramakanta as well as his own real estate business would have made him a formidable candidate indeed. Unfortunately, he could not find any satisfactory employment with the Nawabs.[39] Luckily for him, there was another potential employer available for a man with his education and experience—the East India Company.

By the early 19th century, the EIC had emerged from a 'small collective' of mercantile interests in London to one of the most powerful territorial polities in the world.[40] In eastern India alone, it held sway over a population of more than 30 million.[41] To keep up with the demands of governance, the Company engaged in a major expansion of its revenue and judicial services in Bengal. While the EIC had only employed around 80 officials in Bengal in the 1740s, its cadre had swelled to nearly 300 by the turn of the century.[42] Company bosses in London even considered their officials in India to be merchant-cum-civil administrators who collected revenue, administered justice, and helped draft official policy.[43]

The EIC at London, however, did 'very little' by the way of training Company men for a career in India.[44] Instead, the Company employed a large number of native scribes to help officials in everyday governance.[45] This is because their knowledge of Persian (the language of administration, revenue, judiciary, and commercial transactions) made them indispensable to the administration.[46] Scribes were also employed privately as language teachers (*munshis*) by Company officials to aid them in deciphering Persian revenue and judicial documents.[47] This dependence led to a fluid and informal network of association between Company officials and their scribes in matters of employment under the Company. As Frederick Lehmann, P.J. Marshall, and Subhas Mukhopadhay's research on late-18th-century native employment showed, the eligibility of Kalyan Singh, Shitab Singh, Rai Durlabh, Raj Ballabh, Ganga Govind Singh, and Prankrishen Singh to high posts such as Naib dewan, dewan, and Roy Rayan was due to their personal association with Company officials and the scribal backgrounds of their families rather than any specific bureaucratic eligibility criterion.[48]

The EIC was, however, wary of the dependency of its officials on scribes and *munshis*. Responding to the need for Company officials to undergo some form of administrative training as well as be well-versed in non-Western languages, Governor General Richard Wellesley founded the Fort William College in 1800.[49] Between 1800 and 1802, the college opened Persian, Arabic, Hindustani, and Bangla Departments. This stress on languages was not unanimously welcomed by the British mercantile elite; and old Company hands at Calcutta and London were divided over its value for business and profit. Wellesley, however, was not a businessman but a statesman who was interested in politics and governance; and ultimately, his views prevailed.[50]

At Fort William College, all students were provided with a lavish monthly salary and expected to clear two examinations every year.[51] Students would have to clear papers in Hindu and Muslim laws, EIC regulations, political economy, geography, mathematics, modern European languages, Greek, Latin, the English classics, general history (both ancient and modern), the history of antiquities of Hindustan and the Deccan, botany, chemistry, and astronomy.[52] However, in spite of the rigorous plan of coursework, the college's effectiveness was limited since its students continued to depend on *munshis*. For example, early graduates such as Charles Metcalfe and James Princep learnt Persian under *munshis*.[53] Metcalfe, in particular, was critical of the college's cur-riculum as an aid to district administration. On the other hand, he had 'a soft corner' for his *munshi*.[54] In time, another early graduate of the college, John Digby, would employ Rammohun as a *munshi*.[55] Under Digby, Rammohun would begin to cultivate reading and writing skills in the English language.[56]

John Digby enrolled in the Fort William College in 1800 to learn Persian, Bangla, and Hindustani.[57] Unlike Metcalfe, Digby had no talent for Indian languages. A brief survey of his student records at Fort William College underscores this point. His first exam in 1801 in Hindustani placed him in the 'lowest class'.[58] (An indication of the very poor standards of the 'lowest class' was its peculiar ranking system. Candidates were ranked in the alphabetical order of their names in the lowest class but in terms of their performance in the examinations in the first, second, and third classes.) The next year marked an improvement. Digby was ranked on the basis of his performance, but he was 11th of

12 candidates in Bangla.[59] Persian proved to be his greatest challenge. In 1803, he sat for the Persian examinations in January and July. He was ranked 49th in a class of 53 in January and at the bottom of his class in July.[60] Although his performance in Persian improved by the time of his final year of examinations (securing the 32nd rank), it can be surmised that he would still require the help of an experienced *munshi*.[61]

While Digby was struggling with his Persian examinations, Rammohun gained some experience as a *munshi* when Thomas Woodforde (the register of the appellate court of Murshidabad) employed him in 1802. Rammohun knew Woodforde in the capacity of a client of his money-lending business. He had lent him 5,000 rupees that year.[62] In 1803, Woodforde appointed him the dewan of Decca–Jelalpur after being appointed as acting collector.[63] However, he resigned after Woodforde left the Company.[64] The instance of a *munshi* being absorbed into Company service highlights the lack of bureaucratic eligibility requirements for the highest native post in the districts, and the swift resignation shows that native employees were attached to the person of the Company official and their careers were affected likewise.[65]

Digby graduated from Fort William College in 1804 and employed Rammohun as his *munshi* soon afterwards.[66] In 1805, Digby also appointed him the acting *sheristedar* (Deputy of the dewan) of the Faujdari court of Ramgarh for three months.[67] This proved to be a turning point since it gave him the opportunity to demonstrate his skills in revenue accounting as well as his familiarity with the Company's regulations.[68] By the end of 1808, Digby was convinced that he was eligible for the dewan's post.[69]

Digby's opportunity to appoint Rammohun as dewan came only a few months later when he was transferred to Rangpur as acting collector in 1809.[70] Rangpur was an important posting. Its economic importance lay in its trade of tobacco and opium.[71] For this reason, Governors General from Hastings to Cornwallis had been keen on improving trade relations with the neighbouring countries of Bhutan and Nepal.[72] Although a frontier district, it had been at the centre stage of Company politics in the late 18th century due to its unfavourable geo-political climate. Bordered by the unfriendly zamindaris of Cooch Behar and Dinajpur, Rangpur had been the site of peasant rebellions in 1783.[73] The rebellions were considered to be a serious threat by Company officials and even debated in Parliament during the impeachment proceedings against Warren Hastings as a case of over-reach and misgovernance by the Company.[74]

Digby was formally appointed collector in October 1809 and appointed Rammohun as dewan the very next month.[75] In accordance with Company procedure, Digby informed the Board of Revenue at Calcutta of the appointment thus:

> Having accepted the resignation of Ghulam Shah, late dewan of this office I have appointed Rammohun Roy in his room, a man of a very respectable family and excellent education; fully competent to discharge the duties of such an office, and from a long acquaintance with him I have reason to suppose that he will acquit himself in the capacity of the dewan.[76]

Ghulam Shah's resignation also demonstrated the continuing occurrence of the dewans being attached to the Company man in the districts than being subject to any official policies outlined by the bureaucracy in Calcutta. So, it was not unusual that Rammohun's appointment as dewan was as much a result of his education as his informal association with Digby.

The Board, however, rejected Rammohun's appointment by citing his lack of bureaucratic experience.[77] Annoyed, Digby wrote about his prior appointment in Ramgarh for three months and stressed the importance of personal association as the main criterion for employment as dewan.[78] Digby was not behind the times as far as official convention and policy on this matter was concerned. Just a month earlier, the Board had received a petition from a former native employee echoing a similar argument.[79] And a few months before that, in April 1809, the Board had informed the Governor General's Council that the collector of the neighbouring district of Dinajpur will exercise his own choice in the appointment of the dewan.[80]

However, in Rammohun's case, the Board did not accept Digby's choice but recommended the appointment of another dewan. Burrish Crisp, the acting president of the Board, even authored a note on how Rammohun did not apparently possess the requisite eligibility criterion for the post.[81] Crisp was an important voice in Company administration. A child prodigy in Persian, he had found employment with the Company at 15.[82] Initially appointed in 1774 with the strong recommendation of Warren Hastings, Crisp had quickly worked his way up the official ladder into the Sudder Dewani Adalat in Calcutta.[83] Interestingly, he also had very definite views regarding native employees. For instance, in 1811, he rejected any possibility of a re-establishment of an old native employee post *kanungo* (revenue accountant).[84]

Digby, however, had no intention of taking Crisp's views seriously. Instead, he continued to employ Rammohun in the Rangpur Collectorate as dewan for the next six years, until his furlough in 1814. Cheekily, he even informed the Board of Revenue that their orders had been disobeyed only on the eve of his departure for England. The Board reproved Digby and strongly recommended that their choice of dewan must be followed henceforth.[85]

But the question is: why did the Board of Revenue reject Rammohun's appointment? In his revised edition of Sophia Collet's classic biography, Dilip Kumar Biswas argued that his appointment was rejected as malicious payback for petitioning against the powerful collector of Bhagalpur, Sir Frederick Hamilton.[86] Biswas opined that Hamilton belonged to a clique in the Board of Revenue that took revenge by blocking his appointment. While Biswas refers to the writings of Rammohun's friend Col. James Young for this information, we note that Young had no specific experience of the case.[87] There is, however, a context for the argument that Hamilton may have had powerful allies in the Government at Calcutta. He was a hereditary Scottish peer and would have been in India for 13 years by 1809.[88]

To explain why this chapter does not agree with Biswas's interpretation and how this has a bearing on the broader argument of the centrality of the native employee in Rammohun's political thought, we revisit the case.

In April 1809, Rammohun petitioned Governor General Lord Minto against Hamilton.[89] In response, Hamilton produced his own version of events.[90] Both agreed that the complaint concerned a specific incident earlier that year when Rammohun's *palki* (palanquin) had passed by Hamilton without acknowledgement, but their accounts of what happened next differed.

In his petition to Minto, Rammohun claimed that he had not seen Hamilton as his *palki* passed and would not have recognized him as the collector of the district even if he had. He, however, heard 'gross abuse' from him.[91] On hearing the 'abuse', the *palki* stopped and his *palki*-bearer explained to Hamilton that the mistake had been unintentional.[92] The *palki* then continued for 'about 300 yards' before Hamilton overtook it 'on horseback' and demanded to be saluted in 'Mughal style' (prostration).[93] Hamilton left soon after Rammohun saluted him.[94] The 'Mughal style' salute was deeply humiliating for him since it affected his self-esteem 'in the eyes of the natives' (in this case, his *palki*-bearers). He complained that such behaviour on the part of a Company official reflected the failure of the 'liberal policy' of the British government.

Hamilton's account did not contain any reference to the salute. It also related a different version of events. In this version, Rammohun had at first deliberately ridden past and then sent one of his *palki*-bearers to salute him.[95] Hamilton interpreted this as a slight and confronted Rammohun with a 'reproach' and a warning of the future *possibility* of 'abuse' from other Company officials.[96] On being informed that neither Rammohun nor the *palki*-bearer had recognized him, Hamilton politely recommended the *palki*-bearer's dismissal but was instead confronted with unprovoked anger ('Should I cut off the servant's [*palki*-bearer's] ears?')[97]

Hamilton's account presents a reversal of roles from Rammohun's account in which Hamilton (and not Rammohun) had been the recipient of Rammohun's (and not Hamilton's) unprovoked anger and that Hamilton (and not Rammohun) had tried to diffuse the situation. The reversal of roles also shows that both accounts were written with different *intentions*.

In this context, the inclusion of specific (but not overlapping) additional information in both accounts helps decipher the authorial intention of each. Hamilton alleged that Rammohun had filed an unsuccessful suit on the incident at the Supreme Court in Calcutta. This information was not present in Rammohun's account.[98] In this case, Hamilton's reference to an alleged Supreme Court case can be read as an attempt to nullify the impact or implications of the case altogether. Similarly, Rammohun's account of the humiliating 'Mughal style salute' placed a seemingly isolated event on a much larger canvas of the EIC's attitude towards native employees by strategically pitting Hamilton's misbehaviour against contemporary British political terminology ('liberal policy').[99] This is the earliest example that we find of this strategy. The rest of the book shows the development of this core idea into a sophisticated programme of reform in later writings.

An unintentional impetus to the success of Rammohun's strategy was the discovery made by the Governor General's office that Hamilton had lied about the allegedly unsuccessful Supreme Court suit. Consequently, the government issued an advisory to the magistrate of Bhagalpur to 'caution Sir Frederick Hamilton against any similar altercation with any natives in future'.[100] This advisory was a leap in judgement since the discovery of the lie did not contradict his story about the incident concerning Rammohun's *palki*. The government was, therefore, quite certain that Hamilton had been at fault. If Hamilton had indeed been a part of a powerful faction then the Governor General's office ought to have favoured his case.

But why was Rammohun's account believed over Hamilton's? An important clue may be found in the information contained in both accounts about Rammohun's background and association with the Company. Rammohun's account stressed that he was a part of an *older* tradition of courtly employment in administration.[101] Hamilton's account had also provided some information on Rammohun by inaccurately identifying him as Digby's dewan.[102] This gave the impression that Rammohun was not only a member of the old Hindu elite scribal community in Bengal but also a native employee.

Additionally, there may have been an important precedent to Calcutta's swift decision in favour of Rammohun. At least one other native employee petition against Hamilton had been received by the government in Calcutta by the time of Rammohun's petition. In May 1805, the native employees of the Bhagalpur collectorate had successfully petitioned the Governor General's Council against their dismissal by Hamilton.[103] However, the crucial difference between Rammohun and the native petitioners of 1805 was that while the latter petitioned as legitimate employees of the Company who had been unfairly dismissed, the former was mistakenly attributed to be an employee at the time of complaint. While the Governor General's office was not aware of the distinction, it is quite likely that Rammohun's potential future employer, the Board of Revenue, was. A brief history of the responses of the Board of Revenue and the Governor General's Council to subsequent complaints against Hamilton will further clarify this argument.

After Rammohun's petition, two further complaints were made against Hamilton in 1824 and 1827. The cases were concerned with his role in district revenue administration. Both were initially reported to the Board of Revenue at Calcutta. The Board forwarded them to the Governor General's Council which then forwarded them to London. Both times the Court of Directors assessed the situation as evidence of Hamilton's 'unfitness' to be a high official.[104] However, in 1830, matters came to a head when a complaint alleging embezzlement from an unfair land auction was made against Hamilton. After an investigation, the Board recommended Hamilton's dismissal to the Governor General's Council.[105] The case was again forwarded to London and the Court approved the dismissal as 'fresh proof of his [Hamilton's] unfitness'.[106] Hamilton proceeded to England immediately afterwards and was never again employed by the Company. He died in England in 1853.[107]

There are four points that emerge from these cases. First, at the core of each was an administrative process in which the Governor General's Council did *not* give the final assessment. Their only role was to forward the cases to London. Second, the Board of Revenue conducted enquiries and recommended the next course of action to the Court of Directors. Third, the Board kept a record of complaints and referred to them as a cumulative process of assessments. Our information on the 1824 and 1827 cases comes from the Board's reference to them in 1830. Fourth, it was the Board (*and not the Governor General's Council*) which recommended Hamilton's dismissal. This shows that the Board of Revenue, more than the Governor General's Council, was responsible for complaints against Hamilton and that the Board's decision-making process was based on administrative precedent and cumulative evidence. From this perspective it is likely that the Board dismissed Rammohun's appointment in 1809 because they had been ignored in his petition earlier that year. By consistently rejecting his appointment, the Board asserted its position that his direct petition to the Governor General had effectively ended any chances of an official career for him as dewan with Digby.

Our discussion also highlights the direct role of the Court of Directors in the proceedings of the Board of Revenue. Since the powers of the Board were criticized by Rammohun in *Exposition* (as will be seen further on) it is worth noting the relationship between the Board of Revenue and the Court. The Board (consisting of four members and a president in the civil service) was based in Calcutta but formed by the order of the

Court of Directors.[108] Further, the Court (than the Governor General's Council) assigned the Board's administrative responsibilities of collecting revenue and controlling all revenue appointments.[109] This explains the context of the Court's close involvement in matters of district revenue administration in Bengal. Until 1793, the Board even had the right to administer their own courts. When Lord Cornwallis annulled this right (arguing that it was contrary to the Permanent Settlement's basic organizing principle of separating revenue administration from the judiciary), he compensated the Board's loss of power by granting greater establishment resources to exert an even greater control over revenue collection and appointments.[110]

A consequence of greater powers for the Board in revenue administration after 1793 was greater bureaucratic surveillance over the collectors. Fluid networks of association between Company officials and native employees gradually became subject to new forms of control by the early 19th century. So, while Woodforde appointed Rammohun as his dewan in 1802 without comment from the Board, the situation had changed by 1814 as Digby was being strongly recommended to appoint the Board's choice of dewan.

Rammohun retired and settled down in Calcutta in 1814. From this point onwards, he was indirectly associated with the Company through his son, Radhaprasad; nephew, Govindaprasad; business associate, Ramhari Mitter; Shibnarain Roy, the son of Rajblochan Roy, a close friend; and Rajblochan's dependent, Ramadhan Chatterjee.[111] In 1822, Digby (now collector of Burdwan) employed them in the collectorate.[112]

At Burdwan, Rammohun's son, Radhaprasad, had the important responsibility of checking the treasury papers.[113] Radhaprasad's role created controversy when J.R. Hutchinson, magistrate of Burdwan, alleged that he had been involved in stealing treasury deposits.[114] The Board of Revenue also sent a representative, a certain Mr Edmund Malony, to Burdwan to look into the case.[115] Digby defended Radhaprasad by showing that he could not have 'interfered' with the treasury since he never handled cash deposits directly.[116] Malony was, however, not convinced and cited Rammohun's prior employment under Digby as evidence of the latter's flawed judgement.[117] The Board of Revenue subsequently condemned Digby and Radhaprasad.[118]

Surprisingly for the Board, the Supreme Court later acquitted Radhaprasad of all charges.[119] Radhaprasad's younger brother, Ramaprasad, no doubt took note of this case when he opted to become a pleader in the Supreme Court and a *vakeel* (native lawyer) of the government later on.[120] To Rammohun, Radhaprasad's case showed that by issuing condemnations even before the Supreme Court had declared its verdict, the Board of Revenue had emerged as an extraordinarily powerful government body.

As the previous chapter highlighted, *Exposition* was primarily concerned with district administration in Bengal. Here, we discover that the Board had clearly emerged as the most important Company institution in the districts. So it is understandable that Rammohun's criticism of the Board was the focus of his discussion of revenue administration in *Exposition*.[121] He argued that the Board's regulations prevented the collector from being accountable to the natives. The collector wielded disproportionate administrative power over the native population such that 'legal redress' was 'impossible under the present system'.[122] Rammohun stressed that cases against collectors rarely reached the courts. Quoting an 1828 regulation that 'the decisions of the Collector [in the districts] shall have the force of a decree', he argued that such policies had led to a long-term climate of 'alarm and fear amongst the natives'.[123]

Rammohun noted with approval that William Bentinck as Governor General of Bengal had also become the head of the Board of Revenue. However, he was very critical of Bentinck's reforms in revenue administration in 1830 in which the posts of the collector and judge were combined to form a new post known as revenue commissioner, and strongly recommended a roll-back of the decision to appoint revenue commissioners.[124] This may have been due to a belief that the post was an extension of the administrative scope of a Board which sanctioned an inordinate degree of power to the collectors in the districts.

In this context, the Hamilton petition can be seen as a precedent to Rammohun's argument against collectors in *Exposition*. By presenting Hamilton as an example of a Company official who had abused his predominant position in the districts, his petition had highlighted administrative failures. In *Exposition*, he argued that it was not the man-on-the spot but the native employee who ought to be the main official in the districts. This was done by unflatteringly presenting the collector as an inefficient but highly paid 'establishment cost' whose everyday administrative duties were 'chiefly performed by native officers.'[125] The crucial role of the native employees in everyday governance made them the most practical solution to the problem of the expensive and over-reaching Company official. He suggested that all collectors be 'dispensed with' and native employees be appointed in their place. A specific typology of native employees was also specified in *Exposition*:

> The desirable object [of] reducing the revenue establishment may be accomplished in the following manner: under the former government the natives of the country particularly the Hindus were exclusively employed in the revenue department in all stations and they are still so under the present system.[126]

It is clear that *Exposition* referred to an older scribal elite who had historically been a part of Bengal's administration. As we have seen in this chapter, Rammohun himself was a member of this community. There were, however, two problems with this suggestion. First, though the scribal elite still played an important role in district administration, they were on the verge of being replaced by the new generation of natives, 'bred up in communications and intercourse with the Europeans and progressively becoming imbued with their habits and in the course of time very nearly to them.'[127] To clarify why he was against this development, we take a step back to recall that his critique of the collectors had highlighted their 'European' ethnicity to draw attention to the problem of employing an unfamiliar official to an important post. From this perspective, a native employee 'imbued in the habits' of a 'European' collector would be a disaster since it would destroy the crucial importance of the 'local' native employees and render them with the same difficulties as the collector. His critique of the EIC's employment of European collectors feeds into the implicit argument that the older generation of native employees were more accountable for their actions to the population of Bengal. Second, the old native employee posts which he was most likely referring to—Kanungos, Naib dewans, and Roy Rayans—had been officially abolished by the Company in Calcutta by the second decade of the 19th century.[128] This was in accordance with the Permanent Settlement Act of 1793 which specifically banned high posts for natives in administration.[129]

As the previous chapter showed, Rammohun was pushing hard for a re-appraisal of the critically important role of the scribal elite in Company administration. The next section further substantiates this argument by focusing on the post of the dewan in Rangpur and Calcutta as the historical context of his association with the EIC from 1802 to 1814. The working assumption is that an examination of the historical context of the dewan allows for a perspective of his ideas concerning the centrality of the native employees in administration.

Dewans and Their Role in Revenue Collection, 1766–1814

The dewan's post in Company administration was conceptualized in 1766 by the Court of Directors as a response to practical problems in revenue collection which came to light after the grant of the dewani of Bengal.[130] The Court observed that Company men were 'unfit to collect revenue by themselves' since they were unable to 'follow the subtle native [who] through all arts conceals the real value of the country [and] perseveres [to] elude all payments.'[131] This observation emphasized an important anxiety: on the one hand, the Company had superseded the Bengal Nawabs. On the other hand, Company officials clearly lacked the resources and know-how of a dewan.

The solution to the problem was the allotment of the role to a body of native employees instead who could perform the tasks of the dewan. The post was not, however, conceptualized as a continuation of a Nawabi post but altered to suit the interests of the Company. While 'previously' the dewan had been the 'chief financial officer' of the treasury in Bengal, the post was now subject to the oversight of Company officials.[132]

The ambiguities of this post were further deepened by the rapidly changing political climate in Bengal. In 1766, the Company shared power with the Naib dewan of Murshidabad, Mohammed Reza Khan. This arrangement had been negotiated by Robert Clive as a 'dual monarchy.'[133] Under this set-up, the Company collected revenues but 'the administration of justice, the appointment of officers, zamindars, in short whatever comes under the dominion of civil government' was under the charge of Reza Khan. However, this context changed within a short period. In 1771, 'dissatisfied with the administration of Reza Khan as far as the influence he holds in that position', the Court of Directors 'divested him of that rank'.[134]

The collapse of the dual monarchy heralded a new political context in Bengal where the Company was in charge of civil administration for the very first time. The Company however had a very specific understanding of civil administration. As early as 1773, the Court of Directors weighed in on the matter by opining that 'the collection of revenues was without question the first objective of government'. Nevertheless, the Court did not provide any practical instructions or guidelines on how revenue was to be collected but instead 'left the full details to the man-on-the-spot'.[135]

Unfortunately for the collectors in the districts, the decision to 'leave the details' to them also meant ignoring their complaints. In 1770, the first collector of Rangpur, John Grose, was alerted to severe problems in revenue administration when his colleague George Robertson reported that the dewan was attempting to dismantle the network of revenue collection in the district by actively preventing the village accountant's (*patwari*) records for revenue collection from being made available to him.[136] Robertson was in a particularly difficult position. Since the collectorate had not yet been officially carved out from the neighbouring Dinajpur, the native employees probably found his questions concerning their records to be annoying and lacking in official authority.[137] Robertson even authored a report recommending the regulation of the dewan's post and the institution of a formal system of native employee administration in Rangpur. Calcutta did not, however, introduce any new policies to regulate the post in spite of receiving the damaging report.

Calcutta's responses to its collectors improved by the end of the decade, but not by much. This can be seen in the case of Richard Goodlad, the collector of Rangpur. Goodlad described a breakdown in the everyday work of the revenue office in 1779 and opined that this was mainly due to an ambiguous hierarchy between the collector and dewan.[138] The dewan Ganga Prasad was annoyed at not being appointed collector instead and consequently did not pay any attention to revenue collection rates of the Company. For his part, Ganga Prasad did not agree to this version of events but opined that the demands for revenue were unrealistic.[139] However, Goodlad did not respond to this argument but wrote to Calcutta for a warrant against Ganga Prasad (who promptly fled Rangpur).[140] The case against Ganga Prasad went cold as no new evidence emerged of his whereabouts.

After Goodlad's retirement, George Bogle was appointed as the collector of Rangpur. In 1782, in a surprising turn of events, Bogle disregarded his predecessor's experiences and requested the Committee of Revenue to sanction Ganga Prasad's appointment as dewan. What was even more surprising was that the committee agreed (without mentioning the charges against him or his previous warrants).[141]

Calcutta's lukewarm response to problems regarding the dewan and their refusal to regulate the post can also be seen in cases in Calcutta itself. In 1778, the Calcutta Committee of Revenue (not to be confused with the Committee of Revenue) was divided over the right of its dewan, Radhakanta Ghosh, to imprison defaulters of revenue without prior orders.[142] This case echoes Goodlad's complaint against Ganga Prasad's ambiguous attitude to the predominance of the Company official, but with a significant difference. While Goodlad *complained* against Prasad's perceived over-reach, the Calcutta Committee *debated* whether Ghosh's actions were a legitimate exercise of administrative discretionary powers. The confusion over the status of the dewan's authority shows that while the post was officially subject to supervision, in practical terms, Company officials in Calcutta were still confused about just how far the dewan was subordinate to them.

An important reason for the confusion could have been the vital financial role of the dewan in everyday administration. In the late 18th century, significant sums of money were sent by Calcutta to the districts to be allocated by the dewan.[143] However, dewans were not always prompt with receipts, records, and accounts. In 1784, Francis Goodwin, the superintendent of the zamindari *daftar* (court), wrote an urgent letter to Peter Moore, the collector of Dinajpur, that Lakikant, his dewan, had not transmitted any revenue record but 'given excuses'.[144] Goodwin had appointed Lakikant to the post of dewan, strongly suspected him of wrong-doing but was powerless to take any action.

Unfortunately, Peter Moore's position as collector was not any better than Goodwin's. His dependence on his dewan can be gleaned from the following case: in the aftermath of the bitter and disastrous Rangpur rebellion of 1783, Moore requested the Committee of Revenue to confirm the appointment of a certain Roopnarain Ghose as dewan.[145]

Interestingly, Ghose was not only confirmed as Moore's dewan but also re-employed by the next two collectors. His tenure, however, proved to be disastrous for the zamindars. In 1787, the zamindars petitioned Governor General Lord Cornwallis that Ghose had unilaterally increased revenue rates without any prior sanction from Calcutta.[146] In response, John Shore wrote to D.H. McDowall, the collector of Rangpur, demanding an explanation.[147] Although McDowall defended his dewan, Shore was not convinced.

As president of the Committee of Revenue, it is likely that Shore also knew that collectors in Rangpur had changed thrice in as many years but Ghose's appointment as dewan had remained intact. Soon afterwards, the Governor General personally intervened to involve the preparer of the reports of the Revenue Department, Jonathan Duncan.[148] After consulting the *kanungos* Duncan wrote to McDowall informing him that the amount of extra revenue had been excused by the government.[149] These were the circumstances in which the zamindars' petition was accepted by the Government at Calcutta but *against* the opinion of the most important Company official in the district—the collector. Thus, the dewan was brought to justice only after the direct intervention of the two most powerful EIC officials in Bengal at the time—the Governor General, Lord Cornwallis, and the President of the Committee of Revenue, John Shore.

Independently of the case, Shore was also critical of dewan's post as 'a source of immense power and means of mischief'.[150] However, Shore's assessment did not translate into Company policy. Although the proceedings of the Committee of Revenue were forwarded to London, the Court of Directors did not acknowledge that any regulations were needed. This was not an oversight, but a deliberate policy. For example, in 1787, the Court introduced 'Regulations for Collectors in the Bengal Presidency' and opined that the dewan could 'hear, receive, examine and decide complaints or petitions' only when 'authorised' by the Collector.[151] This regulation, in spite of its claim to being an updated policy, only echoed the Committee of Revenue's regulation in 1773.[152] It was as if a long-term policy of official silence from London and Calcutta on regulating the dewan had been put into practice. Interestingly, officials in Calcutta did not pressurize London to introduce regulations either. This was probably because the official silence on the dewan was useful for maintaining revenue collections. For example, in the takeover of the French factories in 1786, the Company agreed to continue 'the custom of jurisdiction between the dewan and the *ryot*' and decreed that 'there shall be no innovation in this respect'.[153] The dewan of the French East India Company would, therefore, continue to perform his role *without any changes*, solely because of his commercial usefulness to the EIC.

This policy of official silence was being followed at a time when the most disastrous case yet involving a dewan had come to light. The case involved the dewan of the Committee of Revenue in Calcutta, Ganga Gobind Singh. Singh was an extraordinarily powerful native employee. As P.J. Marshall opines, Singh 'certainly wielded more power than any other Indian was to do before the twentieth century'.[154] Singh was also close to Warren Hastings and was reportedly 'the only man whom Hastings trusts'.[155] This connection also bore rich financial dividends. By the time of the case against him, Singh's wealth was estimated to be 320 lakh rupees.[156] In 1785, Singh, his son Prankrishen (as *Naib* dewan or deputy), and an associate Ghulam Ashraf were charged with forgery of revenue documents, embezzlement of government revenues, and land fraud in Dinajpur.[157] The Committee concluded that Ganga Gobind had 'an intention to defraud the government annually of Rs. 42,274' and recommended that the dewan be jailed.[158] Crucially, the Committee insisted that the post of the dewan be henceforth regulated.[159] However, the charges as well as a call to regulate the post of dewan were not accepted by Governor General Macpherson.[160] The case against Ashraf, however, continued and was sent to London on appeal. This, however, also reopened the case of Ganga Gobind Singh and Prankrishen. Consequently, the Court of Directors ordered the release of Ghulam Ashraf but did not offer an opinion on the dewan.[161] Calcutta did not conduct any fresh proceedings.[162]

In spite of such high-profile and damaging cases, the Cornwallis code of 1793 did not introduce regulations for the dewan. This was probably because the Company at Calcutta had begun to disengage with its officials in the districts on all matters pertaining to the dewan.

However, this did not mean that Company officials at Calcutta did not have any perspective on the dewan. As the memoirs of George Valentia show, Company bureaucrats in the city had a very definite perception of what dewans were capable of in 1803.[163] Valentia was a guest of Cornwallis at Calcutta. His account of the dewan revealed a perception of a dominant native employee who lent money illegally to gullible Company officials and then extorted official favours.[164] While officials in Calcutta constructed an image of a dewan who fooled Company servants and embezzled Company revenues, this perception can also be read as a different take on the fluid networks of communication between the Company officials and the dewan which had been an important part of Digby's letters to the Board.

Valentia's record of official opinions in Calcutta regarding the dewan also sheds light on why Rammohun's personal association with Digby would have been viewed with suspicion by the Board of Revenue. It also explains why the Board instituted a rigid bureaucratic surveillance on its officials in the early 19th century and had begun to recommend their choice of dewan to the Company officials in the districts.

Calcutta's perception of the dewan hardened during the period of Cornwallis's tenure in government. This can be seen by considering the differences between Shore's perception in 1787 and Valentia's account of official ideas of the dewan in 1803. Shore's idea was that the dewan's *post* required regulation. Valentia on the other hand wrote of the dewan as an unscrupulous *being*. The implication of this was not only that the post of dewan ought to be abolished but that all higher posts for natives as well. Interestingly, both views prevailed when the post was abolished, along with other high posts for natives in district administration, in the Regulation of 1813.[165]

The question that arises here is: why was the Board still interested in controlling the dewan's post in 1814 when it had officially ceased to exist? The most likely answer is that the practical problems in revenue collection which had led to the creation of the dewan's post in 1766 had not been resolved but in fact continued into the early 19th century. Ultimately, the Board of Revenue was forced to acknowledge the importance of the dewan in spite of the grievances of their top officials.

To Rammohun, the outgoing informal dewan at Rangpur, privy to Digby's public correspondence and knowledgeable of the revenue regulations, the Board of Revenue's acceptance of the dewan's existence even after abolishing the post was a tacit acknowledgement of the continuing importance of native employees. This was the context of his association with the Company in 1814. Its importance can be found in *Exposition* which consistently emphasized that native employees were critical to Company administration. This chapter shows that the emphasis was justified. From the very inception of the EIC's government in Bengal in 1766, Governors General in Calcutta, the Court of Directors in London, and collectors in the districts were only too aware of the important (and ambiguous) role of native employees.

***

Conclusion: The Institutional Context of Rammohun's Political Thought

Rammohun's period of association with the Company from 1804 to 1814 was witness to two concurrent administrative developments: first, the official discourse from Calcutta which abolished high posts for native employees; and second, the continuing employment of native employees in posts which had been abolished. Therefore, in *Exposition*, Rammohun emphasized the importance of the creation of a native employee service with its own networks of hierarchy, administrative power, and pay, and strongly suggested the need for high salaries and a system of internal promotions. This amounted to a radical transformation of the native service within a single structure of payment and eligibility. His ideas were not restricted to high-ranking officials such as dewans (revenue assistant to the district collector), *kanungos* (revenue accountants), amils (the Indian predecessor of the European collector), *sezawals* (assistants in revenue collection), *naibs* and *sheristedars* (deputies of the dewan and *kanungos*), but *all* natives who worked in the Company such as the clerical staff (*naiks, mohururs* and Persian *mohururs*).

Rammohun's emphasis on native employees was shaped by his experiences at different tiers of governance: provincial capitals (Murshidabad and Benares), districts (Decca-Jelalpur, Jessore, Ramgarh, and Bhagalpur), and frontier territories (Rangpur); for 11–12 years, in formal and informal capacities (as a *munshi*, acting *sheristedar*, and dewan). This was the most likely context of the consistent references to 'experiences' cited in *Exposition* to support his assertion that the process of governance was inefficient, expensive, and harmed the Company's accountability to the natives.[166]

Rammohun did not, however, advocate reform based on only his period of association with the Company but with a system of government in an earlier phase of Company rule (1784–93); for this was the only period which was assessed positively in *Exposition*.[167]

From his vantage point as the last generation of dewans of the old scribal elite, Rammohun's argument was a case for a government run by native employees educated in older scribal traditions but in a system of government in Bengal which had been introduced by the Company.

Rammohun's discussion of the importance of native employees also highlights their central role in his political thought. As the previous chapter showed, there is strong evidence of this in *Exposition*. For example, *Exposition* suggested ways in which native employees could occupy high posts in government and have an important role in rural political organizations such as the Panchayat. The viability of his argument lay in its emphasis on economy. In the place of an overpaid, inefficient, and disproportionately powerful single collector, he proposed a cost-effective *system* of administration by regulated native employees. His arguments would have touched a raw nerve with Company officials, many of whom still behaved as trading merchants of a 'Company line' than rulers and officials of a vast territorial Empire.[168] Such attitudes were so prevalent that countering them was one of the principal aims of institutions such as the Fort William College where officials would be *taught* to be rulers, governors, and administrators.[169] Read against this institutional background, Rammohun's arguments appear to be radically revisionist: why teach an EIC official to govern when a vast army of efficient and able native administrators was present and ready to work?

Exposition was written in 1832 in London, for a British readership. However, Rammohun's thought was also articulated in other writings such as *Tuhfat-ul-Muwahidin* and tracts on Hindu scripture. These writings did not repeat the arguments of *Exposition* but were concerned with a distinct but related project—ethics. His political thought in *Tuhfat* and writings on Hindu scripture is the subject of the next chapter.

Notes

1. Roy, *Exposition*, 34.
2. Collet, *Rammohun Roy*, 58.

3. Collet, *Rammohun Roy*, 58.

4. Collet, *Rammohun Roy*, 496.

5. The references to dynamism in courtly culture can also be read as an argument against the static polity which was attributed to Bengali history by Rammohun's contemporary, James Mill, Head Examiner of the Department of Correspondence in the EIC.

6. Collet, *Rammohun Roy*, 2.

7. Kumkum Chatterjee, 'Scribal Elites in Sultanate and Mughal Bengal', *Indian Economic and Social History Review* 47, no. 4 (December 2010): 453.

8. Collet, *Rammohun Roy*, 12.

9. Home, 'Supplementary Notes', 28. Radhanagar was under the jurisdiction of the Burdwan district in Rammohun's lifetime.

10. Home, 'Supplementary Notes', 28.

11. Chatterjee, 'Scribal Elites', 470.

12. Collet, *Rammohun Roy*, 496.

13. Kumkum Chatterjee, *The Cultures of History in Early Modern India: Persianisation and Mughal Culture in Bengal* (New Delhi: Oxford University Press, 2009), 157–9. The scribal elite comprised of a significantly higher number of Kayasthas and the Baidyas than the Brahmins.

14. Chatterjee, 'Scribal Elites', 450–7.

15. Banerji, *Rammohun Roy*, 11.

16. Banerji, *Rammohun Roy*, 13.

17. Banerji, *Rammohun Roy*, 13.

18. Banerji, *Rammohun Roy*, 13. In Chattopadhyay, *JB*, p. 17, Nagendranath Chattopadhyay opined that Rammohun left home to study Sanskrit and Persian in Benares and Patna respectively. However, we have no historical evidence to support this argument. He probably learnt Persian at a madrasa near his home. As a revenue farmer, Ramakanta would have been keen to educate his sons in the language. According to Kumkum Chatterjee, the zamindars of Bengal often set up madrasa schools in their estates in the late 18th century. Rammohun may have learnt Sanskrit from Hariharananda Bharati, a tantric sanyasi whom he had met in his teens in Radhanagar.

19. Banerji, *Rammohun Roy*, 18.

20. Banerji, *Rammohun Roy*, 15. Apart from Rammohun, Ramakanta's two wives, Rammohi and Tarini Devi, and sons, Jagmohun and Ramlochan, were also alloted properties of their own. Ramakanta himself retained ownership of some property as well as his ancestral home at Radhanagar. After his death, the house passed on to his youngest son, Ramlochan. Tarini Devi looked after the property after Ramlochan's death in 1810.

21. Banerji, *Rammohun Roy*, 41.

22. Banerji, *Rammohun Roy*, 41.

23. Banerji, *Rammohun Roy*, 41.

24. Banerji, *Rammohun Roy*, 19.

25. Banerji, *Rammohun Roy*, 19.

26. Banerji, *Rammohun Roy*, 19.

27. Banerji, *Rammohun Roy*, 19.

28. Banerji, *Rammohun Roy*, 20.

29. Banerji, *Rammohun Roy*, 20.

30. Banerji, *Rammohun Roy*, 20.

31. Banerji, *Rammohun Roy*, 20.

32. Banerji, *Rammohun Roy*, 20.

33. Banerji, *Rammohun Roy*, 33.

34. Banerji, *Rammohun Roy*, 23.

35. Banerji, *Rammohun Roy*, 33.

36. Banerji, *Rammohun Roy*, 33.

37. Home, 'Supplementary Notes', 35.

38. Banerji, *Rammohun Roy*, 33.

39. Chattopadhyay, *JB*, 13. It is likely that Rammohun found some form of employment with the Nawabs but this did not satisfy his professional ambitions.

40. Stephen Vella, 'Imagining Empire: Company, Crown and Bengal in the Formation of British Imperial Ideology: 1757–84', *Portuguese Studies* 16 (2000): 276.

41. Vella, 'Imagining Empire', 276.

42. P.J. Marshall, 'British Society in India under the East India Company', *Modern Asian Studies* 31, no. 1 (February 1997): 98.

43. Kopf, *British Orientalism*, 16–17.

44. Kopf, *British Orientalism*, 46–8.

45. P.J. Marshall, 'Indian Officials under the East India Company in Eighteenth Century Bengal', *Bengal: Past and Present* 84, no. 3 (1967): 103.

46. Chatterjee, 'Scribal Elites', 457.

47. Roy, *Exposition*, 7.

48. Fredrick Lehmann, 'The Eighteenth-Century Transition in India: Responses of some Bihar Intellectuals' (PhD diss., University of Wisconsin, 1967), 124; Marshall, 'Indian Officials', 105; Satish Chandra Mukhopadhay, *The Career of Rajah Rai Durlabham Mahindra, Rai Durlabh, Diwan of Bengal, 1710–70* (Bagda: C. Mukherjee, 1974), 5 and 188.

49. Sisir Kumar Das, *Sahebs and Munshis: An Account of the College of Fort William* (Calcutta: Orion Publications, 1978), 1–23.

50. Thiessen, 'Anglo Indian Vested Interests', 38.
51. John Bowen, 'The East India Company's Education of Its Own Servants', *The Journal of the Royal Asiatic Society of Great Britain and Ireland*, no. 3/4 (October 1955): 107.
52. Bowen, 'The East India Company's Education of Its Own Servants', 108.
53. Robert Haldane Rattray, *The Exile: A Poem* (Calcutta, 1837), 251.
54. Das, *Sahebs and Munshis*, 110.
55. As quoted in Home, 'Supplementary Notes', 31.
56. Chattopadhyay, *JB*, 33.
57. Collet, *Rammohun Roy*, 15.
58. *Primitae Oriantales: Containing the Theses in the Oriental Languages pronounced at the Public Disputations on the 29th March, 1803 by the Students of the College of Fort William in Bengal with Translations* (Calcutta: College of Fort William Press, 1803), xxvii.
59. *Primitae Oriantales*, xxx.
60. *Primitae Oriantales*, xxvii.
61. *Primitae Oriantales*, 17.
62. Banerji, *Rammohun Roy*, 22.
63. Thomas Woodforde to the Board of Revenue, March 7, 1803, *LD*, 27.
64. Thomas Woodforde to the Board of Revenue, March 7, 1803, *LD*, 27.
65. Collet, *Rammohun Roy*, 412. Rammohun then joined the writer's establishment at Benares as 'native assistant'. While the job description of native assistant is not specified, he is listed as native employee.
66. *General Register of the Hon. East India Company's Servants in the Bengal Establishment, 1790–1842*, ed. Ram Chunder Doss (Calcutta: Baptist Mission Press, 1844), 140–1.
67. John Digby to the Secretary, Board of Revenue, 30 December 1809, in *The Correspondence of Rammohun Roy*, ed. Dilip Kumar Biswas (Calcutta: Saraswat Library, 1992), 24 (henceforth, *Corr.*).
68. John Digby to the Board of Revenue, 31 January 1810, *LD*, 43.
69. John Digby to the Board of Revenue, 31 January 1810, *LD*, 43.
70. John Digby to the Secretary, Board of Revenue, 30 December 1809, *LD*, 42.
71. Jon Wilson, '"A Thousand Countries To Go": Peasants and Rulers in Late-Eighteenth Century Bengal', *Past and Present* 189, no. 1 (November 2005): 83.
72. Bray, 'Krishnakant Basu, Rammohun Ray and Early-Nineteenth Century Contacts in Bhutan and Tibet', *Tibet Journal Special Issue* 34, no. 3 (2009): 1–6.
73. Wilson, 'A Thousand Countries To Go', 81.
74. Wilson, 'A Thousand Countries To Go', 83.
75. John Digby to the Secretary, Board of Revenue, 30 December 1809, *LD*, 42.

76. John Digby to the Secretary, Board of Revenue, 30 December 1809, *LD*, 42.

77. John Digby to the Secretary, Board of Revenue, 30 December 1809, *LD*, 42.

78. John Digby to the Board of Revenue, 31 January 1810, *LD*, 43.

79. Petition received by the Persian Secretary, Bengal Revenue Council, 8 September 1809, BL, IOR, Bengal Revenue Proceedings, P/55/24.

80. Board of Revenue to G.H. Barlow, Governor-General in Council, 28 April 1809, BL, IOR, Bengal Revenue Proceedings, P/55/20.

81. Brajendranath Banerji, 'Rammohun Roy: From New and Unpublished Sources', *Calcutta Review* 50 (January 1934), 62.

82. Linda Colley, *The Ordeal of Elizabeth Marsh: A Woman in World History* (New York: Pantheon Books, 2007), 433.

83. Colley, *The Ordeal of Elizabeth Marsh*, 434.

84. Rosane Rocher and Ludo Rocher, *The Making of Western Indology: Henry Thomas Colebrooke and the East India Company* (London: Routledge, 2012), 95.

85. Nirmalya Bagchi, *Rammohan Charcha* [Discussion on Rammohun] (Calcutta: Subarnarekha, 1995), 108.

86. Collet, *Rammohun Roy*, 15.

87. Dilip Biswas, 'Editorial Remarks', *Corr.*, 18.

88. *General Register*, 158; *Complete Baronetage*, vol. 2, ed. George Cockayne (Exeter, 1902), 454.

89. Rammohun Roy to the Governor-General, April 1809, *Corr.*, 11.

90. Frederick Hamilton to the Governor-General, May 1809, *Corr.*, 9.

91. Rammohun Roy to the Governor-General, April 1809, *Corr.*, 2.

92. Rammohun Roy to the Governor-General, April 1809, *Corr.*, 2.

93. Rammohun Roy to the Governor-General, April 1809, *Corr.*, 3.

94. Rammohun Roy to the Governor-General, April 1809, *Corr.*, 3.

95. Frederick Hamilton to the Governor-General, May 1809, *Corr.*, 9.

96. Frederick Hamilton to the Governor-General, May 1809, *Corr.*, 9.

97. Frederick Hamilton to the Governor-General, May 1809, *Corr.*, 9.

98. Rammohun Roy to the Governor-General, April 1809, *Corr.*, 10.

99. Rammohun Roy to the Governor-General, April 1809, *Corr.*, 3.

100. Biswas, 'Editorial Remarks', *Corr.*, 10–11.

101. Rammohun Roy to the Governor-General, April 1809, *Corr.*, 5.

102. Frederick Hamilton to the Governor-General, May 1809, *Corr.*, 9.

103. *Bengal Ms. Records*, vol. 4, 1802–1807, ed. William Hunter (London: W.H. Allen, & Co. Ltd., 1894), 233.

104. John Loch Astell to Bengal Revenue Dept., 26 August 1809, BL, IOR, Board's Collections, F/4/1239/40500.

105. Bengal Revenue Dept. to Court of Directors, 13 April 1830, BL, IOR, Board's Collections, F/4/1239/40500.

106. John Loch to Bengal Revenue Dept., 26 August 1829, BL, IOR, Board's Collections, F/4/1239/40500.

107. *General Register*, 158. Hamilton's son would later join the EIC as Magistrate of Meerut in 1834, rise to Lt. Gov. of the North-Western Provinces in 1841, and eventually be commended by Parliament for services to the Company in the 1857 revolt.

108. *The Fifth Report from the Select Committee of the East India Company, Bengal Presidency*, vol. 1 (London: J. Higginbotham, 1812), 25.

109. *Fifth Report*, 25.

110. *Fifth Report*, 25.

111. Brajendranath Banerji, 'A Chapter in the Personal History of Raja Rammohun Roy', *Calcutta Review* 60 (August 1931): 173.

112. John Digby to the Board of Revenue, 22 September 1824, *LD*, 419.

113. John Digby to the Board of Revenue, 22 September 1824, *LD*, 419.

114. J.R. Hutchison to John Digby, 14 July 1823, *LD*, 343.

115. Report of E. Malony to the Government of Bengal, 14 August 1824, *LD*, 357.

116. Board of Revenue to John Digby, 21 September 1824, *LD*, 408.

117. Board of Revenue to the Secretary to the Government, 19 October 1824, *LD*, 455.

118. Radhaprasad Roy's Petition to the Governor-General of Bengal, 23 July 1828, *LD*, 511.

119. Radhaprasad Roy's Petition to the Governor-General of Bengal, 23 July 1828, *LD*, 508–19.

120. John Bowring, *Autobiographical Recollections of Sir John Bowring with a brief memoir by Lewin B. Bowring* (London: Henry S. King, & Co. 1877), 395.

121. Roy, *Exposition*, 38.

122. Roy, *Exposition*, 69.

123. Roy, *Exposition*, 69.

124. Roy, *Exposition*, 28.

125. Roy, *Exposition*, 97.

126. Roy, *Exposition*, 97.

127. Roy, *Exposition*, 110.

128. Board of Revenue to G.H. Barlow, Governor-General in Council, BL, IOR, Bengal Revenue Proceedings, 15 January 1807, P/54/60.

129. Franklin Wickwire and Mary Wickwire, *Cornwallis: The Imperial Years*, vol. 2 (Chapel Hill: University of North Carolina Press, 1980), 89.

130. Harry Verelst, *A View of the Rise and Progress of the English Government in Bengal: Including a Reply to the Misrepresentations of Mr. Bolts, and Other Writers* (London: J. Nourse, 1772), 427.

131. Verelst, *A View of the Rise and Progress*, 427.

132. Verelst, *A View of the Rise and Progress*, 427.

133. Notes on the Bengal *Nawabs* and papers concerning administrative matters, Notes on Muhammad Reza Khan, 1765–1803, BL, IOR, Home Miscellaneous, H/584, pp. 183–200.

134. Notes on the Bengal *Nawabs* and papers concerning administrative matters, Notes on Muhammad Reza Khan, 1765–1803, BL, IOR, Home Miscellaneous, H/584, pp. 183–200.

135. Quoted in R.B. Ramsbotham, *Studies in the Revenue Administration of Bengal, 1769–1787* (London: Oxford University Press, 1926), 12.

136. George Robertson to John Grose, 19 June 1770, *Bengal district records, Rangpur, 1770–1789*, vol. 1, ed. W.K. Firminger (Calcutta: Bengal Secretariat Record Room, 1914), 6–7 (henceforth, RDR).

137. Bankey Bihari Misra, *The Central Administration of the East India Company, 1773–1834* (Bombay, 1959), 123. Rangpur would only officially separate from Dinajpur in 1777.

138. Richard Goodlad to Warren Hastings and the Gentlemen of the Council of Revenue, 17 April 1779, *RDR*, vol. 1, 72.

139. Richard Goodlad to Warren Hastings and the Gentlemen of the Council of Revenue, 17 April 1779, *RDR*, vol. 1, 72.

140. Richard Goodlad to Warren Hastings and the Gentlemen of the Council of Revenue, 31 May 1779, *RDR*, vol. 1, 81.

141. Warren Hastings to George Bogle, 25 July 1780, *RDR*, vol. 2, 56.

142. George Bogle to Charles Purling, 7 April 1778, *RDR*, vol. 1, 37.

143. D. Anderson to Richard Goodlad, 11 June 1781, *RDR*, vol. 2, 130.

144. Francis Gladwin to Peter Moore, 3 July 1784, *RDR*, vol. 3, 182.

145. Peter Moore to Samuel Charters and Gentlemen of the Committee of Revenue, 3 June 1784, *RDR*, vol. 4, 173.

146. D.H. McDowall to William Cowper, President and Members of the Committee of Revenue, 11 June 1786, *RDR*, vol. 6, 62.

147. D.H. McDowall to William Cowper, President and Members of the Committee of Revenue, 11 June 1786, *RDR*, vol. 6, 62.

148. Jonathan Duncan to D.H. McDowall, 15 February 1787, *RDR*, vol. 6, 130.

149. Jonathan Duncan to D.H. McDowall, 15 February 1787, *RDR*, vol. 6, 130.

150. Charles John Shore Teignmouth, *Memoir of the Life and Correspondence of Lord Teignmouth*, vol. 1 (London: Hatchard and Son, 1843), 74.

151. *General regulations, for the conduct of the collectors, in the Revenue Department. Passed by the Right Honourable the Governor-General in Council, on the 8th June, 1787* (Calcutta: The Honourable Company's Press, 1787), 1–23.

152. Proceedings of the Governor-General and the Council of Revenue, 7 April 1786, *RDR*, vol. 5, 70.

153. B. Alpin, the Secretary of the Board of Revenue, Circular, Provisional Convention entered into between Viscomte Soullac and Lieutenant Colonel Cathcart, 25 July 1785, *RDR*, vol. 5, 103.

154. Marshall, 'Indian Officials', 111.

155. Marshall, 'Indian Officials', 112.

156. Marshall, 'Indian Officials', 112.

157. Notes on Ganga Govind Singh and Pran Kishen, *Diwan* and *Naib Diwan* to the Committee of Revenue at Calcutta, 1785–89, BL, IOR, Home Miscellaneous, H/584, pp. 97–112, 599–660.

158. Home Miscellaneous, pp. 97–112, H/584, 599–660.

159. Home Miscellaneous, pp. 97–112, H/584, 599–660.

160. Home Miscellaneous, pp. 97–112, H/584, 599–660.

161. Home Miscellaneous, pp. 97–112, H/584, 599–660.

162. Home Miscellaneous, pp. 97–112, H/584, 599–660.

163. Viscount George Valentia, *Voyages and Travels to India, Ceylon, Abyssinia and Egypt*, vol. 1 (London: William Miller, 1803), 26–7.

164. Valentia, *Voyages and Travels to India*, 26–7.

165. *Circular Orders of the Sudder Board of Revenue at the Presidency of Fort William including the rules of practice for the guidance of the Board and of the Commissioners of Revenue together with a selection from the circular and standing orders of the late Board of Revenue from the year 1788 to the end of August 1837, selected by the Board*, ed. William Peters (Calcutta: Baptist Mission Press, 1838), 21.

166. Rammohun was associated with the Company at Murshidabad for two years whilst a Munshi to Woodforde (1802–February 1803). This can be surmised from his appointment as Woodford's dewan in March 1803 and at Benares for 3 months (May–July 1803). He worked with Digby as Munshi from 1805 to 1809 and as dewan from 1809 to 1814. This is how the total period of his association is approximated as between 11 and 12 years.

167. Roy, *Exposition*, xiii.

168. Thiessen, 'Anglo Indian Vested Interests', 24.

169. Thiessen, 'Anglo Indian Vested Interests', 25.

3   An Ethical Public

From 1815 to 1830, Rammohun published a series of printed tracts on religion in Calcutta. His intended audience was not just a closed group of associates but a rather vague and amorphous social group—the 'public' (*sarvvasadharan lok*). He relentlessly appealed to the 'public' to critique current interpretations of religion and reject unethical social practices. But what did he mean by the term 'public'? This chapter will draw on recent research on the history of the book to argue that the 'public' referred to the Bengali public sphere.[1]

In the early 19th century, the Bengali public sphere was shaped by diverse oral practices and performance narratives. The presence of parallel traditions of orality and print led to a 'direct exposure' of the print medium for 5,000–10,000 people.[2] This was not an exclusively Bengali phenomenon but representative of early colonial India as a whole.[3] V. Narayan Rao has even coined the term 'oral-literate' to describe the writers, storytellers, and bards whose ideas appealed to both written and oral traditions, and noted that a key feature of

oral-literate authors was an abiding commitment to the wide circulation of their works.[4]

Drawing from Rao, I argue that Rammohun was oral-literate and
wrote for a public which was well-versed in oral traditions (such as
storytelling and reading aloud from printed works). Further, a recurring feature of his writings was that they were short tracts in vernacular
Bangla. This is so that they could be easily circulated. The *circulation*
of material was key to the success of his project since it would gener-
ate interest in his works. As Stuart Black argued, printing presses had a
'limited' impact in Indian society until they were 'socialised' in vernacular
languages by the general population.[5] Rammohun's works may have
been an attempt to socialize the public into using print.

Rammohun's printed appeals to the public were based on an important assumption: that they were ethical. This chapter will interrogate
this assumption with three main arguments: first, that his writings on
ethics first appeared in *Tuhfat-ul-Muwahidin* (a short Perso-Arabic tract
written in c.1803 in Murshidabad); second, that *Tuhfat's* arguments
influenced later writings on Hindu scripture (written in Bangla and
English in Calcutta, 1815–30); and third, that he had a broad audience
in mind for his writings (hence, the appeal to the 'public').[6] These arguments are, however, contrary to the ideas of current scholarship. We,
therefore, turn to the scholarly disagreements on these points.

Conceptualizing the 'Public'

To Dermot Killingley, a historian of religion, 'the very idea' that
Rammohun's writings may have interested, informed, or been keenly
followed by a broad audience 'calls for criticism'.[7] This perspective is also
shared by Bruce Robertson (also a historian of religion).[8] Both argue
that the main readers and respondents of his works on Hindu scripture were either upper-caste members of Hindu society such as pandits
(Mrityunjay Vidyalankar, for example) or Orientalist scholars (such as
H.H. Wilson).

Killingley and Robertson's arguments are rooted in a material con-
text. Mrityunjay Vidyalankar had been the head pandit of the Bangla
Department of the Fort William College for 15 years (1800–15).[9]
In 1816, he joined the Calcutta Supreme Court as head pandit and would

have been at this post when he began his critique of Rammohun's writings.[10] H.H. Wilson was also based at the Fort William College and had a high opinion of Rammohun's scholarship. Wilson even sought his help with the precise dating and interpretation of the works of the early medieval Hindu thinker Shankara, and the English translation of the Puranas.[11]

Wilson was also in charge of a vernacular printing press—the Hindustani Press. He employed Ram Comul Sen as its head native employee.[12] Sen was educated in Persian and Sanskrit, and later learnt English.[13] He proved very adept at his job. By 1814, he had managed to become the manager of the press, a post that was not only well-paid but also virtually guaranteed a higher social status in intellectual and literary circles in Calcutta.[14] Eventually, Sen emerged as a powerful voice in institutions such as the Asiatic Society.[15] He was also one of Rammohun's most vocal critics, and co-founded the Dharma Sabha to protest against his ideas of sati.[16]

Rammohun's stress on the 'public' was not, however, without a material context. He published in a variety of printing presses—elite and popular.[17] As Anindita Ghosh has shown, elite presses published books on science, literature, grammar, and language while popular presses published 'petty pamphlets' on 'fables, farces, almanacs, sensational and low-print literature'.[18] Ghosh argues that the literary worlds of 'elite' and 'popular' were discursively sealed. The elite presses did not approve of low-print literature but made no attempt to regulate their content; and for their part, publishers of low-print literature did not give any priority to elite literature.[19] Since Rammohun's works appeared in both typologies of press, I argue that his publishing preferences reveal an intention to appeal to a broad audience—elite and popular.

My arguments concerning the popular reception of Rammohun's writings is based on the publishing data gleaned from the Calcutta School Book Society's (CSBS) catalogue of popular works, 1820.[20] The catalogue is a record of the titles of Bangla, Sanskrit, and Persian writings produced in Calcutta for popular consumption (with the inclusion of information on publishers and pricing wherever available).[21] The CSBS published the catalogue in its *Second Report*. The catalogue included works from popular and elite presses. Our focus here is the Bangla catalogue.

The Bangla catalogue listed the titles of 65 tracts. Almost immediately, Ghosh's perspectives on the difference between elite presses and low-print literature comes to the fore. Eight tracts (12.3 per cent of the Bangla catalogue) had identical English titles since the Sanskrit pandits employed by CSBS refused to translate the titles of low-print literature. Interestingly, more than half the authors were anonymous (33 tracts, 50.7 per cent). This is especially significant when we consider that Rammohun's writings constituted nearly a quarter of the catalogue (15 tracts) and all but one was publicly attributed to him. This made him the most visibly productive author in the popular press.

The catalogue did not only refer to Rammohun's works which had first appeared in 1820 but also to older writings such as *Vedantasar* (an abridged version of his first work in Bangla, *Vedanta Grantha*) which had initially appeared in 1816. In 1820, two popular presses Ganga Kishore Bhattacharya and Lulu Ji reprinted 1,000 copies of the tract, thus making it the most widely circulated of his Bangla works. Significantly, *Vedantasar* was not the only pre-1820 tract to be reprinted by the popular press. Others included his translations of Isho Upanishad, Kena Upanishad, Katha Upanishad, Mundaka Upanishad, and Mandukya Upanishad.

Surprisingly, Rammohun's tracts were reprinted in large numbers but not priced. This point is significant when we consider that Mrityunjay Vidyalankar's *Vedanta Chandrika* (1817) also appeared in the catalogue but was priced at 1 rupee. Also, *Vedanta Chandrika* was a critique of *Vedantasar*. Its continuing circulation in 1820 is evidence of continuing public interest in the debates around Hindu scripture. This argument is bolstered by the fact that 500 copies of Rammohun's response to *Vedanta Chandrika* were also reprinted by Lulu Ji in 1820.[22]

After his death, Rammohun's Bangla writings were reprinted by the Tattvabodhini Sabha (under Debendranath Tagore).[23] The Tattvabodhini Sabha press is, however, an unreliable indicator of the popularity of his works since it had a mandate to popularize his ideas. However, his works were also reprinted, priced, and sold by a burgeoning industry of private publishers who clearly perceived a market for them.[24]

Francesca Orsini has shown that the success of private publishers depended on being able to identify works which appealed to an older tradition of oral-literacy.[25] This is because such works appealed to a larger number of readers. I argue that the publication of Rammohun's works by private publishers was due to their reference to a context which readers would have been familiar with—the work of an oral-literate author. This point is further consolidated when we consider the publication and reprinting of his Bangla tract, *Brahma pautalik samvad* [Dialogue between a theist and an idolater], published in 1820 under a pseudonym, Brajamohun Majumdar. It was reprinted in 1846 by private publishers for 4 annas, but still attributed to the pseudonym.[26] A favourable price comparison with the reprints of the Isho Upanishad (4 annas) and Katha Upanishad (3 annas) indicates that it was not his name that prompted the sale of his works, but rather what accounted for their popularity was the manner in which he made his arguments.

Rammohun's popularity in the popular press also prompted elite presses to publish his works. For instance, the Baptist Missionary Press published 500 copies of *An apology for the pursuit of final beatitude independently of Brahmunical observances* (1820). Similarly, the Hindustani Press (then under the stewardship of Ram Comul Sen) published 500 copies of *Translation of the Abridgement of the Vedanta* and *Translation of the Isho Upanishad* respectively.[27] We note that these publications were not made by allies, followers, or friends but by individuals or groups who were deeply critical of his ideas.[28] Their decision to publish may have been prompted by a potentially large market for his works.

In addition to elite presses, educational associations such as CSBS commissioned Rammohun to write textbooks on geography and Bangla grammar (the former was never published while the latter was only published posthumously).[29] The CSBS also sought his help to translate a Sanskrit text on astronomy (however, his contribution was not acknowledged in the final published work).[30] These projects give us an important insight into Rammohun's priorities as an intellectual. They show that throughout his time in Calcutta (1815–30), the most productive period of his life, his focus remained on free tracts published from popular presses. Further, the contemporary publication data reveals that he was a popular author with the public and so cannot be seen as an elitist thinker. The first major disagreement in current historiography about his restricted and elite audience is hence qualified.

A Reappraisal of *Tuhfat*

We now turn to the second disagreement in current scholarship concerning Rammohun's writings, namely that his writings on Hindu scripture were unrelated to *Tuhfat*. I argue that this disagreement is due to the current perspective of his ideas on religion as an interpretation of Hindu scripture. This perspective has also led to a problem—the comparative ignorance of *Tuhfat* simply because it did not refer to Hindu scripture. For example, Killingley opines that *Tuhfat* was written in an 'Islamic tradition' only to argue that it can be seen as 'a project that was abandoned in later writings' since all subsequent works were on Hindu scripture.[31] Similarly, Robertson tentatively suggests that *Tuhfat* was concerned with a particular interpretation of Islamic theology before dismissing it as 'unremarkable, perhaps of interest only because of its amateurish eclecticism'.[32] Neither spells out the intellectual context of *Tuhfat*.

Drawing on Killingley and Robertson's perspectives, Brian Hatcher further argues that Rammohun introduced an elite religion ('Bourgeoisie Hinduism'). Further, 'Bourgeoisie Hinduism' was institutionalized in the Brahmo Sabha and developed further by the Tattvabodhini Sabha.[33] In Hatcher's view, Rammohun interpreted Hinduism as a private, contemplative, and elitist religion. However, this view is not consistent with the publication data available on his chief work for the Brahmo Sabha, a book of Brahmo songs and hymns, *Brahmasangeet* (1828).

Brahmasangeet was not only published by the Tattvabodhini Sabha but also private publishers in 1835 and 1844.[34] In 1853, James Long observed in his catalogue of Bangla works that it had become a 'much used' text in Bengali society.[35] Note that Long did not make a similar observation for any other text (or tract) in his catalogue. Rammohun's book on Brahmo songs was also reprinted by private publishers in 1889.

In the context of our argument, Hatcher's view of 'Bourgeoisie Hinduism' solidifies the approach towards *Tuhfat* adopted by Killingley and Robertson by perceiving Rammohun as a primarily Hindu thinker and ignoring *Tuhfat* altogether. Historians of religion perceive *Tuhfat* as unrelated to the wider body of Rammohun's work. Their arguments have deeply influenced historians of ideas such as Bayly and Sumit Sarkar.

However, historians of ideas do not ignore the importance of the intellectual context of *Tuhfat*. Indeed, Sarkar opines that a lack of research on late-18th-century intellectual history has led to an ignorance of the intellectual influences of *Tuhfat* and argues that its 'uniqueness cannot be taken as finally settled till much more is known than at present'.[36]

Sarkar's point also has another implication, as seen in the work of Barun De. De opined that 'Rammohun's political and economic ideas merit veneration only by those who worship the history of India's liberalism'.[37] This is not an isolated perspective. We find that Andrew Sartori also makes the same argument by confidently asserting that 'Rammohun's religious, social and political activities in the early 19th century were a form of classical liberalism' and further suggests that *Tuhfat* was a product of a classical liberal epistemology, liberal tropes ('priestly cunning'), and liberal interpretations of property (which we will look into more detail in the next chapter).[38] Such arguments avoid a discussion of an important context—mainly that Rammohun's intellectual exposure to liberal ideas occurred in Calcutta 11 years *after Tuhfat* was written. One way of assessing De's and Sartori's interpretations is as evidence of a lack of research on the intellectual context of *Tuhfat*.

However, in recent years, historians of ideas have attempted to place *Tuhfat* in its intellectual context. Kashshaf Ghani argues that *Tuhfat* was the product of a late-18th-century madrasa education and opines that contemporary madrasas in Bengal and North India would have emphasized a training in Sunni Islamic traditions of jurisprudence (*kalam*) and theology (*fiqh*).[39] He notes, however, that Rammohun's ideas were influenced not only by Sunni traditions of scriptural interpretation but also by radical thinkers such as the medieval philosopher and poet Abu al-Ala al-Maʿarri.

According to Ghani, Rammohun was influenced by Maʿarri's critique of religion. Maʿarri conceptualized religion as 'a product of the human mind which men believe through forces of habit and education, never stopping to consider it to be true'.[40] He argued that the belief in god was intuitive and advocated the rejection of all religious practices. Ghani opines that this argument is *the* context of *Tuhfat*.[41]

However, Ghani does not develop his ideas on Maʿarri any further. This may be due to an unresolved tension in his work, mainly that he is unable to reconcile concepts of *kalam* and *fiqh* with Maʿarri's radical rejection of theology. This tension can be seen in his discussion of apparent mistakes and linguistic problems in *Tuhfat*. We briefly touch upon these below since they directly pertain to the argument of this chapter.

Ghani's main point of disagreement with *Tuhfat* is with the interpretation of *mujtahid* (religious leader) and *muqallid* (religious follower).

He observes that Rammohun's interpretation of these terms deviated from the contemporary Sunni legal and theological tradition (which argued that there are no *mujtahids* but rather everyone is a *muqallid*). Ghani opines that presence of such fundamental errors would have only confused the reader. Interestingly, this criticism does not refer to Maʿarri's idea of religion as a critique of the unequal relations of power between a religious leader and follower/disciple. Instead, he ignores the radical thinker, argues that Rammohun's misinterpretation of these terms may have been due to a poor command of Persian, and asserts that Arabic words were indiscriminately deployed in *Tuhfat* to make up for a lack of Persian vocabulary.[42] In the final analysis, he opines that *Tuhfat* is primarily an indigenous form of liberalism ('a deep rooted liberal, humanitarian and rational current in Indian society').[43]

Ghani's attempt to place *Tuhfat* in its intellectual context throws up four main problems. First is the question of contextualizing the works of radical Islamic thinkers in Rammohun's thought. When and where did he come across radical thought? And how do we account for ideas such as by Maʿarri? Second is that an uncertainty over the syllabi of madrasa education in the 18th century can derail the project of placing *Tuhfat* in its intellectual context. Third is the question of the use of Arabic terms in a Persian text. Was Rammohun's command over Persian weak; or was he referring to a Persian intellectual text/tradition in which Arabic plays an important role? Finally, there is the problem of the assessment of *Tuhfat* as an indigenous liberal text. I argue that Ghani's perspective ignores the other problems mentioned above and effectively amounts to an admission of the severe lack of evidence for placing *Tuhfat* in its own context.

At this point, one cannot help wondering if there are any scholarly perspectives to the problems raised in our discussion. There is one: in *Recovering Liberties*, C.A. Bayly also attempted to place the *Tuhfat* in its intellectual context and opined that the text was an example of the philosophy of *akhlaq*. He further argued that Rammohun was inspired by *akhlaq*'s emphasis on the 'political morality' of rulers to author petitions which criticized the Company's governance. Unfortunately, Bayly did not develop this line of enquiry any further but abruptly narrowed the scope of his argument by asserting that *akhlaq* was 'analogous to liberalism'.[44]

However, independently of studies on Rammohun Roy, the tradition of *akhlaq* has been placed in its own context by Muzaffar Alam.

Alam argues that *akhlaq* is primarily concerned with ethics (defined separately for the individual, household, and government) and governance (the primary task of governments is investing in the welfare of their subjects and ensuring social stability).[45] At its core, *akhlaq* is a persuasive argument for the role of ethics and government. Although *akhlaq* philosophy is a broad tradition, *Akhlaq-i Nasiri* (1235), written by Nasir ad-Din Tusi, is its principal text.

Akhlaq-i Nasiri is frequently assessed as 'the best-known ethical digest to be composed in medieval Persia if not in all of medieval Islam.'[46] Its approach to ethics and society was shaped by two main intellectual traditions—Hellenistic philosophy (particularly Aristotle's conception of government) and medieval Islamic thought (such as Kindi, Abu Nasr Farabi, Avicenna, Avempace, and Averroes).[47] In keeping with *akhlaq* tradition, Tusi also defined ethics separately for the individual, the household, and the government.

Tusi divided *Akhlaq-i Nasiri* into three distinct 'discourses' or sections. G.W. Wickens argued that the first discourse, 'the corrections of dispositions' (*tahdhib-i akhlaq*), was the most important section of the text, 'in terms of space and priority'.[48] This discourse argued that all individuals were accountable to god through their everyday conduct and stressed that ethical actions would lead to greater happiness.[49] This was why all ethical individuals were rational (*'aqil*).[50] Note that *'aqil* did not refer to an individual who possessed any specific education but to two characteristics: belief in the soul (*jauhar-i basit*) and in god.[51] The connection between the soul and god was intricate, unchanging, and absolute. The soul also directed the actions of the human body to the extent that 'the body is a tool and an instrument for the soul'.[52] While all living creatures (vegetables, animals, and plants) had souls, the human soul was unique since it possessed the power of speech (*quwat-i nutq*) which resulted in the ability 'to distinguish between good and bad'.[53] This conception of 'rationality' extended to all human beings, and not just a particular type of person or religion.

The second discourse, 'the regulation of the household' (*tadbir-i manazil*) was concerned with the dynamics of the household.[54] The household was the basic 'economic' unit and the main basis of an individual's lived experience—the location of wealth, property, and family.[55] Tusi advocated generosity in donating wealth; prudence in looking after one's property; and temperance when dealing with other members of the household.[56] The household was regulated and, in effect, *governed.*

The third discourse, 'the government of cities' (*siyasat-i mudun*), was about the relationship between an individual and the political unit of the city, state, or empire.[57] Tusi argued that all individuals were members of a wider society and governed by monarchical authority.[58] 'Society', he theorized, 'was the fabric of everyday life but prone to conflict.'[59] Ideally, if there was 'love' between the various members of society, political authority ought not to have been required to prevent conflict.[60] In practical terms, however, this was not the case and intervention by monarchical authority was absolutely critical to prevent social conflict and ensure justice.[61] Thus, Tusi advocated the necessity of government (*siyasat*) in the context of a society which could not always be ethical.[62] The government was responsible for the welfare of its subjects. Its primary role was to create the conditions by which ethical practice became possible.

In conclusion, we find that *Akhlaq-i Nasiri* is an argument for individual and societal ethics. The concept of god and soul was central to Tusi's ideas of ethical practice. He continually stressed that an ethical individual was one who recognized the presence of both.

The question that now arises is: how did the *Akhlaq-i Nasiri* influence Indian intellectual traditions? In this context, Alam has shown that it was an important text for the Mughals.[63] Babur, the first Mughal Emperor, introduced it at the imperial court; and his grandson Akbar institutionalized it as the political philosophy of the empire and even arranged for it to be structured into madrasa syllabi to educate aspirants for a future employment in Mughal government service on 'non-religious themes'.[64] Akbar's educational reforms had important consequences for madrasas throughout the empire. In Bengal, a madrasa education became more 'culturally acceptable' to Hindus (particularly Kayasthas and Khatris). Even madrasa faculty, though initially Iranians, later featured Hindu teachers.[65] This process continued under Akbar's successors—Jahangir, Shah Jahan, and Aurangzeb.

Unfortunately, the importance of *Akhlaq-i Nasiri* after the death of Aurungzeb in 1707 has not yet been traced in current historical scholarship. However, as the next section will show, references to the text can be found in the late 18th century.

Akhlaq Texts in Early Colonial Bengal

The EIC's intervention in Bengal in the late 18th century prompted an intense engagement with the Persian language. Influential officials such as Warren Hastings and Henry Vansittart held it in high esteem and recommended its learning.[66] This is understandable since Persian was the language of administration at the time (and continued to be so until 1835). However, EIC officials were not only interested in Persian from an institutional point of view, but also considered it to have an aesthetic and poetic value.[67]

The Company's interest in Persian received an 'impetus' in the 1780s with the arrival of William Jones to Calcutta. Jones 'championed' the publication of Persian, especially grammar, poetry (Hafiz and Sa'adi amongst others), and Mughal works (such as *Ain-i Akbari*).[68] In 1771, his book on Persian grammar referred to the language as 'rich, melodious, and elegant'.[69] Institutionally, the foundation of the Asiatic Society of Bengal in 1784 aided the publication of Persian manuscripts by 'scholar–officials' (James Anderson, John Stonehouse, William Chambers, Thomas Law, William Kirkpatrick, Francis Gladwin, and Alexander Hamilton). As Beatrice Tessier has shown, scholar–officials were deeply influenced by Jones's research; and 'with the sole exception of Hamilton', all the others 'enjoyed' cultivating Persian poetry.[70]

Scholar–officials also drew from their interest in Persian poetry and literature to write textbooks for new Company recruits.[71] *The Persian Monshee* (1795) was one such textbook. Jointly authored by Francis Gladwin and William Chambers, it was intended to serve as an introduction to Arabic and Persian.[72] The text featured a large number of translation exercises (from English to Persian) which drew from familiar (Biblical) passages as well as medieval Persian poetry and literature. Interestingly, it also included passages from *Chahar Chaman*, a Persian text authored by Chandar Bhan 'Brahmin', the most well-known Mughal bureaucrat of the 17th century.[73]

Chandar Bhan was a product of a certain intellectual context. He recommended texts such as *Akhlaq-i Nasiri* and Persian poets such as Hafiz and Sa'adi as essential reading for a career in Mughal bureaucracy.[74] This is also reflected in Chandar Bhan's writings, where, as Rajiv Kinra notes, 'It is quite difficult at times to distinguish his administrative self from his poetic self'.[75] Kinra argues that such modes of writing were not due to authorial eccentricities but representative of Mughal bureaucracy where 'the language of poetry was the language of politics'.[76] Chandar Bhan's recommendations were taken seriously and *Chahar Chaman* was 'widely circulated' and read in madrasas throughout the Mughal Empire.[77]

In this context, *The Persian Monshee* also has another significance. Note that parts of the text were written in collaboration with William Chamber's Munshi.[78] This fact is important because the text also instructs Company officials on the desirable educational qualifications of Munshis.[79] I surmise that Chamber's Munshi almost certainly included familiar texts from his madrasa education (this could help explain its inclusion of Chandar Bhan's work).

The Persian Monshee also gives us a glimpse of late-18th-century madrasa syllabi in Bengal and constitutes material evidence of the fact that the writings of Mughal bureaucrats and the intellectual context they would have been familiar with continued to be studied during this period.

In 1801, Gladwin was appointed as the first professor of Persian at Fort William College.[80] Two years later, John Baillie, an avid Persianist, joined the faculty.[81] Baillie even bought a manuscript of *Akhlaq-i Nasiri* for his private collection.[82] *Akhlaq-i Nasiri* was thus recognized by the Orientalists as an important text.

The *akhlaq* tradition and Persian poetry were also recognized as important intellectual contexts outside scholarly circles. The CSBS published selected translated passages from *Akhlaq-i Nasiri* as well as Sa'adi's *Gulistan* and *Bustan* for its *Persian Reader* series (1825–35). Also included was Gladwin's translation of *Pandnama* (significantly, his translation of its title, 'A compendium of ethics', was retained).[83]

The CSBS's choice of selection of Persian texts not only informs us of how Perso-Arabic literature and philosophy were perceived at the time but also reveals that this literature was widely circulated. This is because its publications were not only meant for Company officials but also schools in Bengal—Calcutta, Barrackpur, Burdwan, Chinsura, Dinajpur, and Murshidabad—and even in territories as far away as Agra.[84] The Hindu College primarily depended on its publications (although it was not able to pay for most of them) and the Church Missionary Society in Calcutta acknowledged their aid in free books.[85] That the *Persian Reader* series was quite popular can be seen from sales/publication figures.

The *Ninth Report* (1832) noted that 231 copies had been sold that year and the *Tenth Report* (1834) recorded an official approval for a print order of 2,500 copies.[86]

The CSBS did not just publish English translations of Persian texts. From its very inception in 1818, native intellectuals associated with the organization such as Radhakanta Deb, Ram Comul Sen, and Taranicharan Mitra pushed for Bangla translations as well. In this context, the trio proposed a book project in Bangla—*Persian moral tales*. Their qualifications to write such a book were not in any doubt. Taranicharan Mitra was a Sanskrit pandit but knew Arabic and Urdu so well that he had even written books in these languages for the CSBS.[87] Mitra had been Head Munshi of the Hindustani Department at Fort William College since 1809.[88] Ram Comul Sen not only had a working knowledge of Persian but may have also been keen to publish Bengali translations since he had donated a copy of Gladwin's *The Persian Monshee* to the CSBS library that year.[89] The book project was quickly approved and sold well: 500 copies were printed for the first edition, 1,500 for the second, and 4,000 for the third. Significantly, it was recommended for 'distant stations' in Bengal.[90]

The circulation of publications to 'distant stations' was an important aspect of CSBS operations in Bengal. The intended recipients of 'distant stations' were not Company officials but 'native adults'. In *Third Report* (1820), the highest decision-making body of CSBS (referred to as the 'Committee') published an ambitious plan to 'facilitate the circulation of the society's works in the districts and generally render them more accessible'. While previously the CSBS had worked with 'auxiliary associations' and schools in the districts to provide books at cost price, the organization was now willing to cooperate with 'any individual, or body of individuals engaged in superintending native schools in the interior of the country'.[91] The Committee took steps to popularize their plan by placing advertisements in the government gazettes and even requested Company officials in the districts to distribute the catalogues as widely as possible amongst the natives. The CSBS also planned to publish a catalogue of books in Bangla.

The CSBS catalogue of books in Bangla would have been bound to include *Persian moral tales*. This is because Radhakanta Deb, Ram Comul Sen, and Taranicharan Mitra were also members of the Committee.[92] We note that all three men were bitter critics of Rammohun. Their interest in popularizing Persian stories shows that the discussion of texts written in the language was not limited to Rammohun and his associates. Rather, Persian was seen in an intellectual context—a landscape of ideas on ethics and everyday life; and through CSBS, they planned to popularize the ideas of early modern Persian texts and reach a readership which may not have been familiar with these ideas previously.

The Persian cultural context was a known, observable feature to CSBS native subscribers, Company officials, and Fort William College faculty in the early 19th century. *Akhlaq-i Nasiri* was translated into English and sections of the text were reprinted in textbooks for schools and colleges. At the heart of this process was the Fort William College Persian faculty. As the previous chapter noted, Rammohun was associated with Fort William College in 1801 and employed as a Munshi in 1805 by one of its early graduates, John Digby. Whether from the madrasa or Fort William College, Rammohun would have been acquainted with *Akhlaq-i Nasiri*. As the next section will show, it was also an important influence on *Tuhfat-ul- Muwahidin*.

Akhlaq-i Nasiri and Tuhfat

Tuhfat-ul-Muwahidin (henceforth, *Tuhfat*) is Rammohun's first known work.[93] It is also the only Perso-Arabic tract in his oeuvre. Significantly, its choice of language(s) restricted its readership to only those select few in Bengal who had been educated in Persian (for instance, the scribal elite).

The scope of *Tuhfat*'s argument was not, however, restricted to a select few. A case in point is its title which translates to 'A gift to the believers of one god'. The title summarizes Rammohun's main argument that 'everyone' intuitively believed in one god. This argument was paraphrased by the use of the word 'nature'.[94] This argument is also similar to the first discourse of *Akhlaq-i Nasiri* which stressed that the knowledge of the existence of god was intuitive and 'self-evident'.[95] Further, as Wickens noted, *Akhlaq-i Nasiri* also addressed a wide target audience since the scope of its argument was not restricted to any particular community or religion but all human beings.[96]

Tuhfat argued that in spite of one's intuitive belief in one god, 'everyone' had nevertheless been brought up to believe in *many* gods.[97] This argument was paraphrased by the use of the word 'habit'. [98]

The key difference between 'nature' and 'habit' was that while the former stayed the same, the latter could change.[99] To this extent, challenging the legitimacy of religious 'habits' was an important argument in the text. Rammohun insisted that the arguments of the religious leaders (or *mujtahids*) were simply appeals to inherited social conventions.[100] In the final analysis, he concluded that the 'habits' advocated by *mujtahids* were illegitimate, unethical, and contributed to social conflict amongst their followers (*muqallids*).

From Ghani's research we know that Rammohun's argument was influenced by Maʿarri's critique of religion. On the question of how Rammohun came across Maʿarri's ideas, our earlier discussion of madrasa syllabi in late-18th-century Bengal showed that it focussed on 'non-religious themes'. Thus, the ideas of Maʿarri would not have contradicted the prevailing intellectual context of the madrasas.

Rammohun was not against all religious practices. Rather, his aim was to reject only those religious practices advocated by the *mujtahids*. He noted that religious practices which otherwise contributed to 'welfare' caused conflict when interpreted by *mujtahids*.[101] In this case, he appealed to the *muqallids* to 'distinguish between the truth and untruth and the true propositions from the false ones':

> God has endowed each individual with intellectual facilities and senses. This should be used to discern the good from the bad, and man does not need to follow his fellows without reason if he has been invested with the power of intellectual thought.[102]

Rammohun's argument is rather vague since the terms and phrases such as 'intellectual faculties' and 'power of intellectual thought' are neither explained nor defined. We only know that if 'god has (already) endowed each individual' with them, then it cannot be a reference to a specific form of intellectual training or education. An additional point of congruity is important here. Like Tusi, Rammohun also argued that while all living creatures (vegetables, animals, and plants) had souls, the human soul was unique. This is because only the human soul possessed 'the faculty of rationality'. [103]

I argue that the passage quoted above can also be interpreted with reference to *Akhlaq-i Nasiri*'s argument concerning god, the human soul, and ethical practice.[104] Tusi argued that a 'rational individual' (*aqil*) was one who was aware of the relationship between god, the soul, and everyday ethical practice.[105] Crucially, *aqil* did not refer to a particular form of education.[106] I tentatively suggest that Rammohun's argument was that god endowed 'intellectual facilities' to the soul, which in turn affected everyday conduct. His reference to 'the power of intellectual thought', for example, could be a reference to *aqil*. With *aqil*, 'each individual could discern the good from the bad' without 'the need to follow his fellows' (specifically, the *mujtahids*).[107] In fact, by referring to the concept of *aqil*, we find that *Tuhfat* sketched out an argument for the emancipation of the *muqallids* from *mujtahids*. This argument can thus be read as Rammohun's *Tuhfat* or 'gift' to the *muqallids*.

We now turn to another distinct argument—the use of the Persian language in *Tuhfat*. Rammohun's linguistic usage has attracted sharp criticism as scholars opine that his command of Persian was 'poor', his grammar 'juvenile', and style 'abstruse'.[108] Moreover, the author of *Tuhfat* himself admitted that Arabic (and not Persian) was his language of choice. So, the question is: why didn't he write the entire text in Arabic?

Rammohun insisted that the use of Persian was necessary 'to make it more intelligible to readers who don't understand Arabic' (*ajam*).[109] This point is revealing when we recall that *Akhlaq-i Nasiri*, though a Persian text, frequently employed Arabicisms. This was not an authorial eccentricity but related to the type of arguments employed—a syllogistic mode of argument for which Arabic was more suited. However, as Wickens, the translator of the *Akhlaq-i Nasiri*, noted, the use of syllogisms also made for complicated reading.[110] In this context, historians have oft commented on the *Tuhfat*'s syllogistic structure.[111]

Tentatively, I suggest that Rammohun would have preferred to use Arabic because it was more suitable for syllogistic arguments. As to why he wrote in Persian, this was an attempt to render the text more accessible to readers.

Accessibility was an important concern to Rammohun. He explained his arguments by referring to the poet Hafiz. Consider, for example, the argument that a belief in one god was more suitable for social stability since the presence of many religious sects led to social conflict. This was explained with reference to Hafiz's verses on the disputes within the 72 different sects of Islam:

> The disputes of the seventy-two sects are to be excused,
> Because they not finding the truth,
> Have trotted the way of fables and nonsense.[112]

The concern with the prevention of social conflict and ethical practice was also stressed with another verse from Hafiz:

> Be not after the injury of anyone,
> For the rest you may do as you will,
> For in our way and conduct,
> There is no other sin but this (injuring others).[113]

In the final analysis, *Tuhfat* articulated an argument for a more stable, peaceful society. This argument also shares an important conceptual similarity with *Akhlaq-i Nasiri*. Both conceptualized a society based on fairness, consideration for others, and the existence of a government and laws to protect one's person and property.[114] But the difference in their arguments lies in the degree of emphasis. While *Akhlaq-i Nasiri* devoted two detailed discourses to government, law, and property, *Tuhfat* only but briefly touched upon these concepts and prioritized arguments concerning ethical practice.

Rammohun did not refer to, translate, or popularize *Tuhfat*. Consequently, historians are doubtful of its influence on subsequent writings.[115] These doubts are, however, misplaced.[116] In the next section, I will argue that *Tuhfat's* ideas feature prominently in subsequent writings on Hindu scripture in Calcutta (1815–30). These writings questioned the legitimacy of the Brahmins (whom the *Tuhfat* had referred to as *mujtahids*) and stressed the importance of everyday ethical practices (an argument which *Tuhfat* had prioritized).

Writings on Hindu Scripture, 1815–30

After completing *Tuhfat* in 1803, Rammohun became associated with the EIC's district administration for the next 11 years. A better part of this time was spent in the Rangpur district. It was here that he began to translate the Vedanta and the Upanishads.[117] He also renewed his acquaintance with Hariharananda Bharati, a wandering sanyasi who had renounced his birth name (Nandakumar Vidyalankar) and livelihood (a teacher of Sanskrit philosophy).[118] He had first met Hariharananda in Radhanagar (while still in his teens) and maintained a close friendship ever since.[119]

Hariharananda taught Rammohun the Mahanirvana Tantra (henceforth, MnT), a late-18th-century text of which he had also produced the first known commentary.[120] Although referred to frequently by Rammohun and a host of Bengali social reformers in the 19th century, MnT has also been the subject of much speculation, suspicion, controversy, and has only recently been unambiguously accepted as a genuine work.[121]

MnT comprises of more than 2,000 verses of dialogue between Shiva, the Hindu god of destruction, and his wife and consort, Parvati; and claims inspiration from the Vedic corpus. Towards the beginning of the text, Shiva even declares that MnT essentially reinforces Vedic doctrine. However, such a stance is unusual since Tantra texts are typically critical of the Vedas. Even more surprising is MnT's identification with a Vedantic interpretation of an invisible, benevolent Brahman than one informed by personal cults of goddesses and gods (such as Kali, Sakti, or Shiva).[122]

To Rammohun, MnT was an important source by which his own arguments concerning religious knowledge could be justified and elaborated on.[123] MnT would go on to emerge as a steady discursive companion in his forays into interpreting scripture. He referred to it in a number of works including *Translation of the Isho Upanishad* (1816),[124] *Second Defence of the Monotheistic System of the Vedas* (1817),[125] and *An Apology for the pursuit of Final beatitude independently of Brahmunical observances* (1820) to make his case against the 'illusion' of idol worship and emphasize the need to recognize the 'reality' of an invisible Brahman. [126]

Rammohun also referred to MnT to substantiate his arguments on religious worship. In his view, worship had not only been unfairly monopolized by the Brahminical community but also mistakenly viewed as a practice that was only concerned with rites and rituals. His opinions on the subject appeared in *Translation of a Sanskrit tract inculcating the*

Divine worship (1827). The 'Sanskrit tract' in the title was the Gayatri Mantra, (which was 'recited daily in prayers' during this period in Bengal).[127] He argued that the Gayatri Mantra could be performed through oral recitation by all members of society and all castes, 'whether a Brahmin or not', and did not require either rites or rituals.[128] Tellingly, he pointed out that his argument was not unique since it had also been reiterated by MnT.[129]

MnT was not only concerned with religious knowledge and worship. Nearly half of it was on social practices and legal procedure. It borrowed heavily from MDhS and Dayabhaga and provided detailed stipulations on upholding caste, living in a marriage, inheriting property, and rejecting sati. These discussions were not only atypical of Tantric literature but also selectively contradicted DhS and Dayabhaga. So, MnT's discussion of caste rules and regulations and its presentation of the householder as the *homo religiosus* of Hindu society was along DhS lines; but its stipulations concerning marriage, property, and sati were not. On the subject of marriage, it held consent to be critical to the entire process but did not place any emphasis on factors which the DhS considered important, such as age and caste.[130] Similarly, while discussing property it held that only the eldest son can inherit, a point of view that was a clear departure from Dayabhaga which insisted that women could also inherit. On the question of sati, while MnT rejected the idea that the practice was necessary, MDhS, the most authoritative of the DhS, was silent on the matter.[131]

Rammohun selectively borrowed from MnT in matters of social and legal practice.[132] On the one hand, he was ambivalent about the importance of caste[133] and rejected the view that only the eldest son could inherit property.[134] On the other hand, he agreed with the MnT's views on marriage[135] and sati.[136] Ideas such as these may have featured in his regularly organized evening congregations on religion at his home in Rangpur.[137] His meetings, however, courted controversy. A certain Gaurikanta Bhattacharya, the dewan of the local court, was so incensed with his ideas that he wrote an entire book, *Gyananjan*, to criticize them. (A revised version of Bhattacharya's book appeared in 1838, suggesting that interest in this period of Rammohun's life continued long afterwards.)[138] I think Rammohun's sojourn at Rangpur had an important impact on his thought. It was there that he embarked on his project of translation of Hindu scripture, met his first major critic, and encountered new texts such as MnT. In the long run, his encounter with MnT proved to be very fruitful as the text served as a dependable reference for a number of projects—from property laws to religious worship.

In 1814, Rammohun left the Company and shifted out of Rangpur into Calcutta and began a new phase of his intellectual career. At Calcutta, he soon made a name for himself as one of the city's most successful businessmen, with an income of over 10,000 rupees annually. He lived lavishly and in style. Even the British were impressed. In May 1823, Fanny Parkes (a British diarist who had arrived but a year ago with her husband) visited his home. Parkes has left us with an enthusiastic and vivid account of the extravagant displays of fireworks, dance, and music that she had witnessed.[139]

Rammohun had not, however, forgotten his interest in Hindu scripture. He soon set about publishing interpretations and translations of the Vedanta and Upanishads.[140] During this time, Hariharananda, who had travelled with him to Calcutta, introduced him to his younger brother, Ramchandra Vidyavagish. Impressed by Ramchandra's knowledge of the DhS, Rammohun encouraged him to study the Vedanta with his pandit, Shivaprasad Sharma, and monetarily supported him for many years. Vidyavagish proved to be a quick learner and later became Rammohun's chief assistant in publications on Hindu scripture.[141]

Rammohun's interest in supporting Ramchandra's studies on the Vedanta stems from the fact that it was also his main area of study. *Vedanta Grantha* (1815), his first published work in Calcutta, tackled the subject matter of the Vedanta Sutras. The Vedanta Sutras is a core text in Hinduism, primarily concerned with interpreting the Upanishads.

Vedanta Sutras has two textual peculiarities which renders it a difficult read. First, it is organized into notes and headings (but in no particular order); and second, its writers are ambiguous about their arguments.[142] In this context, commentaries (such as the Advaita Vedanta) have always occupied an important position in the canon for providing clarity and context. Advaita Vedanta was written in Sanskrit in the 7th century CE by Shankara.[143]

Vedanta Grantha claimed to be a literal Bangla translation of the Advaita Vedanta. This claim is not entirely true because some of its more complex arguments were also abbreviated.[144] The simplification was probably done to reach out to a broad readership for Rammohun was well aware that most readers would find *Vedanta Grantha* difficult to read and even pleaded with them to persevere. 'Only after 2–3 months can you get a sense of *Vedanta Grantha*', he wrote, 'but it is time worth investing in.'[145] The key concept that he wanted his readers to know about, and reflect on, was the *brahman*. 'The question of the *brahman* is an important one, and has value', he opined. He continued, 'To understand *brahman* is to understand all the shastras and learn something fundamental about one's self. It takes faith to achieve the best results.'[146]

Rammohun's stress on the importance of *brahman* is understandable for it is also a critical point of discussion in Shankara's Advaita Vedanta. According to Shankara, *brahman* is of two types—*paramarthika* (absolute truth) and *vyavaharika* (practical truth). The latter has external attributes (*upadhi*) which can be comprehended by human beings while the former is unknowable. Ultimately, Advaita Vedanta is a method by which knowledge of *vyavaharika* could be gained.[147] However, *Vedanta Grantha* ignored such distinctions between *paramarthika* and *vyavaharika*.

Rammohun's reluctance to cite important distinctions in Shankara's thought was a pattern rather than an exception. For example, the various distinctions between *brahman*, *atman* (self), and *isvara* (god) were also ignored.[148] In fact, for approximately one-tenth of Advaita Vedanta, he even contradicted Shankara without acknowledgement. These were not noted in Bengali society because his contemporaries were not familiar with the text of Advaita Vedanta. As Killingley opines, *Vedanta Grantha* had created a context in which 'having stepped into the shoes of Shankara as an authentic expositor', Rammohun could then advance positions which completely deviated from Advaita Vedanta.[149] For example, he asserted that the Advaita Vedanta's discussion of the relation between the soul and god is an important argument.[150] This assertion is untrue. Consequently, his argument that the soul cannot exist without god is neither related to Vedanta Sutras nor Advaita Vedanta and other commentaries (such as by Ramanuja and Madhava for example).[151]

One does wonder what Rammohun hoped to achieve by falsely claiming a literal translation of Advaita Vedanta and then pushing forward arguments which were beyond the scope of Vedanta Sutras. And did his arguments then have a textual basis to them? I argue that a reading of *Akhlaq-i Nasiri* can help explain Rammohun's simplification of the concept of *brahman* and his idea of the soul. An exploration of this thematic also helps us recognize the importance of his religious works as projects of ethics. This is because *Akhlaq-i Nasiri* argued that the realization of the existence of god and soul was a necessary condition for ethical practice.[152]

Akhlaq-i Nasiri provided Rammohun with a conceptualization of an ethical society. Tusi defined society as the awareness of one's connection to a wider community; argued that it was not possible for an individual to *not* live in society; and concluded that an ethical society was one in which *everyone* was aware of the need to be ethical.[153] I suggest that this argument influenced Rammohun's ideas of worship (*atma vidya*) in *Vedanta Grantha*. He even rejected Shankara's argument that the purpose of worship was the realization of the self (*atman*—which in Advaita Vedanta is the source of man's consciousness) and insisted instead that 'worship' referred to ethical practices in society.[154]

Rammohun was making an argument that was not present in the textual canon that he claimed to translate and interpret. But there was also a specific reason for his interest in the Vedanta Sutras and Advaita Vedanta: both were associated with Shankara. In the early 19th century, most Bengali households would have recognized Shankara as a religious scholar but one who was more revered than read.[155] To this extent, Rammohun reached out to Hindu Bengali householders (*grihastha*) in his writings by referring to texts, ideas, and contexts which they would have been familiar with.

Rammohun championed the role of the householder in *Vedanta Grantha* by asserting that a householder's lived experience was the most important pre-requisite for gaining knowledge of *brahman*.[156] He argued that the householder who understood the concept of *brahman* would henceforth be 'godly' (*Brahmanishtha*).[157] In fact, any householder following his tracts would have read that he was to aspire to the ideal of a 'godly householder' (*Brahmanishtha grihastha*). The emphasis on the householder was markedly different from Shankara who insisted that only those who renounced society (sanyasi) could aspire to become 'godly'.[158] Indeed, he ignored Shankara's arguments concerning renunciation altogether and instead continued to develop his own argument.

Three years after *Vedanta Grantha*, a small write-up on the house-holder appeared in his introduction to the Bangla translation of Mandukya Upanishad (1818). The householder, he opined, had a duty to listen to discussions on the Vedanta and reflect on its meaning. All those who persevered would ultimately arrive at the conclusion that an individual's mind, ego, body, intellect, as well as the *brahman* itself had the Supreme Being at their heart. After this realization, the householder would henceforth pursue the singular goal (*sadhana*) of having their soul merge with the *brahman* after death.[159] A householder following such a goal would be then known as a *sadhak* (devotee).

As he had stressed in *Vedanta Grantha*, Rammohun fervently asserted that everyday 'material' domesticity contributed to the house-holder's goal of merging with the *brahman*.[160] He also outlined duties towards the family. A householder was expected to practice temperance and serve his teachers. He seemed to have assumed that a devoted *sadhak* would naturally engage in ethical conduct and so did not pay more attention to developing a concept of ethical practices in the household. The overall impression that readers would have had was that the 'godly householder' was still a concept in the making and details would be worked out soon.

To this extent, Rammohun's other writings also referred to the role of the householder in similar terms through his works *Translation of the Abridgement of the Vedanta* (1816),[161] *Translation of the Isho Upanishad* (1816),[162] *Translation of Mundaka Upanishad* (1819),[163] and *Translation of Katha Upanishad* (1819).[164] Collectively, his writings championed the role of the householder and dismissed the idea that asceticism could be seen as a more intense form of religious experience.

The consistency and rapidity with which Rammohun published his arguments should not lead one to believe that they were not challenged in print. Indeed, his contemporaries also published detailed rebuttals. In 1820, an anonymous writer who simply signed his name as 'an artist' (kavitakar) asserted that an ascetic's experience of religious life was far more complete than that of a householder and that Rammohun was only able to argue otherwise because he had deliberately misinterpreted scripture.[165]

Rammohun, in turn, published a critique of kavitakar's views within the year in a Bangla tract, *Kavitakarer sahit vichar* [Debate with Kavitakar, 1820]. He rejected the allegation that Hindu scripture had been deliberately misinterpreted. Instead, he appealed to kavitakar to read his introduction and translation of the Isho Upanishad (1816) before offering an opinion.[166] He opined that kavitakar's views about religious life and asceticism were wrong and pointed out that early Indian Hindu thinkers such as Yajnavalkya, *Angira*, and Vasistha had been householders.[167] He was also 'disgusted' with the tone of the tract and complained that kavitakar had written a piece that was 'full of angry insults.'[168] 'My relative wanted to respond to these insults,' he wrote, 'but I stopped him with the following quote from the Mahabharata (MBh): "Unsavoury truths are never beneficial for society (*lokatta*) or religion."'[169]

Rammohun would not have wanted to admit it, but kavitakar had picked up on an 'unsavoury truth'—the absence of any detailed tract on the concept of a 'godly householder' in his writings until then. In fact, it took him more than a decade after the publication of *Vedanta Grantha* to produce a short Bangla tract on the subject—*Brahmanishtha grihastha lakshan* [Hallmarks of a Godly Householder, 1826]. This tract was probably aimed at upper-caste Hindu conservatives such as kavitakar who disagreed with his ideas. For instance, Rammohun conceptualized the householder as a Brahmin man. Although he did not make a direct reference to MDhS, conservative Brahmin householders would have immediately recognized its influence on his work.

On the surface, Rammohun's choice of text for discussing the householder does not appear to be unusual. In fact, the MDhS's discussions on the householder are so extensive that its translator, Patrick Olivelle, has even opined that the text presented the householder as the *homo religiosus* of Hindu society.[170] From an MDhS perspective, the most important fixture of a householder's everyday life were the Vedas. All householders had a 'daily commitment' to perform five domestic Vedic rites[171] and engage in Vedic study.[172] As far as social practices were concerned, householders were to look after their parents and teachers[173] as well as exercise temperance in everyday conduct with priests, relatives, dependents, and children.[174]

In *Brahmanishtha grihastha lakshan*, Rammohun followed the MDhS's discursive trail and also insisted that all Brahmin householders must meticulously perform five domestic Vedic rites every day, read scripture, and exercise temperance.[175] His assertion that householders must perform certain rituals every day was rather puzzling. For more than a decade, he had consistently argued that rituals were inadequate and unnecessary modes of worship.[176] So, why did he now author a tract which contradicted these arguments altogether?

Rammohun never explained his reasons, but I think that *Brahmanishtha grihastha lakshan* can be read as a failed example of his approach of reaching out to potential readers by presenting an argument through a familiar reference. Try as he might, it would have proved discursively impossible to argue that MDhS dissuaded its readers from performing rituals. He opined that all Brahmin householders who were unable to perform Vedic rites could spend some time every day in the study of the Vedas, Upanishads, and the Pronob Mantra (Om) but did not (or, *could not*) substantiate this argument any further.[177] Perhaps this is why it took so long for him to produce the tract and why it was never referred to in any other work.

One does however wonder if his concept of a 'godly householder' may have been an inspired interpretation of another text. After all, references to householders also occur in the Mahabharata (MBh). In MBh's Rajadharmaparvan, Yudhishthira, a key character, was even 'persuaded' to reject a life of renunciation and instead informed that a householder was 'superior' to an ascetic.[178] Like the MDhS, MBh too emphasized the 'domestic religiosity' of a householder and accorded it 'a central role' in society.[179] Such similarities are not coincidental but the product of a shared historical context. As Olivelle has shown, the 'timeframe, geography and socio-political environment' of the MBh and the MDhS is very similar and their authors belonged to the Brahmin caste.[180] Similar words, concepts, ideas, and narratives thus abound. Further, MBh not only stressed on the householder but also contained extensive debates around the subject of social ethics. As Rammohun frequently referred to MBh, we can be sure that he would have been familiar with its arguments on these subjects.[181]

As we shall see in Chapter 6, to Rammohun, ethics referred to an individual invested with prescriptive responsibilities. A 'godly householder' in this sense would have referred to a householder who was devoted to the idea of *brahman* through ethical actions. So, could MBh have provided

Rammohun with such a conception? Unfortunately, it couldn't have. MBh did not conceptualize the householder in these terms. Rather, as Bimal Krishna Matilal eloquently argued, all discussions on ethics and morality in MBh were always framed in terms of binaries and dilemmas.[182] For instance, MBh's Santiparvan dwelt at length on the binary between the many compromises made by a king and the 'moral absolutes' of an ascetic but did not expound on the prescriptive rules of ethical conduct.[183] Rammohun himself was of the opinion that Hindu scripture did not provide any information on prescriptive ethics ('maxims of moral duty').[184] So the question remains: from which text did he develop the argument concerning an ethical householder?

I argue that the *Akhlaq-i Nasiri* may have been the chief inspiration behind the concept of a 'godly householder' invested with ethical responsibilities. Specifically, the second discourse, 'the regulation of the household' (*tadbir-i manazil*) conceptualized the household as the locus of an individual's lived experience and outlined the qualities of an ethical householder.[185] Since Tusi's ideas of an ethical householder were epistemically indispensable to the belief in god, I suggest that 'godly householder' is also a good description of his ideas. This text may not have been as agreeable to Hindu Bengali householders though, and Rammohun did not refer to it in *Vedanta Grantha*.

Vedanta Grantha's similarities with *Akhlaq-i Nasiri* also highlight an important common intellectual context: *Tuhfat*. *Tuhfat* and *Vedanta Grantha* also share several discursive similarities. Both are arguments for the belief and worship of one god. Both argue that everyday ethical practice is the best form of worship (and do so by de-legitimizing the role of religious leaders) and finally, both root their arguments in the public social practices of contemporary Bengali society. These similarities are not immediately apparent because the tracts were written in different languages and cited different textual influences.

The key difference between *Tuhfat* and *Vedanta Grantha* is that the former could only be read by those who had been educated in Persian while the latter was made accessible to a broader audience. Unlike *Tuhfat*, *Vedanta Grantha* was summarized in abridged English and Bangla editions, *Translation of the Abridgement of the Vedanta* (1816) and *Vedantasar* (1815). This marked a turning point in his methods, and one that we must discuss in some detail before we return to our discussion on the *Tuhfat*.

Rammohun's decision to produce abridged translations of *Vedanta Grantha* improved the visibility of his ideas considerably. English language newspapers were impressed with the *Translation of the Abridgement of the Vedanta*. On 1 February 1816, *The Government Gazette* announced its arrival as 'a phenomenon in the literary world'.[186] On the same day, *The Missionary Register* published a glowing review.[187] A week later, the *Gazette* reported that its readers were curious for more details and opted to reprint the tract in full.[188]

Readers may have been curious about Rammohun's writings because of their accessibility. Indeed, certain authorial strategies were employed to aid the process of textual comprehension. For example, his English translations introduced new conceptual vocabularies: *Advaita Vedanta* was interpreted as 'the rational worship of the god of nature' which was 'confirmed by the dictates of common sense'.[189] For Bengali readers, familiar mythical figures such as Vyasa, the (mythical) author of MBh, were referred to highlight the reasonableness of his ideas.[190] Not all strategies passed off without comment and some provoked harsh criticism. For instance, kavitakar (mentioned earlier) argued that his appeals to Vyasa were so suspiciously frequent that they must be untrue.[191]

Rammohun, however, needed to defend his methods and hence sharply disagreed by insisting that Vyasa had been invoked correctly, and with respect.[192] His case was considerably strengthened by the fact that the Vedanta Sutras are traditionally ascribed to Vyasa, 'the greatest of Indian theologists, philosophers and poets'.[193] Vyasa also has a specific status in the hierarchy of authorship in Hindu scripture. As V. Narayan Rao explains, 'The Veda is the text of the highest authority [in Hindu scripture] but also above human authorship. The next level of authorship is Vyasa.'[194]

Rammohun's textual strategies in *Abridgement of the Vedanta* and *Vedantasar* paid off; for as contemporary newspapers reported, his tracts were read, discussed, and debated by an audience of nearly 500 people in Bengal.[195] Perhaps, this was why MBh and Vyasa would also be referred in other works (such as his interpretation and translation of the Upanishads). In contrast, *Tuhfat* was neither mentioned again in any other work nor translated into Bangla or English. But was this to do with the specific style of argument of *Tuhfat*?

In this context, consider the structure of *Tuhfat*. Rammohun used a syllogistic structure of argument. An investigation of the syllogistic structure of the tract has not been undertaken in detail in current scholarship. Therefore, as an exploratory point, let us consider its first paragraph (which argued the case for the existence of one god).

> I travelled the remotest parts of the world, in plains as well as in hilly lands and I found the inhabitants thereof agreeing generally on believing the existence of One Being who is the source of all creation and the governor of it.[196]

Rammohun further noted that inhabitants who believed in many gods fell to arguing with each other over contrasting representations of god and ultimately engaged in violence and conflict.[197]

Syllogistically, 'the existence of One Being' is a universal categorical proposition, that is, it argues that since the proposition of the belief in one god is universally true, all propositions which contradict it are false. Thus, if a proposition is universally true, then it is unquestionably true. Similarly, if a proposition is universally false, then it is undeniably false. Further, a false argument can be shown by identifying contradictions.

Tuhfat's point about identifying contradictory arguments as evidence of false arguments was retained in his writings on Hindu scripture. Consider *Abridgement of the Vedanta* (1816). This tract elaborated on *Vedanta Grantha*'s ideas of 'worship'. Rammohun rejected the idea that the plethora of rituals associated with worship of idols of Hindu gods and goddesses in contemporary Bengal had any epistemic connection with 'worship' since Hindu texts (such as MDhS) had different prescriptions for rites and ritual. Instead, readers were advised to consider ethical practices ('charity and humility') as 'worship'. These assertions were not, however, accepted by his critics who argued that idol worship was sanctioned by various authors and commentators of Hindu scripture.[198] In response, Rammohun opined that their interpretation of Hinduism was not viable and led to confusion over contradictory rituals for different idols. Instead, he stressed that an emphasis on ethical practice was more reasonable because it avoided such contradictions.[199] In Calcutta, these ideas were widely considered to be unique, so much so that charges of forgery were levelled against him (and rejected, politely but firmly).[200]

Rammohun's method of identifying contradictions in arguments also applies to writings other than Hindu scripture, such as *Padri o shishya samvad* [A Padre and His Disciples, 1821]. This short dialogical tract originally appeared in Bangla but was later translated into English in 1823. The emphasis on Christianity ought not to surprise us. After all, Rammohun wrote four lengthy tracts on the Bible between 1820 and 1823 and was particularly interested in discussions of ethics in the four Gospels of the New Testament. I argue in Chapter 6 that he was so moved, inspired, and influenced by Christian ethics that he even referenced and integrated Biblical dictums into his own writings on Hindu scripture. In this chapter, we touch upon just one aspect of the *Padri o shishya samvad*—Rammohun's method of argument. Significantly, his arguments were made by using humour and satire.

Humour was also an important new method in Rammohun's writings on Hindu scripture and primarily employed to reach out to readers and audiences. For example, English and Bengali translations of the Isho Upanishad (1816) and Katha Upanishad (1819) humorously criticized ritual by referring to contemporary Hinduism as 'observances of a peculiar form of diet'.[201] *The Universal Religion: Religious Instructions founded on sacred authorities* (1819) criticized ritual vegetarianism by humorously opining that 'it is certainly far more preferable to adorn the mind than to think of purifying the belly'.[202] The phrase 'adorn the mind' brings to mind his reference to *atma vidya* (worship) in *Vedanta Grantha*, making it a clear case of humour being used to advocate a key argument on ethics.

Along with humour, Rammohun's writings on Hindu scripture also employed another method: that of referring to contemporary social practices and theological concepts to provide a familiar context to his ideas for his audience. Even early writings such as *Utsavanader sahit vicar* [Reply to Utsavananda, 1816] and *Gosvamir sahit vichar* [Reply to a Goswamin, 1818] contained references to familiar household rituals (*puja*); contemporary sects (Saiva, Sakta, and Vaishnava); theological concepts such as salvation (*mukti*); texts such as Bhagavata Purana and Bhagvadgita; and verses such as Gayatri.[203]

Rammohun's method of identifying contradictory arguments, employing humour and satire, and referring to familiar socio-religious terms made his writings more accessible. This was probably why his works were read, critiqued, and reviewed in Bengali society. But that doesn't mean that everyone agreed with him. Rather, his writings were oft challenged by critics. Some of his responses to critics often found their way into the prefaces and introductions of his translations and interpretations of scripture while others took the form of specific tracts. For our discussion, we will consider four such works—*Gosvamir sahit vichar* (1818), *Chari proshner uttar* (1822), *Pathyapradan* (1823), and *Bhattacharyer sahit vichar* (1817). *Bhattacharyer sahit vichar* also appeared in English as *Second Defence of the Monotheistical System of the Vedas* in 1817, but the Bangla version is referred here because it contains information which was excluded in the English translation.[204]

Gosvamir sahit vichar (1818) is a short Bangla tract. 'Goswami' here is an unknown Vaishnavite and the tract is a criticism of his faith. It is structured as a dialogue between Rammohun and Goswami. Rammohun began by sharply disagreeing with the content and purpose of Vaishnava traditions, arguing that they only served to distract devotees from contemplating on the nature of the Supreme Being.[205] On his part, Goswami seemed to have realized that a reference to a Vedic context was important in any debate with Rammohun. He responded that while Vaishnavism did not disregard the authority of the Vedas, one has to provide a description of the Supreme Being or be lost in abstraction.[206] He then asked Rammohun how the Vedas described the Supreme Being and was told to read his translations of the Kena Upanishad and Mundaka Upanishad for answers.[207]

According to Rammohun, a thorough reading of his tracts would reveal that the Supreme Being was not perceivable by humankind.[208] He also disagreed with Goswami's idea that religion could only be comprehended when taught by a teacher (as far as he was concerned; only reading, reflection, and debate was required) and that the Bhagavata Purana adequately described the central tenets of the Vedanta. In the end, he revealed his central problem with Vaishnavism. The Vaishnavas practised idol worship. According to him, this interpretation of divinity was false as the Vaishnavas were not worshipping the Supreme Being but only a glorified image.[209] Goswami presented a few more arguments; these were also discarded and the debate swiftly came to an end. *Gosvamir sahit vichar* reveals much about the reader, the 'public' that Rammohun had in mind and also tells us much about his method by which he chose to engage his audience—debates around scripture.

While *Gosvamir sahit vichar* ended on a polite note, critics could also turn aggressive and hostile, and none more so than the man who went by the name of Dharma Shanstapana Kankhi (the person who wants to protect the established religion). On 6 April 1822, the pseudonym was used for the first time in an article against Rammohun's project in the Bangla newspaper *Samachar Darpan*. Significantly, Dharma Shanstapana Kankhi did not refer to Rammohun by name but sarcastically as 'the one who knows the essence of devotion' (*bhakta tattva gyani*) and challenged him to answer his queries.[210]

Bhakta tattva gyani was denounced as an outsider (*nogorantobashi*) and a hypocrite for continuing to wear the Brahminical sacred thread (while questioning the veracity of idol worship and superstition); for justifying his consumption of non-vegetarian food (by berating against ritual vegetarianism in scripture); and for single-mindedly pursuing his own ambition to be recognized as a religious leader by publishing scripture in Bangla.[211] So, why did he pretend to selflessly serve and worship the Supreme Being when he was clearly only using scripture and upholding religious conventions to serve his own ends?

Rammohun responded to Dharma Shanstapana Kankhi the very next month in his Bangla tract, *Chari proshner uttar* (1822). He argued that he had no ambitions to be a religious leader. Rather, his writings were meant to be a public good since they introduced the ideas of the Vedas to a broader audience in society. He reminded his critic that the Vedas themselves sanctioned the injunction to wear the sacred thread. Further, he opined that eating meat was not a problem as long as one exercised temperance.[212] He humorously argued that Dharma Shanstapana Kankhi was not a protector of the established religious order but 'a destroyer of religion' (*dharma shangharak*).[213]

Meanwhile, Dharma Shanstapana Kankhi's work must have made quite an impact in the public sphere, for Calcutta conservatives now began to take notice and came forward with funding and commissions. Consequently, on 1 February 1823, Dharma Shanstapana Kankhi produced *Pasanda Pidana* [Torment to the Heretic].[214] *Pasanda Pidana* listed Nandalal Thakur as the author, for he had commissioned the tract.[215] Perhaps this authorial change may have also contributed to its unusual length of over 200 pages.

As Thakur, Dharma Shanstapana Kankhi became even more vicious. He now claimed that Rammohun (or rather, *bhakta tattva gyani* as he insisted on calling him) was apparently 'so full of evil (*papatma*) that even if he committed a hundred sins, it wouldn't make a difference to his karma; just as a drop of water does not make a difference to an ocean'.[216] Rammohun's 'sins' were long and numerous: he had rejected traditional eating regulations; declared that Sri Chaitanya, the Vaishnavite saint, was not divinely ordained but just an ordinary human being (and mocked his followers to boot); and opposed caste regulations.[217] But worst of all, he had flamboyantly disregarded caste rules and conventions in the full light of the public sphere.[218] 'So many accounts of his activities were being circulated by people that they cannot all be baseless,' he complained.[219]

Dharma Shanstapana Kankhi even brought up the question of what Rammohun's parents may have thought of his project. 'His parents, devout Vaishnavites as they were, must have done a great deal of good *karma* to beget a son like him, who brings such glory to the family name.'[220] This argument was problematic because it was untrue. Rammohun's father had died in 1803 and his mother in 1822 in Puri, Orissa, the year before *Pasanda Pidana* was published.[221] Dharma Shanstapana Kankhi was not aware of these details as he probably did not know Rammohun personally.

Pasanda Pidana was well received in Bengali society.[222] Undaunted, Rammohun responded in a voluminous Bangla tract of over 250 pages, *Pathyapradan* (1823). The title (which translates to 'Medicine for the sick offered by one who laments his inability to perform righteousness') not only expressed his opinion of his critic but also set the tone for the arguments of the main text:

> My critic's entire tract is only concerned with snide and derogatory comments. Once we know this fact, that jealousy and the intense desire to put somebody down has been used under the garb of *shastric* debates, we realise that *dharma shangharak* [Rammohun referred to Dharma Shanstapana Kankhi by this name] just wants to express his anger against me. But, *dharma shangharak* and others know that I am capable of using worse words for him and his dependents. But I am refraining from doing so, for then, it is I who will lose face.[223]

Rammohun then continued along a line of argument that Dharma Shanstapana Kankhi would have found familiar: the relations between parents and children. He recalled that 'parents continue to be affectionate with their children even when they are violently rebuffed', and proceeded to refer to his critic as a child. He resolved to be affectionate and hoped that his critic would realize that a Shastric approach is about being compassionate towards others.[224] When Dharma Shanstapana Kankhi did not respond, it was clear that Rammohun had had the last word. But one question was left unanswered: who was Dharma Shanstapana Kankhi? Rammohun himself took the view that Kasinath Tarkapanchanan, (then an assistant pandit at Fort William College) could have been the real author.[225]

Rammohun's perspective has been clarified by Brajendranath Banerji. In 1942, Banerji produced an intellectual biography of the pandits of Fort William College. His research revealed that Tarkapanchanan had been recruited by William Carey to teach Bangla to Company officials in Fort William College and that he was a highly reputed Sanskrit scholar whose works were published by the Baptist Mission Press (and also appeared in *Samachar Darpan*).[226] After discussing his work at length, Banerji concluded that Tarkapanchanan was Dharma Shanstapana Kankhi and that Rammohun was the author of *Pathyapradan*.[227] Although Banerji continued to work on the subject (and by 1959 had produced no fewer than five new editions of his intellectual biography), his opinions regarding Tarkapanchanan's authorship did not change. In 1973, a new edition of Rammohun's collected Bangla and Sanskrit works by Ajit Kumar Ghose confirmed Banerji's views by reprinting *Chari proshner uttar* and *Pathyapradan* in its corpus of works by Rammohun, and listing *Pasanda Pidana* as the work of Tarkapanchanan.

According to Banerji, Tarkapanchanan's primary area of interest lay in *nyaya* philosophy. *Nyaya* is a school of philosophy concerned with epistemology, logic, and language. In 1821, Tarkapanchanan published *Podartho Kaumadi*, a book on the characteristics of language (*bhasha parichay*).[228] From Amiya Sen's research we now know that his academic background also provides a valuable clue as to why he would be opposed to Rammohun's project. Sen points out that the proponents of *nyaya* were traditionally opposed to the Vedanta in the early 19th century.[229] To this extent, Banerji's bibliographic survey of Tarkapanchanan's works reveals that he was also a part of this tradition, having authored a tract criticizing Vedantic philosophy—*Atma tattwa kaumadi* in 1822.[230]

Rammohun also opined that Dharma Shanstapana Kankhi taught *nyaya* to the colonial officials.[231] I think that there is a case to be made for Tarkapanchanan's involvement as the mind behind Dharma Shanstapana Kankhi.

The debate with Rammohun and Tarkapanchanan was also a debate about the use of language in religion. Language and polite discourse were the building blocks, indeed the *grammar* of Rammohun's view of a compassionate and caring religion. He not only preached compassion in print and but also enacted his ideas in public. As Tarkapanchanan's tract reveals, Rammohun openly disregarded eating restrictions and social divisions and instead favoured a society that was less rule-bound by caste and ritual. He deliberately employed a Shastric vocabulary so that his critics could be informed that he was *not* inventing a new system from the ground up. He even wrote that he valued imagination and innovation but only as long as they could be placed within a Shastric framework.[232] The next chapter will explore his interpretation of Shastric thought. Here, we focus on another aspect of his writings— language and phraseology.

Rammohun structured his prose writings in ways that would appeal to a wider audience of readers, listeners, cynics, and supporters. In a linguistic analysis of his writings, Pradyumna Bhattacharya showed that Rammohun followed a policy of progressively using simplified grammar, sentences, and word structure to make his writings more comprehensible.[233] These changes yielded results and made his prose more stylistically refined. As Banerji observed, although Rammohun was writing at a time when Bangla prose was yet in its infancy (and only tentative beginnings on the subject had been made by the Sanskrit pandits of Fort William College), his writings were well-populated with a rigorous conceptual vocabulary.[234]

Rammohun even specified his ideas on the use and purpose of language in *Bhattacharyer sahit vichar* (1817). The 'Bhattacharya' in the title is Mrityunjay Vidyalankar, a proponent of the use of Bangla for exploring new fields of enquiry and the best-known Bengali prose writer during this period.[235] Mrityunjay had experimented with various prose styles in Bangla since the 1800s, at a time when (most) contemporaries at Fort William College would have struggled to frame meaningful sentences.[236] During his lifetime, he published hugely popular works such as *Batris Simhasan*, *Hitopadesa*, and *Rajavali*. His posthumous publication, *Prabodh Chandrika*, was so well received in the 19th century that Calcutta University brought out a special commemorative edition in the 1870s.[237]

In 1817, Mrityunjay published *Vedanta Chandrika* for an exclusive, elite readership and his tract quickly became popular amongst his followers. *Vedanta Chandrika* was a critique of *Vedanta Grantha* but with a caveat: its author did not reveal his identity. From the relative safety of his authorial anonymity, Mrityunjay mocked Rammohun and argued that any reader of *Vedanta Grantha* would lose faith in the Vedanta. In response, Rammohun demanded that the specifics of Mrityunjay's argument be spelt out in greater detail in a revised and updated edition. 'Which pages of *Vedanta Grantha* does Mrityunjay have a problem with?' he asked.[238] In this context, he argued anyone reading *Vedanta Chandrika* would mistakenly think that the Vedanta was only concerned with disparaging and derogatory remarks (*durvakya*) about Rammohun's activities.[239]

To Rammohun, the use of derogatory remarks was unacceptable in a discussion on Vedanta. As he explained, the primary purpose of language was to clarify the meaning of a text and not obscure it. By employing *durvakya*, Mrityunjay had also misrepresented the *Vedanta* by turning it into vicious bazaar gossip (*hatori bajari kotha*) and a discourse on hate and societal discord. Instead, he directed Mrityunjay to employ compassionate language (*kripa purba*) so that *Vedanta* would be understood by all readers as 'a compassionate view of the universe where one need not hate anyone or anything.'[240]

Mrityunjay would not have agreed with Rammohun's suggestions or even his use of the Bangla language. He was of the opinion that Bangla could not be used for discussions on Shastric debate and often employed a highly Sanskritized version of the language in *Vedanta Chandrika* while discussing specifics. Rammohun, in turn, argued that a large number of Sanskrit words had been deliberately used to confuse the public (*sarvva-sadharan lok*). Instead, he suggested that Mrityunjay should employ more colloquialisms so that the general public could also read it.[241]

Rammohun was not being cheeky with his suggestions. In a stylistic analysis of the two tracts, Pradyumna Bhattacharya concluded that *Vedanta Chandrika* did in fact consistently employ longer words than *Bhattacharyer sahit vichar*. According to Bhattacharya, Rammohun's concern with Bangla sentence structure, aesthetics, and insistence of a simplified grammar shows that he did have a wider public readership in mind.[242]

Rammohun concluded *Bhattacharyer sahit vichar* with some black humour. Mrityunjay, he argued, deliberately hid the true nature of Hindu scripture but still hoped to convince his readers because he dressed like a saint (*rishi*). On the other hand, Rammohun wrote about scripture in a way that the public could understand but did not dress like a saint.[243] Now, who would readers consider more authentic? Mrityunjay or him? He casually remarked that the Supreme Being (*parameshwar*) already knew that Rammohun only wanted the public to interpret scripture as per their own life experiences, economic means, and faith whereas whatever Mrityunjay was doing was for his own selfish reasons.[244]

Rammohun's responses to his critics reveal the distinctiveness of his style. His responses are sharp, witty, and dramatic. But they also tell us something about his arguments. He was uncompromisingly rigid with his views and very careful in his employment of language. Each response also hinted at a deep structure of argument, one that is carefully worked out but never fully revealed. We turn to the deep structure of his argument now, and unsurprisingly, it takes us right back to the *Tuhfat*.

I argue that the deep structure of Rammohun's writings on Hindu scripture continued to be informed by *Tuhfat*. For example, the category of 'nature' was also used in his writings on Hindu scripture. A comparative textual analysis of *Tuhfat* and Isho Upanishad explores this argument in some detail.

Rammohun's translation of the Isho Upanishad was published in 1816 at Calcutta. Significantly, its introduction and preface mainly dealt with observations on contemporary Bengali social practices than on an introduction to the text. This was not unusual. As Killingley observes, Rammohun's introductions and prefaces were largely concerned with his own opinions of religious practices in contemporary Bengali society.[245] The English and Bangla translations were also written in prose, as opposed to the original Upanishadic verse.

The Isho Upanishad's introduction in the Bangla version included some material which was not included in the English translation. It is also an excellent example of the methods by which Rammohun reached out to the public and set out his agenda for reform by describing and critiquing contemporary practices. Here we find him taking aim at

Bengali Brahmanical orthodoxy and their unwillingness to reform certain DhS sanctions. He pointed out that all religious practices in contemporary times were not the product of DhS prescriptions. For instance, the worship of certain goddesses (Jagaddhatri and Ratanti) as well as cults (Vaishnavism) was the product of social conventions that had gradually developed across the centuries in Bengal, rather than of DhS prescriptions.[246]

The stylistics of Isho Upanishad was different from *Tuhfat*. While the latter's arguments were organized in a formal system of propositional assessment, the former was written in an informal conversational style. Isho Upanishad featured irony, sarcasm, and appeals to 'common sense'.[247] Rammohun also introduced an element of drama (with selective capitalization and italicization of sentences) to argue that the practice of religious observances is not desirable.

> Let man desire to live a whole century, practising, in this world, religious rites, because for such A SELFISH MIND AS THINE besides the observances of these rites, there is no other mode the practice of which would not subject thee to such evils. THOSE THAT NEGLECT THE CONTEMPLATION OF THE SUPREME SPIRIT *either by devoting themselves solely to the performance of ceremonies of religion, or by living destitute of religious ideas*, shall after death, ASSUME THE STATE OF DEMONS *such as that of the celestial gods and of other created beings* WHICH ARE SURROUNDED BY DARKNESS OF IGNORANCE.[248]

Isho Upanishad and *Tuhfat* employed different literary styles but a methodological continuity can be seen in the employment of the categories of 'nature' and 'habit'. For example, the introduction to Isho Upanishad also highlighted the differences between 'nature' and 'habit'.

Rammohun opined that contemporary Bengali society was not aware that their religious practices of worshipping multiple denominations of gods and goddesses ('habit') were but a part of the 'attributes of the Supreme Being' ('nature'). Just as Isho Upanishad, *Tuhfat* too referred to 'habit' as the practice of 'giving attributes'.[249] Thus, the employment of 'nature' and 'habit' in Isho Upanishad demonstrates a conceptual continuity from *Tuhfat*. This explanatory scheme is also found in other translations of Hindu scripture. Rammohun referred to contemporary religious practices with bitter irony in his preface to *Vedanta Grantha* to emphasize that they ought to be avoided.[250]

Isho Upanishad did not only employ the categories of *Tuhfat* but its deep structure was also influenced by it. Consider, for example, *Tuhfat's* interpretation of the origin and analysis of social conflict. *Tuhfat* argued that religious practices advocated by the Ulemas and Brahmins led to social conflict.[251] The English and Bangla versions of Isho Upanishad also criticized the Brahmins for promoting practices which led to conflict.[252] We conclude that *Tuhfat* and Isho Upanishad were a part of a political project of reform and displayed a will to act against ecclesiastical authority.

Isho Upanishad was, however, produced in a different context than *Tuhfat*. Its publication in 1816 coincided with a bitter familial dispute which ultimately culminated in an acrimonious judicial suit filed in the Calcutta Supreme Court in 1817 by his nephew Govindaprasad Roy (his elder brother Jagmohan's son). Govindaprasad alleged that Rammohun had usurped his property but was proven wrong and compelled to tender an apology.[253] Strangely enough, Rammohun's mother, Tarini Devi, was also a part of the failed suit.

Tarini Devi had no legal quarrels with Rammohun. However, her relationship with him was fraught with tension over his writings on Hindu scripture. Rammohun probably suspected this to be the primary motive for her involvement. Accordingly, his lawyers produced a lengthy questionnaire in court to challenge her. The questionnaire began with straightforward questions such as: 'Had Tarini Devi cut ties with Rammohun because she did not agree with his views on religion?' But then, it moved on to the matter of Tarini Devi's own motives. Consider, for instance the question: 'Did Tarini Devi intend to bankrupt Rammohun with her case against him?' And finally, the questionnaire attempted to portray her as an unreliable witness at court with such provocative questions as: 'Was Tarini Devi's desire to financially ruin Rammohun so strong that she would even be willing to commit perjury by providing false evidence in court?' And even, 'Did Tarini Devi believe that it would be a blessing (*punna*) if anyone were to destroy him?'[254]

We shall never know what Tarini Devi would have thought of these queries. But we can gather that Rammohun was estranged from his mother and family over his writings on religion and scripture. He was also deeply unhappy with these personal developments and legal entanglements.[255] As he wrote rather revealingly in his introduction to *Translation of an Abridgment of the Vedanta* (1816), 'I, born a Brahmin, have exposed myself to the complainings and reproaches, even of some of my relations, whose prejudices are strong and whose temporal advantage depends upon the present system.'[256] This context, I believe, added another discursive layer to his written tracts—a directness which was not present in works before 1816, such as in *Tuhfat* or *Vedanta Grantha*. As he nonchalantly declared to his readers, 'At any rate, whatever men may say, I cannot be deprived of this consolation: my motives are acceptable to that Being who beholds in secret and compensates openly!'[257]

The directness of Rammohun's prose did not diminish with time. Even three years after *Abridgment of the Vedanta* and two years after Govindaprasad instituted a failed suit against him, he did not return to the careful and cautious style of reasoning of *Tuhfat*. Take, for instance, *Tuhfat*'s systematic denunciation of priests, Brahmins, and religious leaders and compare it with a new kind of style of writing, one which referred to the Brahmins as 'those fools who are immersed in ignorance that is the foolish practices of rites' and whose followers were 'like blind men guided by a blind man'.[258] He also wrote to readers directly, appealing to the 'common sense perspective of man' to make his point.[259] The term 'common sense' articulated the basic argument that Hindu scripture was a unified body of thought, concerned with political and social ideas. This strategy was not without success. As the *Asiatic Journal* reported, Rammohun's style of argumentation earned him a 'well-founded reputation' in Calcutta.[260]

However, Rammohun's 'well founded' reputation came at a cost since his directness and sharp views annoyed many in Bengali society. Critics alleged that his writings insulted contemporary religious sentiments.[261] Along with his written works, his other activities were also affected by the hostility towards his ideas and methods of writing. Unable to deal with the vicious social criticism (*lokninda*), the Atmiya Sabha discontinued its meetings.[262] But alongside the criticism and setbacks, one also finds evidence of the small snippets of success. In April 1820, the *Madras Government Gazette* responded to its readers' demands and entered into an arrangement with the printing presses in Calcutta to secure more copies of Rammohun's works.[263] Three months later, in July, the judges of the Supreme Court in Calcutta witnessed a rather surprising development when a defendant in a case refused to take an oath by swearing on the Ganges, as was the convention at the time. Instead, the defendant publicly declared his affiliation to Rammohun's ideas and insisted that he will *only* take an oath on the Vedas.[264] It does lead one to wonder about the range of his writings. How broad would his interpretation of the Vedas have to be in order to evoke responses from such diverse quarters?

Rammohun frequently referenced the Vedas in his translations of Hindu scripture. The Vedas were interpreted as all-encompassing texts which discussed a range of concerns. His writings emphasized that the Vedas were not concerned with only theology but also discussed topics and disciplines such as astronomy, medicine, and botany.[265] This may have attracted more followers and supporters. But alongside the acclaim, his interpretation and translations also invited criticism at Calcutta and Madras.

Two aspects of Rammohun's translations were contentious: first, their authenticity; and second, the point of translating ancient scriptures at all. In response, he argued, 'The point of being able to perceive the existence of god is to be able to do so in a way that is best calculated towards substantial material advantages.'[266] Thus, he related scripture to the everyday 'material' world of his readers. He also opined that scripture had a contemporary political relevance. 'I regret to say that the present system of religion adhered to by the Hindus is not well calculated to promote their political interest,' he wrote in a letter to Digby, 'and I think it necessary for some change to take place in their religion at least for the sake of their political advantage and social comfort.'[267] He took the view that thinkers in Bengali society were more likely to agonize over the details of scripture and ignore contemporary political realities. Instead, he suggested that scripture can be a method by which one could creatively engage with the political problems of the day.[268]

Rammohun did not only translate and interpret scripture but actively defended his ideas in *An Apology for the Pursuit of Final Beatitude Independent of Brahmunical Observances* (1820) and *Humble suggestions to his countrymen who believe in one true God* (1823).[269] Though forceful and direct, these writings also betray a very visible anxiety to be *the* correct translation of scripture. He was right to be anxious, for his works coincided with a larger intellectual context in Bengal—a public sphere which consisted of parallel traditions of oral debate and written vernacular and English newspapers and journals.

Rammohun hoped to inaugurate his own project of ethics in the Bengali public sphere. The public was certainly aware of his ideas. This can be seen in the newspaper reporting of a case which occurred in 1817, two years after *Vedanta Grantha* had been published and involved the final words of a Calcutta resident, Radhamohun Ghoshal-Bhattacharya. Ghoshal-Bhattacharya had refused to have any religious ceremonies performed, confessing 'with shame' that he had encouraged such ceremonies and rituals throughout his life for 'selfish motives' and now understood them to be 'a mere mockery of the true god who is the true source of all our faculties and whose nature is incomprehensible'.[270] In the end, he made a 'public confession' of belief in Vedanta.[271]

Ghoshal-Bhattacharya insisted that religion was a public social practice, informed by wider concerns of social welfare. Note that he was a Brahmin, and Rammohun's writings frequently described Brahmanical ritualistic practices as a result of 'self-interested motives'. In this case, the 'public confession' shows that the strategy of reaching out to a broad readership had succeeded in creating observable everyday changes in social practice in Bengali society.

I argue that a close analysis of newspaper reports on Rammohun's writings shows that some contemporary observers also perceived his religious writings as an argument for ethical practice. Take, for example, *Calcutta Journal*'s reporting of the Ghoshal-Bhattacharya case. This newspaper cited the facts of the case in conjunction with an assessment of Rammohun's writings on Hindu scripture as examples of 'a reform in the system of morals'.[272] It also informed readers of an upcoming project, namely the English translation of an abridgement of *Vedanta Grantha*, and opined that it would be available soon.[273]

As this chapter has highlighted, Rammohun did not only want to reach out to an English-speaking readership. He was adamant that his project of translation was meant to be read by the Bengali public. He argued that the Brahmins had lost touch with the 'generality' of the population while his writings were meant for a broad readership. By publishing and *translating* scripture, he argued that he was not a member of a distant elite.[274] However, if the authorial intention was to make a case for the reform of contemporary socio-religious practices, it would have to be unambiguously spelt out in his works.

Rammohun first made this argument in the Mandukya Upanishad (1818) and followed it up the next year in Mundaka Upanishad (1819).

He asserted that the Brahmins ('self-interested guides') had rejected 'nature' (belief in one god) and advocated conflicting religious practices. *Tuhfat* had argued that 'mankind' could easily distinguish between the 'truth and untruth' based on 'natural inclination'. Mundaka Upanishad was arguing the same and presenting the case for one invisible god.

In Mundaka Upanishad, Rammohun argued that the case for understanding the nature of god lay in the correct assessment of two types of knowledge: inferior and superior. Inferior knowledge referred to treatises on astrology, pronunciation, rules for rituals, prosody, and grammar. Superior knowledge referred to the information contained in the Upanishads on the nature of an eternal and unchanging god (Rammohun used the word God interchangeably with Supreme Being).[275]

Readers of his earliest work on Hindu scripture would not have been surprised with Rammohun's argument that the Upanishads provided an account of the ways in which god had created the material universe, life, human bodies, and souls.[276] The human body, the soul, and god were not separate from each other. Indeed, he stressed that the Mundaka Upanishad interpreted god and the soul as two birds who lived in one tree—the body.[277] However, an individual could only come to this conclusion after meditation and reflection, rather than the performance of rites and rituals.

Rammohun's interpretation of the Mundaka Upanishad's anti-ritual stance was broadly true, for as one recent translator opined, 'more than any other Upanishad, the Mundaka Upanishad engages in a direct and frontal attack against both Vedic ritualism and the Vedic texts that embody the ritual tradition'.[278] In the context of early-19th-century Bengal, Rammohun noted, with regret, that most Hindus did not meditate on the nature of the Supreme Being but instead practised rituals. He warned that the mechanistic practice of rites and rituals was merely 'foolish' and ultimately led to a melancholic existence and undesirable consequences (including death, disease, and the possibility of being reborn as an 'inferior animal or plant').[279] Citing the DhS commentator Vasistha, he argued that rites and rituals were not an end by themselves but the means of '*producing good consequences*'.[280]

At first glance, Rammohun's stress on 'good consequences' may appear to be unclear. But I think it ought to be contextualized with his introduction to Mundaka Upanishad which drew a linear relationship between mechanistic religious rituals and unethical conduct ('total destruction of the moral principle [resulting in] criminal intercourse').[281] He was anxious to show that the implications of this point extended far beyond the Mundaka Upanishad and also cited other tracts in which this argument had first appeared. These tracts also reveal Rammohun's position in relation to the public (whom he addressed) and the Brahminical community (whom he criticized).[282] Consider a tract that was published in the same year as Mundaka Upanishad, the translation of the Kena Upanishad.

Rammohun's translation of the Kena Upanishad was concerned with a specific question—the role of reason in contemporary Bengal. In the introduction, he admitted that when faced with contradictions in scripture, one could be tempted to only 'appeal to reason'. However, he warned that reason alone was 'incompetent' since it ultimately led to a nagging, uncomfortable, and all-pervasive 'universal doubt'. Instead, he suggested a judicious mix of reason and scripture, to 'endeavour to improve our intellectual and moral faculties, relying on the goodness of the Almighty Power, which alone enables us to attain that which we earnestly and diligently seek for'.[283] The main text elaborated this point by arguing that all 'learned men' were aware of the simple fact that the Supreme Being is the sole source of language, thought, meaning, sight, and touch ('sense'). Rammohun was presenting a view that reason was epistemically indispensable to a belief in an 'Almighty power'. His interpretation focussed on an 'Almighty power' who had provided every individual with a sense of purpose and direction but was beyond the scope of human comprehension. It is important to note here that scholarly translations of Kena Upanishad have also argued that the text was concerned with an unknowable *brahman* who created life in the universe.[284] As with Mundaka Upanishad, Rammohun's translation was inspired, but broadly true.

Rammohun's introduction to Kena Upanishad as well as Isho Upnaishad followed a similar style. In both tracts one cannot fail to detect an essential concern with critiquing contemporary practices in Bengali society. Rammohun even referred to contemporary religious practices as 'erroneous conceptions' leading to the deprivation of 'common comforts of society' and warned against the effects (they led to 'sacrifice' and 'suicide').[285] It summarized two key aspects of Rammohun's project—the criticism of Brahmanical religious practices and the interpretation of religion as ethical conduct. It did not, however, clarify his role as a transla-tor. When his critics forced him to declare his position, he (untruthfully) declared that he had never 'pretended' to be a reformer.[286]

Rammohun did, however, identify his position as that of a Brahmin. He argued that the main difference between his ideas and that of the Brahmin community was his stress on intuitive belief ('nature') than con-trol and regulation of religious practices ('habit'). His self-identification as a Brahmin was an attempt to legitimize his bold new interpretations of scripture. He also legitimized his reinterpretations by appealing to the DhS.[287] In fact, his writings frequently placed the author of MDhS in the same discursive context as religious scripture and philosophy.[288]

Apart from DhS, Rammohun also identified with two other intel-lectual traditions—religious philosophy and commentary. Consider his translations of Shankara's commentaries of the Upanishads. His trans-lations were inspired and broad based and he did not produce literal translations of Shankara's commentaries (although he claimed that he did). Unsurprisingly, his 'departures' were judged harshly by his critics. Mrityunjay Vidyalankar argued that his ideas were 'an innovation.'[289] Vidyalankar had a point, as our discussion of Rammohun's translation of Katha Upanishad will show.

Rammohun's translation of the Katha Upanishad was published in 1819 at Calcutta. It was an important work since it contained evidence of the success of Rammohun's project of translating scripture.[290] 'A great body of my countrymen', he announced, were 'perfectly satisfied with the truth of the doctrines.'[291] The tract emphasized the importance of pub-lic debate of social practices and outlined his concept of societal ethics, everyday conduct, and laws and regulations in society. As in *Abridgement of the Vedanta* (1816), the Brahmins were seen as advocates of illegiti-mate and unethical religious practices. As in *Tuhfat*, these practices were seen as evidence of the destruction of the 'texture' of social relations. The translation of the Katha Upanishad can also be read as an example of how Rammohun viewed the role of scripture in contemporary society as part of a larger project of reform. For example, the tract made a persua-sive case for abolishing female infanticide in Bengal.[292]

In Rammohun's translation, the Katha Upanishad's narrative centred on a debate between Nachiketa, a Brahmin, and Yama, the god of death. Yama was initially reluctant to answer Nachiketa's questions on Vedic scripture but later won over by the latter's perseverance. Thus, if bettered in a debate, it was possible for even gods to reveal the information that mortals asked for, however reluctant they may be to do so.

> The Liberal minded Yama ... offered Nachiketa an extensive empire on earth. ... When Nachiketa refused, Yama replied, 'the knowledge that you seek cannot be obtained through perishable means [rites and sacrifices] but will be obtained only by he who is well versed in the sacred scriptures. I will perform the worship [for you] whereby I became possessed of this sovereignty of long duration.'[293]

The language of the translation shows that the text was not merely an appeal to an ancient Upanisadic tradition since its narrative context and chief characters were described in contemporary phraseology. Rather, Rammohun had produced an inspired translation. The 'Liberal minded' Yama was clearly the authority in the passage since he was able to offer an 'Empire' to Nachiketa. However, Nachiketa did not want an 'Empire' but 'sovereignty'. When the 'Liberal minded' Yama consented, he explained the 'long duration of sovereignty' to Nachiketa. Nachiketa was seen here as an ethical individual who ultimately emerged victorious despite the unequal relations of power with Yama.

Thus, the translation of the Katha Upanishad addressed a contemporary context by referring to terms such as 'Empire' and 'liberal mindedness'. The new rulers, Rammohun hoped, were 'Liberal minded' enough to grant greater levels of political power to the inhabitants. The way to achieve greater concessions from the ruling authorities, he informed the Bengali public sphere, was a consistent ethical commitment to one's political project.

***

Conclusion: On (Re)Interpreting Religion as Ethical Practices to the Bengali Public

Current scholarship on Rammohun's writings has argued that he was an isolated and elite thinker. This argument assumes that his audience required to be 'print-literate'. However, drawing on recent research on the history of the book, I have argued that Rammohun was 'oral-literate', that is, his writings appealed to traditions of orality and practices of reading aloud.[294] In this case, it is not the print literacy of his readers that is important but rather the degree to which he was oral-literate enough to be able to reach out to his audience.

Rammohun's writings contain important evidence of his oral-literacy. First, they are humorous, informal, dramatic, ironical, sarcastic, and short. This would have made them easy to narrate and read aloud. Second, linguistic practices such as shorter sentences, smaller words, and greater clarity of prose contributed to the ease of readability. Third, their free availability in the popular press would have enabled a wider circulation. These strategies yielded some success since his writings were, in fact, circulated and reprinted in the popular press during his lifetime and by private publishers after his death.

Rammohun's writings had a consistent narrative thread: that the public *must* be ethical. His ideas were influenced by *Akhlaq-i Nasiri*.[295] *Akhlaq-i Nasiri* was a familiar text in early-19th-century Bengal.[296] Its influence can be clearly seen in his first work *Tuhfat-ul- Muwahidin*, particularly its key arguments concerning ethical practice, the human soul, and belief in one god.

Akhlaq-i Nasiri is also important to our argument because it provides a different intellectual context to Rammohun's ideas. Scholarly works on the man consistently present him as a modern thinker, a harbinger of modernity, the father of modern India, and the first Indian liberal. Consequently, a discussion of his intellectual context is almost always restricted to his encounter with modernity.

But Rammohun was also a product of a madrasa education; and as the chapter highlighted, madrasas were important centres of early modern thought where diverse political and literary traditions were taught (of which *Akhlaq-i Nasiri* is just one). While this chapter may have inadvertently suggested that *Akhlaq-i Nasiri* is the only influence on his thought, my arguments are exploratory. Further questions can be asked in this context. For instance, could Rammohun have been influenced by Kamandaka's Nitisara, the influential early medieval Hindu political text? Like the DhS and the MBh, Kamandaka too argued that the householder (*grihastha*) was spiritually superior than the ascetics who renounced material life.[297] In a separate discussion on state power, Kamandaka took a firm stand against political violence and advocated a form of rule which involved the sharing of political power between the king and the 'elements of the state' as well as local forms of administration.[298]

These ideas on politics also appear in and are elaborated by the DhS, the subject of the next chapter. The larger question, which is yet to be researched more thoroughly, is the full influence of early Indian, early medieval, and early modern thought on Rammohun's writings.

Tuhfat's ideas concerning the human soul and its relationship to conduct, worship, criticism of religious leaders, and concern with accessibility were developed and explained in Rammohun's subsequent works in greater detail. *Tuhfat* also introduced methods and techniques (such as the conceptual categories of 'nature' and 'habit') which continued to feature in later writings. The similarities in method and argument were not incidental but evidence of a political project. They show that his writings on religion, whether in Arabic, Persian, Bangla or English, had a common basis.

Rammohun articulated a clear, consistent political project on ethical practice in *Tuhfat* (c.1803) and works on Hindu scripture (1815–30) to a Bengali public; and as the publication data and newspaper reports of the period indicate, the 'public' responded.

Notes

1. Examples of this research include: Anindita Ghosh, *Power in Print, Popular Publishing and the Politics of Language and Culture in a Colonial Society, 1778–1905* (New Delhi: Oxford University Press, 2006) and C.A. Bayly, *Intelligence Gathering and Social Communication in India, 1780–1870* (Cambridge: Cambridge University Press, 2000).

2. Bayly, *Recovering Liberties*, 79.

3. Francesca Orsini, 'Introduction', in *The History of the Book in South Asia*, ed. Francesca Orsini (Oxford: Ashgate, 2013), i.

4. Cited in 'Introduction', xiv.

5. Cited in 'Introduction', xvii.

6. My interpretation of the *Tuhfat-ul-Muwahidin* depends almost entirely on Obaidullah el Obaide's English translation of it in 1883. Though dated, this translation is widely referred in current scholarship (for instance, by Dermot Killingley, Bruce Robertson, Sumit Sarkar, and Brian Hatcher). I have also compared it with J.C. Ghosh's English translation of the *Tuhfat* and qualified all points of disagreement between the two authors. Further, Obaide's reference to, and translation of, Persian and Arabic words has also been compared with Steingass's *Comprehensive Persian-English dictionary*.

7. Dermot Killingley, *Rammohun Roy in Hindu and Christian Tradition: The Teape Lectures* (Newcastle upon Tyne: Grevatt & Grevatt, 1993), 35.

8. Bruce Robertson, *Raja Rammohan Ray: The Father of Modern India* (New Delhi: Oxford University Press, 1995), 72.

9. Kopf, *British Orientalism*, 113.

10. Brajendranath Banerji, *Mrityunjay Vidyalankar* (Calcutta: Bangiya Sahitya Parisad, 1943), 14.

11. Kopf, *British Orientalism*, 201.

12. Kopf, *British Orientalism*, 116–19.

13. Kopf, *British Orientalism*, 116–19.

14. Kopf, *British Orientalism*, 116–19.

15. Kopf, *British Orientalism*, 116–19.

16. Kopf, *British Orientalism*, 116–19.

17. Ghosh, *Power in Print*, 142.

18. Ghosh, *Power in Print*, 107.

19. Ghosh, *Power in Print*, 14–15.

20. *The Second Report of the Calcutta School Book Society*, Memorandum of the indigenous works which have appeared from the native presses, drawn up for the Calcutta School Book Society Committee by the Corresponding Secretary, No. II (Calcutta: School and Mission Presses, 1820), 38.

21. See Table A.3.

22. See Table A.3.

23. Brian Hatcher, *Bourgeois Hinduism, or Faith of the Modern Vedantists: Rare Discourses from Early Colonial Bengal* (New York: Oxford University Press, 2008), 45.

24. Orsini, 'Introduction', xviii. The number of private publishers greatly expanded after 1835 owing to a more flexible legal framework advocated by the 'Metcalfe Minute'.

25. Orsini, 'Introduction', xiv. Discussed earlier in a discussion of the term 'oral-literate'.

26. See Table A.1.

27. See Table A.3.

28. The Baptists (William Carey and Joshua Marshman being prominent amongst them) were initially well-disposed towards Rammohun. But by 1820, the relationship had soured. This context will be explored in greater detail in Chapter 6.

29. Rammohun's geography textbook was commissioned by the CSBS in 1817. It appeared as unpublished in the CSBS's annual reports: *Second Report*, 1819, Appendix no. 18, 97; *Fourth Report*, 1821, Appendix no. 5, 36; *Fifth Report*, 1823, Appendix no. 7, 36. Rammohun's idea of geography in *Exposition*, and emphasis on latitudes and longitudes and physical features, can probably be traced to this unfinished project.

30. *Tenth Report of the CSBS*, Appendix no. 2 (Calcutta, 1834), 27–31.
31. Killingley, *Rammohun Roy*, 45.
32. Robertson, *Raja Rammohan Ray*, 97–109.
33. Hatcher, *Bourgeois Hinduism*, 19–32.
34. See Table A.1.
35. Bayly, *Recovering Liberties*; Chatterjee, *The Black Hole of Empire*; Sumit Sarkar, 'Rammohun Roy and the Break with the Past' in *Rammohun Roy and the Process of Modernisation in India*, ed. V.C. Joshi (Delhi: Vikas Publishing House, 1975), 46–68.
36. Sarkar, 'Rammohun Roy and the Break with the Past', 49–52.
37. Barun De, 'A Biographical Perspective on the Political and Economic Ideas of Rammohun Roy', in *Rammohun Roy and the Process of Modernisation in India*, ed. V.C. Joshi (Delhi: Vikas Publishing House, 1975), 147.
38. Sartori, *Bengal in Global Concept History*, 62–3.
39. Kashshaf Ghani, 'Vestige of a Dying Tradition: *Tuhfat-ul-Muwahidin* in Nineteenth Century Bengal', *Studia Iranica* 44, no. 1 (2015): 60.
40. Ghani, 'Vestige of a Dying Tradition', 72.
41. Ghani, 'Vestige of a Dying Tradition', 73.
42. Ghani, 'Vestige of a Dying Tradition', 61.
43. Ghani, 'Vestige of a Dying Tradition', 78.
44. Bayly, *Recovering Liberties*, 35–7.
45. Muzaffar Alam, *The Languages of Political Islam: India, 1200–1800* (London: University of Chicago Press, 2004), 57–8.
46. Naṣīr al-Dīn Muḥammad ibn Muḥammad Ṭūsī, *The Nasirean ethics*, trans. G.W. Wickens (London: Allen & Unwin, 1964), 9.
47. Wickens, 'Introduction', *Nasirean Ethics*, 10.
48. Wickens, 'Introduction', *Nasirean Ethics*, 10.
49. *Nasirean Ethics*, 37.
50. *Nasirean Ethics*, 36.
51. *Nasirean Ethics*, 36.
52. *Nasirean Ethics*, 37.
53. *Nasirean Ethics*, 42.
54. *Nasirean Ethics*, 153–5.
55. *Nasirean Ethics*, 155.
56. *Nasirean Ethics*, 159.
57. *Nasirean Ethics*, 185.
58. In *Nasirean Ethics*, Wickens noted that although Tusi was influenced by Aristotle's ideas of government, he did not refer to the Greek model of a city-state but rather conceptualized political authority as monarchical.
59. *Nasirean Ethics*, 195.

60. *Nasirean Ethics*, 196.

61. *Nasirean Ethics*, 191.

62. *Nasirean Ethics*, 190.

63. Alam, *Languages of Political Islam*, 129.

64. Alam, *Languages of Political Islam*, 50–61.

65. Chatterjee, *Cultures of History*, 220.

66. Beatrice Teissier, 'Texts from the Persian in the Late Eighteenth-Century India and Britain, Culture or Construct?' *Iran* 47, no. 1 (2009): 133.

67. Teissier, 'Texts from the Persian', 134.

68. Teissier, 'Texts from the Persian', 135.

69. Teissier, 'Texts from the Persian', 136.

70. Teissier, 'Texts from the Persian', 144.

71. Teissier, 'Texts from the Persian', 144.

72. Francis Gladwin, *The Persian Monshee*, vol. 2 (Calcutta: The Chronicle Press, 1795), 1.

73. Gladwin, *Persian Monshee*, vol. 2, 43.

74. Alam, *Languages of Political Islam*, 130.

75. Rajeev Kinra, *Writing Self, Writing Empire: Chandar Bhan Brahman and the Cultural World of the Indo-Persian State Secretary* (San Francisco: University of California Press, 2015), 10.

76. Kinra, *Writing Self, Writing Empire*, 11.

77. Kinra, *Writing Self, Writing* Empire, 4.

78. Gladwin, *Persian Monshee*, vol. 2, 2.

79. Gladwin, *Persian Monshee*, vol. 3, 1.

80. Kopf, *British Orientalism*, 85.

81. Stanley Lane-Poole, 'Baillie, John (1772–1833)', Oxford Dictionary of National Biography, Oxford University Press, 2004. Available at http://www.oxforddnb.com/view/article/1064, https://doi.org/10.1093/ref:odnb/1064. last date of access of link: 27 September 2018.

82. William Irvine, 'The Baillie Collection of Arabic and Persian MSS', *Journal of the Royal Asiatic Society of Great Britain and Ireland* (July 1905): 560–65.

83. *The Persian Reader or short extracts from various Persian writers*, 3 vols (Calcutta: Calcutta School Book Society, 1825) and *The Persian Reader or short extracts from various Persian writers*, 3 vols (Calcutta: Calcutta School Book Society, 1835); *The Persian Reader*, vol. 2 (Calcutta: Calcutta School Book Society, 1825), 149–58; *A Compendium of ethics by Sheikh Sady*, trans. Francis Gladwin (Calcutta: Stuart and Cooper, 1788) and Second edition (Calcutta: Stuart and Cooper, 1796). Note that Gladwin mistakenly attributed the authorship of *Pandnama* to Sa'adi.

84. *Third Report of the Calcutta School Book Society* (Calcutta: Calcutta School Book Society, 1820), 26–7.

85. *Third Report*, 26–7.

86. *Ninth Report of the CSBS* (Calcutta: Calcutta School Book Society, 1832), Appendix No. 2, 26; *Tenth Report*, 47.

87. Brajendranath Banerji, *Fort William Colleger Pandit* [Pandits of Fort William College] (Calcutta: Bangiya Sahitya Parisad, 1943), 16.

88. Banerji, *Fort William Colleger Pandit*, 20–3.

89. *First Report of the CSBS* (Calcutta: Calcutta School Book Society, 1817), 4.

90. *First Report*, 4.

91. *Third Report*, 27.

92. Kopf, *British Orientalism*, 108–9.

93. Banerji, *Rammohun Roy*, 47. Rammohun wrote *Tuhfat* when he was about 30 years old. Whether he was at all interested in religion before this point is unknown. Banerji argued that the evidence seemed to point in a different direction; that in his youth, Rammohun was only but a rich man's son, interested in commerce, business, and property.

94. 'Tuhfatul Muwahhiddin', trans. Maulvi Obaidullah El Obaide, in *Rammohun Roy*, by Kishori Chand Mitter (Calcutta: K.P. Bagchi, 1975), 1. Henceforth, *Tuhfat*.

95. *Nasirean Ethics*, 37.

96. Wickens, 'Introduction', *Nasirean Ethics*, 11.

97. *Tuhfat*, 8–9.

98. *Tuhfat*, 1.

99. *Tuhfat*, 1.

100. *Tuhfat*, 12–13.

101. *Tuhfat*, 8.

102. *Tuhfat*, 20.

103. *Tuhfat*, 8.

104. *Nasirean Ethics*, 36.

105. *Nasirean Ethics*, 36.

106. *Nasirean Ethics*, 37.

107. *Tuhfat*, 20.

108. *Tuhfat*, 'Translator's Preface'; B.N. Dasgupta, *Rajah Rammohun Roy: The Last Phase* (New Delhi: Uppal Publishing House, 1982), 106.

109. *Tuhfat*, 1.

110. *Nasirean Ethics*, 15.

111. Bayly, *Recovering Liberties*, 51.

112. *Tuhfat*, 12.

113. *Tuhfat*, 22.

114. *Tuhfat*, 6.
115. Dasgupta, *Rajah Rammohun Roy*, 106; Sarkar, 'Rammohun Roy and the Break with the Past', 51.
116. The tract was reprinted in 1859, 1898, and 1918, and translated into Bengali in 1899 and 1949 (by Girish Chandra Sen and Jyotirananda Das respectively) and into English in 1884 and 1906 (by Obaidullah el Obaide and J.C. Ghosh, respectively). It was thus a well-known work in 19th and mid-20th century. See Table A.1.
117. Chattopadhyay, *JB*, 33.
118. Brajendranath Banerji, *Ramchandra Vidyavagish and Hariharananda Tirthaswamy* (Bangiya Sahitya Parisad: Calcutta, 1942), 26.
119. Banerji, *Ramchandra Vidyavagish and Hariharananda Tirthaswamy*, 26.
120. Urban, *Tantra*, 67.
121. Urban, *Tantra*, 64.
122. Urban, *Tantra*, 65. When MnT does refer to goddess Kali, it presents her as sweet-tempered, nurturing, and 'domesticated'.
123. Hugh Urban, *Tantra: Sex, Secrecy, Politics and Power in the Study of Religion* (London: University of California Press), 2003, 64.
124. Nag and Burman (eds), *EW* 2:42.
125. Nag and Burman (eds), *EW* 2:105.
126. Nag and Burman (eds), *EW* 2:125.
127. Killingley, *Only True God*, 19–21; 30–45.
128. Nag and Burman (eds), *EW* 2:78.
129. Nag and Burman (eds), *EW* 2:78.
130. Urban, *Tantra*, 66.
131. Urban, *Tantra*, 67.
132. Urban, *Tantra*, 71.
133. For a discussion on this question, see Urban, *Tantra*, 69.
134. Nag and Burman (eds), *EW* 1:32.
135. Nag and Burman (eds), *EW* 2:113.
136. Nag and Burman (eds), *EW* 3:95.
137. Sen, *Rammohun Roy*, 55.
138. Chattopadhyay, *JB*, 33.
139. Banerji, *Rammohun Roy*, 35.
140. Banerji, *Rammohun Roy*, 47.
141. Banerji, *Ramchandra Vidyavagish and Hariharananda Tirthaswamy*, 6. Ramchandra was also a lexicographer and scholar in his own right. He published a dictionary in Bangla from CSBS as well as a text on astrology.
142. Dermot Killingley, 'Rammohun Roy on the *Vedanta Sūtras*', *Religion* 11, no. 2 (April 1981): 151.

143. This was a view which he also expressed in writings on the Upanishads. Each translation of the Upanishads was accompanied by a cover page which insisted that they were merely Bangla and English reproductions of Shankara's commentaries of the Upanishads. The chapter will end with a discussion of one such translation (Killingley, 'Vedanta Sūtras', 151).

144. Killingley, 'Vedanta Sūtras', 155.

145. *BW*, 3–6.

146. *BW*, 3–6.

147. Killingley, 'Vedanta Sūtras', 156–7.

148. Killingley, 'Vedanta Sūtras', 155.

149. Killingley, 'Vedanta Sūtras', 165.

150. Killingley, 'Vedanta Sūtras', 155.

151. Killingley, 'Vedanta Sūtras', 152.

152. *Nasirean Ethics*, 36.

153. *Nasirean Ethics*, 190–5.

154. Killingley, 'Vedanta Sūtras', 151.

155. Killingley, 'Vedanta Sūtras', 165.

156. Killingley, *Only True God*, 1–6; Killingley, 'Vedanta Sūtras', 151.

157. Killingley, *Only True God*, 1–6; Killingley, 'Vedanta Sūtras', 151; Hatcher, 'Pandits at work', 54–9.

158. Killingley, *Only True God*, 1–6; Killingley, 'Vedanta Sūtras', 151.

159. *BW*, 148.

160. *BW*, 148.

161. Nag and Burman (eds), *EW* 2: 70–1.

162. Nag and Burman (eds), *EW* 2: 43–44.

163. Nag and Burman (eds), *EW* 2:3.

164. Nag and Burman (eds), *EW* 2:24.

165. *BW*, 212.

166. *BW*, 212.

167. *BW*, 217.

168. *BW*, 217.

169. *BW*, 212.

170. Patrick Olivelle, 'Introduction', in *Manu's Dharmaśāstra: A Critical Edition and Translation of the Mānava Dharmaśāstra* ed. and trans. Patrick Olivelle (New York: Oxford University Press, 2005), 43.

171. Olivelle, 'Introduction', 12.

172. Olivelle, *Manu's Dharmaśāstra*, 284.

173. Olivelle, *Manu's Dharmaśāstra*, 106.

174. Olivelle, *Manu's Dharmaśāstra*, 133.

175. *BW*, 331.

176. Chapter 6 will focus on this argument in greater detail.

177. *BW*, 331.

178. Mark McClish, 'Householders, Holy and Otherwise, in the Nīti and Kāma Literature', in *Gṛhastha: The Householder in Ancient Indian Religious Culture*, ed. Patrick Olivelle (New York: Oxford University Press, 2019), 556.

179. Patrick Olivelle, 'Introduction', in *Gṛhastha: The Householder in Ancient Indian Religious Culture*, ed. Patrick Olivelle (New York: Oxford University Press, 2019), 36–8.

180. Olivelle, *Manu's Dharmaśāstra*, 38.

181. *BW*, 143; Nag and Burman (eds), *EW* 1:51, 2:78; 2: 117–18.

182. Bimal Krishna Matilal, 'Introduction', in *Moral Dilemmas in the Mahābhārata*, ed. Bimal Krishna Matilal (Simla: Indian Institute for Advanced Study, 1989), 5.

183. Adam Bowles, 'Gṛhastha in the *Mahābhārata*', in *Gṛhastha*, 525.

184. Nag and Burman (eds), *EW* 2:100.

185. *Nasirean Ethics*, 159.

186. 'Government Gazette, 1 February 1816', in *Raja Rammohun Roy and Progressive Movements in India: A Selection of Records, 1775–1845*, ed. J.K. Majumdar (Calcutta: Art Press, 1941), 3.

187. *Missionary Register*, 1 February 1816, *RRPM*, 4.

188. *Government Gazette*, 8 February 1816, *RRPM*, 4.

189. Killingley, 'Vedanta Sūtras', 15.

190. Killingley, 'Vedanta Sūtras', 12.

191. *BW*, 214.

192. *BW*, 214.

193. Nag and Burman (eds), *EW* 2:63.

194. Velchuru Narayan Rao, 'Purana as Brahminic Ideology', in *Purana Perennis: Reciprocity and Transformation in Hindu and Jaina texts*, ed. Wendy Doniger (New York: State University of New York Press, 1993), 87.

195. *Missionary Register*, 1 February 1816, *RRPM*, 4.

196. *Tuhfat*, 3.

197. *Tuhfat*, 3.

198. Nag and Burman (eds), *EW* 2:197.

199. Nag and Burman (eds), *EW* 2:197.

200. *Calcutta Monthly Journal*, August 1817, *RRPM*, 5–9.

201. J.C. Ghose (ed.), *The English Works of Rammohun Roy*, vols 1–6 (Calcutta: Srikanta Roy, 1983), 51–2 and 102.

202. Ghose (ed.), *The English Works*, 160.

203. Killingley, *Only True God*, 19–21, 30–45.

204. Ajit Ray, *The Religious Ideas of Rammohun Roy* (New Delhi: Kanak Publications, 1976), 34.

205. *BW*, 155.
206. *BW*, 155. We are not certain whether the debate did, in fact, take place or whether Goswamin is a general reference to Vaishnavites in Bengal.
207. *BW*, 155.
208. *BW*, 155.
209. *BW*, 167–8.
210. Brajendranath Banerji, *Pandits of the Fort William College* [in Bangla]. Calcutta: Bangiya Sahitya Parishad, 1943.
211. Chattopadhyay, *JB*, 70–2.
212. Chattopadhyay, *JB*, 70–2.
213. As quoted in Banerji, *Pandits*, 53.
214. *BW*, 265.
215. Banerji, *Pandits*, 54.
216. As quoted in Banerji, *Pandits*, 54.
217. Banerji, *Pandits*, 54.
218. Banerji, *Pandits*, 54.
219. As quoted in Banerji, *Pandits*, 54.
220. As quoted in Banerji, *Pandits*, 53.
221. Banerji, *Pandits*, 54.
222. Banerji, *Pandits*, 54. In 1846, a decade after Rammohun's death, the poet Ishwarchandra Gupta wrote a very favourable review of *Pasanda Pidana*, commenting on its popularity and use of language, and was so taken with the tract that he even began a weekly journal that went by the same name.
223. *BW*, 265.
224. *BW*, 265.
225. Banerji, *Pandits*, 46.
226. Banerji, *Pandits*, 46.
227. Banerji, *Pandits*, 48.
228. Banerji, *Pandits*, 46.
229. Sen, *Rammohun Roy*, 53.
230. Banerji, *Pandits*, 47.
231. As quoted in Banerji, *Pandits*, 53.
232. *BW*, 334.
233. Pradyumna Bhattacharya, 'Rammohun Roy and Bengali Prose', in *Rammohun Roy and the Process of Modernisation in India*, ed. V.C. Joshi (Delhi: Vikas Publishing House, 1975), 201. For example, long compounds were split into smaller words—*guner anusare* (each according their ability) instead of *gunanusare*.
234. Banerji, *Rammohun Roy*, 70.
235. Bhattacharya, 'Rammohun Roy and Bengali Prose', 197.
236. Banerji, *Mrityunjay Vidyalankar*, 7.

237. Banerji, *Mrityunjay Vidyalankar*, 6.
238. *BW*, 107.
239. *BW*, 108.
240. *BW*, 108.
241. *BW*, 107.
242. Banerji, *Rammohun Roy*, 70.
243. *BW*, 124–5.
244. *BW*, 124–5.
245. Killingley, *Only True God*, 1–6.
246. *BW*, 75–9.
247. S.N. Mukherjee, 'Class, Caste and Politics in India', in *Elites in South Asia*, ed. S.N. Mukherjee and Edmund Leach (Cambridge: Cambridge University Press, 1970), 37–40.
248. Nag and Burman (eds), *EW* 2:53. Formatting as in the original.
249. *Tuhfat*, 17.
250. Nag and Burman (eds), *EW* 2:44.
251. *Tuhfat*, 9.
252. Nag and Burman (eds), *EW* 2:48.
253. Home, 'Supplementary Notes', 34.
254. Banerji, *Rammohun Roy*, 44.
255. Nag and Burman (eds), *EW*, 4:95.
256. Nag and Burman (eds), *EW*, 2:61.
254. Nag and Burman (eds), *EW*, 2:61
258. Nag and Burman (eds), *EW* 2: 1–2.
259. Nag and Burman (eds), *EW* 2:48.
260. *Asiatic Journal*, May 1819, *RRPM*, 18.
261. Chattopadhyay, *JB*, 70.
262. Chattopadhyay, *JB*, 91.
263. *Madras Government Gazette*, 6 April 1820, *RRPM*, 29.
264. *Asiatic Journal*, July 1820, *RRPM*, 22.
265. Nag and Burman (eds), *EW* 2:88.
266. Nag and Burman (eds), *EW* 4:116.
267. Nag and Burman (eds), *EW* 4:94.
268. *BW*, 75–9.
269. In Chapter 6, the ideas of ethics in these works will be seen in greater detail.
270. *Calcutta Monthly Journal*, December 1817, *RRPM*, 14.
271. *Calcutta Monthly Journal*, September 1817, *RRPM*, 12–13.
272. *Calcutta Journal*, October 1818, *RRPM*, 14–17.
273. *Calcutta Monthly Journal*, September 1817, *RRPM*, 12.

274. Nag and Burman (eds), *EW* 2:85.

275. Nag and Burman (eds), *EW* 2:1.

276. Nag and Burman (eds), *EW* 2:2.

277. Nag and Burman (eds), *EW* 2:6.

278. Patrick Olivelle (ed. and trans.), *The Early Upaniṣads: Annotated Text and Translation* (New York: Oxford University Press, 1998), 434.

279. Nag and Burman (eds), *EW* 2:3.

280. Nag and Burman (eds), *EW* 2:2. Italics in original.

281. Nag and Burman (eds), *EW* 2:1.

282. Nag and Burman (eds), *EW* 2:1.

283. Nag and Burman (eds), *EW* 2:15.

284. Olivelle, *The Early Upaniṣads*, 363.

285. Nag and Burman (eds), *EW* 2:15.

286. Nag and Burman (eds), *EW* 2:83.

287. Nag and Burman (eds), *EW* 2:100.

288. Nag and Burman (eds), *EW* 2:92.

289. Nag and Burman (eds), *EW* 2:84.

290. Nag and Burman (eds), *EW* 2:26.

291. Nag and Burman (eds), *EW* 2:23.

292. Nag and Burman (eds), *EW* 2:5.

293. Nag and Burman (eds), *EW* 2: 26–9.

294. The term 'oral-literate' was coined by V. Narayan Rao. Cited in Orsini, 'Introduction', *History of the Book*, xiv.

295. Chatterjee, *Cultures of History*, 219.

296. Chatterjee, *Cultures of History*, 218.

297. McClish, 'Householders', 464.

298. Upinder Singh, 'Politics, Violence and War in *Kāmandaka's Nītisāra*', *Indian Economic and Social History Review* 47, no. 1 (2010): 29–62.

4 Accountable Governance

Discursively, Rammohun's writings on Hindu scripture operated within a much larger field—a body of early Indian texts known as the Dharmashastras (DhS, as mentioned earlier).[1] Rammohun infused the DhS with a dual identity, hinting that they were not only texts of Hindu scripture but also manuals of good governance. Although academic literature has not explored the theoretical implications or the textual integrity of such hints, recent research on the DhS has proven him right. We now know that the DhS were indeed concerned with statecraft, administration, and judicial procedure as well as religious and social practices.[2]

The DhS are comprised of two separate traditions: *dharma* and *artha*.[3] The former is concerned with scripture and prescriptive rules for rituals; the latter with statecraft, law, governance, and administration.[4] The primary objective is to bring all the inhabitants of a particular area under a single system of *dharma* and within a framework of administration informed by *artha*. To this extent, DhS and their commentaries advocate a system of governance which integrates rituals, social practices, customs, conventional rules, and moral precepts within a framework of administration—judicial and civil.[5] Conceptually, they put forward a new theory of governance. As B.D. Chattopadhyay has shown, the DhS carefully chalk out a plan by which large centralized administrations can progressively allocate political power and administrative autonomy to local governments and thereby structure local autonomy into state administration.[6] The reference to large administrations is not surprising when one considers that the DhS were written with reference to the Mauryan Empire.[7] The Mauryans were early India's largest territorial polity. At the height of their power their empire encompassed all of South Asia (a feat that would only again be achieved 1,500 years later with the Mughal Empire and then later by the British Empire).

The DhS have had a considerable influence on Hindu scripture and literature.[8] Many passages of the Mahabharata (MBh, as mentioned earlier), for instance, contain passages from the Manava Dharmashastra (MDhS). The Puranas, too, extensively borrowed from the DhS.[9] Their influence can also be found in early-19th-century Calcutta. Indeed, as Brian Hatcher opines, the DhS were important to Sanskrit pandits and the native elite who referred to them to 'explore' new social contexts and express different world views, even ones which disagreed with each other.[10] Rammohun's supporters (Ramchandra Vidyavagis and Madanmohan Tarkalankar) as well as his critics (Mrityunjay Vidyalankar, Radhakanta Deb, and Anantaram Vidyavagisaktr) articulated their ideas from an intellectual context which was informed and influenced by the DhS.[11]

I argue that Rammohun's ideas of accountable governance were influenced by the DhS. His ideas were expressed in short English and Bangla tracts and addressed two distinct sets of readers—EIC officials and the Bengali public. Since neither was well versed with the complexities of DhS vocabulary, his arguments were explained to both by referring to terms, concepts, and contexts that they were familiar with. A clearer perspective of his ideas can be gained from a brief examination of his references to the DhS in his writings.

The Political Thinker, the Public, and the EIC

Rammohun referred to the DhS in writings on Hindu scripture, the freedom of the press, judiciary, sati, and property law. This section will focus on his writings on property law. This is because the concept of well-defined property laws was critical to his political thought. As the previous chapter showed, *Tuhfat*, his earliest known work, conceptualized a stable society as that which had defined property laws.

Rammohun published his first tract on property law, *Brief Remarks regarding Modern Encroachments on the Ancient Rights of Females*, in Calcutta in 1822 (henceforth, *Brief Remarks*). This short bilingual piece in English and Bangla was primarily concerned with a legal text, *Dayabhaga*, composed in Sanskrit prose and attributed to the medieval jurist Jimutavahana.[12] By 1822, *Dayabhaga* had been translated into English, but by EIC scholar–officials who wrongly declared that it was unrelated to any historical traditions of legal scholarship in India; and that its author, Jimutavahana, was but a mythic figure.[13] *Brief Remarks* was intended as a critique of such points of view.

Rammohun rightly opined that Jimutavahana was of a tradition of medieval DhS scholars—a fact we now know to be true from Ludo Rocher's research on the subject.[14] Rocher showed that Jimutavahana was indeed a historical character who heavily cited DhS scholars in *Dayabhaga*.[15] Patrick Olivelle's careful tabulation of the number of times that DhS scholars have been cited in the *Dayabhaga* has also underscored this point: Manu, 101; Apastamba, 4; Gautama, 20; Baudhayana, 19; Vasistha, 7; Narada, 41; Yajnavalkya, 41; Vishnu, 45 ; Brihaspati, 64; and Katyayana, 47.[16]

Brief Remarks also referred to Katyayana, Brihaspati, Vishnu, and Yajnavalkya.[17] Rammohun argued that the current system of law discriminated against step-mothers and widows who did not have children. This was in clear violation of DhS stipulations on property and inheritance.[18] Further, a woman's social status and legal rights on property now seemed to be determined by whether or not her husband was alive. The death of the husband could bring about an entirely new gamut of unfair and, indeed, brutal, socio-legal circumstances. As Rammohun explained,

> The consequence is, that a woman who is looked up to as the sole mistress by the rest of a family one day, on the next, becomes dependent on her sons, and subject to the slights of her daughters-in-law. She is not authorized to expend the most trifling sum or dispose of an article of the least value, without the consent of her son or daughter-in-law, who were

all subject to her authority but the day before. Cruel sons often wound the feelings of their dependent mothers, deciding in favour of their own wives, when family disputes take place between their mothers and wives. Step-mothers, who often are numerous on account of polygamy, being allowed in these countries [Bengal], are still more shamefully neglected in general by their step-sons, and sometimes dreadfully treated by their sisters-in-law who have fortunately a son or sons by their husband.[19]

Given this background, it is not surprising that Rammohun was aghast that EIC scholar–officials had ignored the influence of the DhS on the *Dayabhaga*.[20] Although he did not specify which scholar–official's work was being critiqued, we note that Rocher compiled a list of commentaries on *Dayabhaga* from 1475 to 1825 and observed that none but H.T. Colebrooke had written out all DhS references.[21] Rammohun's criticism was thus a reference to Colebrooke.

This does not mean that Colebrooke was not aware of the DhS. Rather, he held that the DhS were an important legal tradition.[22] However, his interpretation of the DhS tradition was deeply flawed because he considered them to be early Indian relics which did not have much influence on subsequent legal traditions in India.[23] Unfortunately, the EIC uncritically applied Colebrooke's flawed interpretation to the entire system of Hindu law in Bengal with the consequence that their interpretation of 'Hindu law' became 'a British administrative invention' rather than a reflection of Indian legal practices.[24]

Rammohun argued that the Company's ignorance of the DhS had led to the legalization of unethical practices.[25] In this context, he referred to the Kulin Brahmins' successful efforts to legalize polygamy in Bengal and blithely noted that 'the evil consequences arising from such polygamy, the public may easily guess'.[26] (Unfortunately, his appeals to regulate polygamy would not be taken up until 1856. Buoyed by calls for legislative intervention against Kulin polygamy, his son, Ramaprasad, would later reprint the tract as an aid to public debate on the matter.)[27]

Rammohun also referred to those who were not aware of polygamy's consequences on Bengali society—EIC officials. In his view, officials were also unaware that polygamy was largely prohibited in DhS literature.[28] He urged EIC officials to seek the opinion of 'humane and liberal Hindus' while deciding on judicial matters.[29] Such pointers were also signposts to Company officials to engage with a politically conscious and educated public in Bengal. He argued that engaging the public would enable the passage of social welfare legislation, and emphasized this point by citing a law introduced by late Raja of Tirhoot, Madhav Singh, to regulate polygamy in response to the 'painful' experiences of his subjects, nearly fifty years ago.[30] The marked emphasis on the time drew attention to the slow rate of change in EIC policy.[31]

Rammohun's ideas on unchecked Brahminical legislative authority may have found an agreeable readership amongst the judges of the Supreme Court in Bengal. William Jones, perhaps the most important judge of the Supreme Court in the late 18th century, had been a harsh critic of the role of Sanskrit pandits and had even written in 1788 to the then Governor General Lord Cornwallis: 'I could not with an easy conscience concur in a decision merely on the written opinion of the native lawyers in any case in which they would have the remotest interest in misleading the court.'[32] In 1794, Jones attempted to break the pandit monopoly on the DhS by producing the first English translation of MDhS. These efforts were not unacknowledged in *Brief Remarks* which even ended with a glowing reference to the Company's 'honest judgement':

> I only maintain that the native community place greater confidence in the honest judgement of European countrymen than that of their own countrymen. But should the natives receive the same advantages of education that the Europeans generally enjoy and be brought up in the same notions of honour they will I trust be found equally with Europeans worthy of trust and confidence of their countrymen and the respect of all men.[33]

At the first instance, the above passage appeared to contradict Rammohun's criticism of the Company's interpretation of the *Dayabhaga* and did not give much importance to the Bengali public. A closer reading, however, suggests that this was not the case. It began with an assertion that the Bengali public was an informed and educated readership, went on to argue that the EIC ought to invest in the education of its subjects, and strongly implied that this task was currently being neglected. Further, Rammohun reiterated his argument that the Company was not only accountable to 'native interpreters of law' but to all its subjects. He did so by requesting the native community 'to place greater confidence' on EIC officials than their 'own countrymen'. When read in this light, the passage appears to explain his arguments on the importance of governmental accountability to the public ('great body of learned Hindus') and highlight the importance of public participation in governance. Implicit in such references is the conceptualization of Bengali society as an *ethical* society. The 'native community' would not be able to place 'greater confidence' on the 'honest judgement' of Company officials unless there were strong ethical reasons to do so. Thus, his ideas of everyday ethical practice in Bengali society went hand-in-hand with his concept of accountability.

The conceptual scope of *Brief Remarks* was wider than a mere critique of current property law. I argue that this tract can also be read as a template for his political thought. A careful reading of a lengthy and dense narrative-footnote printed on the first page of the tract clarifies this argument. Fittingly, the footnote applied a distinct Puranic narrative structure.[34] This unique stylistic choice however requires some explanation.

The Puranas (tales of ancient days) are a genre of Sanskrit and vernacular literature mainly concerned with cosmogony, myth, genealogy of gods, and the lives of rulers. Perhaps no other textual tradition in Indian literature at the time could rival the Puranas for their popularity in Bengali society.[35]

Rammohun deliberately adopted a Puranic narrative structure to circulate his ideas as broadly as possible in contemporary Bengali society than a restricted native elite. In fact, the native elite in the 19th century looked down on the Puranas. For example, Debendranath Tagore appealed to his followers to 'turn away' from the Puranas and focus instead on the Upanishads and Vedas. Similarly, Soshee Chunder Dutt, an influential Bengal writer, assessed the Puranas as 'woven out of a system of mythology, which has perhaps nowhere been surpassed in extent, richness or obscenity.'[36]

Rammohun, however, freely employed the Puranas to explain his ideas to the public, particularly in Bengali writings such as *Vedantasar* (1815). When his critics objected, he retorted that the Puranas were carriers of complex ideas.[37] Three years later, in 1818, his Bengali tract, *Utsavanader sahit vicar* [Reply to Utsavananda] explained Vedanta by referring to the Bhagavata Purana.[38] Later that year, he argued that the Puranas were explanatory texts which 'presented the meaning of the Veda and various moral teachings under the guise of stories.'[39] The use of the Puranas as explanatory texts for the Bengali public was a consistent feature in his writings.

The Puranas were not unknown in official circles either. EIC scholar–officials had undertaken translations of the Puranas since 1784. In the 1830s, Vans Kennedy and H.H. Wilson publicly debated the importance of Puranic narrative in Calcutta periodicals, hinting at an official familiarity with the popularity of the Puranas and their 'simple and easy' stylistics.[40] Neither Bengali society nor Company officials would have been surprised when the narrative-footnote in *Brief Remarks* was presented within a Puranic narrative.

A Puranic narrative also allowed for significant flexibility.[41] As V. Narayan Rao notes, Puranic myths were not concerned with the historicity of their narratives but rather their purpose was to promote 'a new world-view'. 'The Puranas don't just alter facts,' Narayan argues, 'but perceive them in a new way [such that] the very concepts of time and space in Indian history are changed through Puranic narration.'[42] The Puranic narrative was the ideal vehicle to reach out to a diverse audience.

One particular idea in the footnote which Rammohun's readers would have found intriguing was his understanding of the caste system. The traditional caste system was a rigid social hierarchy comprised of Brahmins, Kshatriyas, Vaishyas, and Shudras. However, he referred to the Brahmins and Kshatriyas throughout his narrative without mentioning them by their caste names or even indicating that a social hierarchy was in place. For example, he insisted on referring to the Kshatriyas as the 'second tribe' without giving any indication of who the 'first tribe' might be.[43] And, he referred to the Brahmins as the 'first class' (and avoided any reference to a 'second class') as if to show that he was deliberately moving away from a ritualistic definition of caste.

Rammohun's footnote took the shape of a narrative of political institutions in early and medieval India. The narrative did not, however, begin with chronological, geographical, or textual references but an abrupt declaration that the Kshatriya caste though 'appointed to defend and rule' had failed to perform their duties effectively:

> The second tribe [Kshatriya caste] having adopted arbitrary and despotic practices, the *others* revolted against them and under the personal command of the celebrated Parasurama, defeated the Royalists in several battles and put cruelly to death almost all the males of that tribe.[44] (Emphasis mine)

Rather than a historical context, the reader is immediately directed to the mythical Puranic hero Parasurama (who also appeared in the Bhagvada Purana, Agni Purana, Padma Purana; and Vayu Purana, the oldest of the genre). That Parasurama was not given any introduction in the narrative-footnote is indicative of Rammohun's confidence that his readership was familiar with the character. This was a fairly accurate assumption. Parasurama appears in the text of Wilson's translation of the Vishnu Purana, a project in which Rammohun was involved in at the time of writing *Brief Remarks*.[45] Interestingly, the original text of the Vishnu Purana did not have any reference to Parasurama. Rather, Wilson had included the myth because 'the legend makes a great figure in *Vaishnava* works in general.'[46]

Rammohun's assumption that his readership were familiar with the myth also meant that he did not have to give an account of it. In this context, we recall that Wilson recounted the most popular version of the myth in his translation of the Vishnu Purana. In the absence of direct evidence from Rammohun himself, we have taken Wilson's account as our text.[47]

The Parasurama myth concerned three main characters: Parasurama; his father, Jamadagnya; and mother, Renuka. Jamadagnya, a reclusive ascetic, ordered Parasurama to chop off Renuka's head with an axe when he suspected her of wrongdoing. After Parasurama chopped off her head, he pleaded with Jamadagnya to bring his mother back to life. Jamadagnya agreed and Renuka was subsequently revived.[48]

Although the Parasurama myth has been oft perceived as an account of a matricide, what strikes us here is that the beheading was not fatal. In an analysis of this episode, Wendy Doniger has shown that such narratives are not unusual but in keeping with the general literary tradition of mythological beheadings.[49] Doniger argues that the point of the myth is not the beheading but to illustrate that 'Parasurama is torn between two warring parents. In the end, all wrongs are righted.'[50]

The story of Parasurama did not, however, end there. In a tragic turn of events, Jamadagnya was murdered by the sons of a Kshatriya prince, Kartavirya. The consequences of this were bloody as Parasurama swore revenge against the Kshatriyas. After emerging victorious in a brutal war, he was congratulated by the ghost of his father. The ghost even appointed various Brahmins as kings in place of the earlier rulers.[51]

The Parasurama myth recounted an overhaul of the current political system in which the Brahmin caste was now given political power. While the narrative-footnote in *Brief Remarks* shares important similarities with this account, Rammohun also differed from the myth by asserting that Parasurama led a societal revolt (as opposed to a caste war between the Brahmins and Kshatriyas). He also extended the scope of the myth by not only citing the transfer of power to the Brahmins but also outlining a distinct perspective of a government which shared power between the Brahmins and the Kshatriyas. He insisted that the new government was accountable and that laws were only proposed after seeking societal consensus.[52] His narrative pushed forward the idea that an active and politically conscious society played a leading role in the transformation of law-making into a process of reform.

In academic literature, the narrative-footnote has been cited as evidence of a constitutional liberal programme.[53] *Brief Remarks* does not, however, contain evidence of any affiliation to constitutional liberalism but highlights the importance of the Puranas on Rammohun's political thought. As we shall see later in the chapter, the Puranas were also sources of political theory and government, explained through the medium of popular stories. Let us take the case of a Purana which Rammohun, Company officials, and contemporary Bengali society would have been familiar with, the Vishnu Purana.

The Vishnu Purana referred to a wide array of myths but our concern here is the marriage myth of the celestial gods Mitra and Varuna. In an important monograph on the subject, A.K. Coomaraswamy proposed that this myth encapsulated a theory of government based on the Kshatriya and Brahmin. According to Coomaraswamy, their political relationship was that of 'power and counsel'.[54] However, the Brahmin and Kshatriya shared an unequal relationship since the former's status as a 'spiritual authority' meant that his legitimacy was derived from a 'higher power' or from scripture.[55] In this sense, the Kshatriya was 'ruled' by 'a higher King' and therefore subject to the *laws* beholden by the 'higher King'.[56]

Coomaraswamy argued that the Vishnu Purana popularized political ideas articulated in early Indian texts such as Sathapatha Brahmana and Rig Veda.[57] Revealingly, Sathpatha Brahmana also explained the working relationship between the Kshatriya and Brahmin in the same terms as a marriage and even gendered their roles as feminine and masculine respectively.[58] Since masculinity is typically seen as a function of absolute power and violence, the Kshatriya's femininity was an attempt to subvert his potential to be a violent overlord. But this does not mean that the Vishnu Purana provides us with a literal explanation of early Indian texts. Rather, it expresses complex ideas poetically. The Puranic result of the union of Mitra and Varuna was Agastya, a Brahmin hero.

Early Indian texts conceptualized of a political system which was very different from constitutional liberalism or a republican parliament.[59] The Puranic conception of Agastya is a poetic reference to Sathpatha Brahmana's interpretation of a successful king who embarked on a passage into 'Brahman-hood' to attain inner peace and tranquillity rather than rule for political dominance.[60]

Rammohun stressed that the stability of the state depended on the Brahmins being independent of the Kshatriyas. For 'two thousand years', he noted, impartial Brahmin 'legislators' contributed to political stability in early India. The state, however, collapsed when the Brahmins ('the first class') became employees of the Kshatriyas ('Rajputs').[61] The word 'Rajputs' is but a representative example of those kings who ruled without the independent counsel of their Brahmin advisors. Note that Sathpatha Brahmana warned that the result of a king without counsel was a tyrannical system of government and Rammohun assessed 'Rajput' rule as 'a thousand years' of political instability, 'tyranny and oppression'. The 'Rajputs' ruled as 'petty princes' of a large number of smaller kingdoms. Ultimately, a dissatisfied populace revolted against them and instead appointed new rulers from 'Ghazni and Ghor'. However, the new rulers continued with a 'tyrannical system of government'.[62] This marked the end of *Brief Remarks'* narrative of political institutions in India.

In keeping with the Vishnu Purana's narrative structure, Rammohun's narrative-footnote too was not a historical account.[63] But was the lack of historicity deliberate? One way to answer this question is to re-examine the structure of the narrative. While historians oft presume that a reference to the Puranas is compelling evidence of Rammohun's belief in a narrative of decline from a supposed ancient golden age,[64] recent research on Puranic myths does not support this view. As Doniger explains, 'In the majority of Puranic myths, the golden age is only a temporary passing phase.'[65]

I argue that *Brief Remarks'* narrative-footnote's emphasis on a recurring theme of social revolution and misgovernance (rather than historical context and causal explanation) reveals a *mythic* structure of narrative. As Doniger observed, 'Myths are essentially stories which are united by themes that recur in the narrativity.'[66] Note that the narrative-footnote is united by a single theme, that through the course of Indian history, those governments which were unaccountable to their subjects ultimately succumbed to revolution. This basic argument also mirrors the blunt warning in MDhS that kings can engage in war and military conflict to destroy rivals and enemies but can never introduce a tyrannical government.[67]

The next section will explain the influence of MDhS on Rammohun's thought in greater detail. Here I offer a tentative suggestion. I think that the primary purpose of the narrative-footnote in *Brief Remarks* was to explain the ideas of MDhS concerning political power, good governance, and accountability by referring to popular Puranic historical and mythical figures. His narrative-footnote wasn't simply a reiteration of a standard myth, but rather introduced many deviations from it, so that he could accommodate his arguments from within its familiar context.

Rammohun's deviations from the standard Puranic myth, and inclusion of new terms and concepts to explain his ideas would not have been unusual to his readers in Bengali society who were familiar with an even more flexible version of the Puranic narrative in the local vernacular (also known as folk Puranas).[68] A.K. Ramanujan's study of the subject showed that folk Puranas 'reworked motifs from a Puranic pool' to 'domesticate, localise, incorporate and contemporise' myths to the requirements of the readership/audience.[69] As D.C. Sen pointed out, folk Puranas were extremely popular in early-19th-century Bengal.[70]

In the case of Rammohun's narrative, a folk Puranic flexibility allowed for a vast vocabulary of concepts and categories to enter the narrative, such as British historical categories ('royalists') and liberal political concepts ('executive and legislative authority'). The term 'royalist' is a Cromwellian reference and 'constitution' is indicative of a liberal vocabulary. These are also terms which EIC officials would have been familiar with. Moreover, the deployment of these terms within a popular mythological context reveals an attempt to reach out to a wide audience (Bengali society and Company officials) but with a common message—that the consequences of an unaccountable government were social instability and violent political revolution.

Rammohun's argument was not restricted to a footnote in *Brief Remarks* but developed in two later tracts—*Memorial to the Supreme Court* (published in Calcutta) and *Appeal to the King-in-Council* (published in London). Both were published in 1823.

Rammohun wrote both tracts as petitions in favour of the freedom of the press in Bengal. The press was crucial to his political project. Since 1818, his vernacular papers, the bilingual weekly *Sambad Kaumadi*, and the Persian weekly *Mirat al-Akhbar* had popularized his ideas in Bengali society. For example, *Sambad Kaumadi* rejected excessive expenditure on rituals and pleaded instead that costs be diverted to philanthropic projects such as education.[71]

Sambad Kaumadi also referred to Rammohun's other writings such as the reform of property law.[72] As the next chapter will elaborate, it was his chief vehicle for articulating his ideas on social reform projects (such as abolishing the practice of sati). But *Kaumadi* was not just a vehicle for reformist ideas. James Silk Buckingham, the 'radical' proprietor of *Calcutta Journal*, observed that it also provided information on a wide number of subjects, 'religious, moral, domestic affairs, foreign communications and communications on various hitherto interesting local topics'.[73] Buckingham was a close friend. He had first met Rammohun in 1818, and been in touch ever since.[74]

Buckingham's *Calcutta Journal* was, however, far too radical for the Company's taste. Matters came to a head in 1823 when Buckingham criticized a minister of the Scottish Church for agreeing to be appointed by the EIC as the Clerk of the Stationary. As far as he was concerned, it was 'unbecoming' for a clergyman to accept an EIC post.[75] His opinions alarmed the government, and Lord Hastings, the then Governor General, arrested *Calcutta Journal*'s assistant editor and ordered Buckingham to leave India within two months.[76]

Hastings also proposed new regulations on the freedom of the press but left India before they were approved by his superiors in London.[77] His successor, John Adam, vigorously implemented the regulations by licensing all newspaper content and stipulated harsh fines for 'objectionable material' against the government.[78] That the regulations had a very harmful effect on vernacular newspapers in Bengal can be seen in the paucity of new publications in the years following the regulation.[79] Given this impact, it is unsurprising that the press regulations prompted appeals and petitions from the native community.

Rammohun's appeals were amongst the many native petitions to the government at Calcutta and London to rescind the regulations. His appeals also articulated his political thought by stressing the importance of the press as a vehicle of governmental accountability. This argument had earlier been articulated in the prospectus of *Mirat al-Akhbar* where he intended to 'communicate to the rulers a knowledge of the real situation of their subjects'.[80] However, he did not stop with 'rulers' but also emphasized the absolute necessity to be accountable to the natives.[81] We note that the same argument had featured in the narrative-footnote of *Brief Remarks* (which appeared in the same year as the prospectus of *Mirat al-Akhbar*).

Mirat al-Akhbar assessed the current 'rulers' in the light of earlier governments in Indian history: a mode of political assessment which also appeared in *Memorial to the Supreme Court* (henceforth, *Memorial*) and *Appeal to the King-in-Council* (henceforth, *Appeal*) in 1823. *Memorial* can be read as a development of the narrative-footnote in *Brief Remarks*. This tract argued that Indian governments have been historically accountable to their subjects (and those which weren't were violently overthrown by social revolution).[82] This argument was further developed in *Appeal*.

Appeal first presented Britain as 'the successful defender of Europe from [Napoleonic] continental usurpation'. Following this congratulatory tone, Rammohun swiftly distanced himself from a European political context and cautiously noted that his petition contained a 'painful' assessment of the EIC in India—its 'abuse' of legislative power, 'invasion of civil rights' of subjects, and campaign of 'encouraging a cruel and unfounded suspicion of our attachment to our existing Government'. Significantly, in a direct reference to its political status in India as a representative of British political practices, the EIC was termed as the 'local government'.[83]

Appeal then spelt out the 'painful circumstances' introduced by the 'local government'. Rammohun opined that the Supreme Court was guilty of bias towards the government, stressed that public accountability depended on an impartial legislature, and warned that unaccountable governments have historically triggered social revolution in India. While this argument has similarities with *Brief Remarks*, *Appeal* did not refer to the Puranas (which would have been virtually unknown in Britain); instead it provided examples which British readers would have been more familiar with. Thus, the current judicial system of Canada was cited as a representative example of an accountable government.[84]

Rammohun did not just complain about the Supreme Court in *Appeal*, he also neatly pointed out the three main political implications of Company rule in India. First, the EIC had introduced unfamiliar political institutions in Bengal. Second, its policies reflected the shift in sovereign power from India to Britain. And third, the natives widely *expected* that the EIC would invest in the 'welfare' of its subjects since their 'dutiful subjects have not viewed the English as a body of conquerors but rather ... as a protector.'[85]

Appeal's stress on native expectations of the Company was not unique to the tract. This argument also featured in *Memorial* and revealed that governmental accountability was an important subject of discussion amongst the natives.[86] In this context, both tracts compared the EIC unfavourably with previous governments and positioned it as the inheritor of previous political systems in India. But the question is: if the EIC had inherited a previous political system, then what was it? As the next section will show, to Rammohun, this referred to a DhS theory of state.

Explaining Shastric Ideas to the EIC

Seven years after *Memorial* and *Appeal*, Rammohun's second tract on property law, *Essay on the Rights of Hindus over Ancestral Property* (henceforth *Ancestral Property*), appeared in Calcutta in 1830. *Ancestral Property* was a critique of the EIC's current policy of overriding the *Dayabhaga*'s tenets on the inheritance of property. Rammohun argued that while *Dayabhaga* had upheld the right of the family patriarch to disinherit biological heirs, the EIC had vetoed this stipulation, much to the dissatisfaction, 'surprise and alarm' of Bengali society.[87]

Ancestral Property's critique did not go unchallenged as an anonymous letter published in the *Bengal Hurkaru* quoted a DhS commentary as well as scholarship by EIC officials on inheritance law to argue that Rammohun was wrong.[88] In his response, Rammohun published an open letter arguing that the anonymous writer had misunderstood the tenets of *Dayabhaga* and its relationship to DhS commentaries.[89] Amused by the letter's anonymity, he demanded that the writer declare his name. However, the anonymous writer refused to reveal his identity and responded by continuing to disagree with Rammohun's views. After a flurry of four more letters (in which the two disagreed with each other, and published their responses in the *Hurkaru*), the anonymous writer fell silent while Rammohun reiterated the argument which had first featured in *Brief Remarks*: the point of arguing about the law was to make 'lives more agreeable' rather than simply disagree over competing interpretations in legal texts.[90]

Unfortunately, Rammohun's anonymous critic had not detected a larger political undercurrent. Much like *Brief Remarks*, *Ancestral Property* too highlighted a larger concern. *Ancestral Property* referred to the EIC's government as the 'government of a conquered country' and its officials as 'judicial officers of the conquerors'.[91] I argue that such references were deliberately employed by Rammohun to draw attention to the problematics of the political situation of the Company in Bengal and imply that its recent decision to override *Dayabhaga* also undid earlier efforts to follow a legal system which had the approval of its subjects and thereby gain a measure of legitimacy.

Rammohun argued that the new inheritance laws amounted to a blatant disregard for indigenous legal systems. In this context, he observed that the decision to change the law was in violation of how laws were proposed, legitimized, and observed throughout the world. He observed that globally, political and religious authorities could not legitimize laws. That privilege lay with the general populace.[92]

Rammohun opined that the EIC's arbitrary change in property law had led to problems in the accountability of legal officials. This argument was a critique of current legal procedure. He opined that judges were not currently 'obliged to consult' established legal codes in *Dayabhaga* and thus could not be held accountable for their decisions. He warned that this faulty procedure would inevitably lead to bad results as 'experience shows that unchecked power often leads the best men wrong and produces general mischief' and that the concentration of power in the hands of a single judicial officer employed by the government would lead to the breakdown of the entire system of administration.[93] Note that *Brief*

Remarks also made a similar argument that unaccountable 'Brahmin' legislators employed by the rulers had historically led to the collapse of governments in India.

Much in the same vein as *Brief Remarks*, *Ancestral Property* too argued that *Dayabhaga* was a part of a DhS tradition of law which upheld local autonomy and accountability.[94] The tract also expanded and developed Rammohun's political thought by introducing political concepts and ideas with greater visibility than *Brief Remarks*. While *Brief Remarks* explained his ideas of accountable government in a footnote, *Ancestral Property* included them in the main text.

In *Brief Remarks*, Rammohun had ended his narrative-footnote rather abruptly by insisting that long periods of misgovernance had led to the disintegration of the early Indian 'Empire' into a confused patchwork of warring kingdoms. He had also avoided any discussion on his concept of 'Empire'. *Ancestral Property*, however, updated this narrative by noting that 'at present the whole Empire has been placed under British power'.[95] It also revealed a new political vocabulary for his concept of 'Empire'. Rammohun insisted that 'Empire' was not a British political construct but a historical remnant of the ideas of DhS theorists who formulated laws in response to different social practices and differences in 'language, dress and habits' across regions.[96] 'Empire' thus referred to a large culturally diverse territory, derived from the DhS.

Rammohun's bold interpretation of empire, however, raises the question of how far his ideas reflected DhS doctrine. In this context, recent Indological research has shown that the DhS did indeed integrate a diverse set of local practices into a textual tradition of law-making. This process began with the MDhS, a text with 'a recognised trajectory of pre-eminence' in DhS literature.[97] A DhS commentator, Brihaspati, recognised MDhS as an important authority in the 5th century CE. By 1500 CE, it was held as the most important DhS text of all and from this point on, its 'fame' continued for 'the next 15 centuries' until the EIC intervened in Indian politics and erroneously experimented with the possibility of interpreting it within a frame of reference provided by modern European law.[98]

The MDhS was inspired by Mauryan Emperor Ashoka's state policies in the 3rd century BCE.[99] The text was not, however, composed during the time of an extant Mauryan Empire but two centuries after its collapse. Consequently, MDhS was inspired by the *memory* of certain facets of Mauryan administration (namely, the methods by which Ashoka ordered and organized a state, its officials, and its subjects on the ideology of *dharma*).[100]

MDhS was written in verse as a dialogue between a teacher and student, and almost three quarters of the text are concerned with the activities of Brahmins and Kings.[101] It is extant today in the form of 53 manuscripts and 9 commentaries, and has been translated into English and placed in its historical and linguistic context by Patrick Olivelle in a new standard critical edition in 12 chapters (*adhyayas*).[102] The scope of this chapter's engagement with MDhS is restricted to discussions on statecraft: in chapter 7 (MDhS 7) and a portion of chapter 9 (MDhS 9.252–9.324). The notations 7 and 9.252-9.324 are as per Patrick Olivelle's critical and annotated standard English translation of the MDhS. A close reading reveals the careful conceptualization of a government which integrated different local polities within the framework of a large administration on very similar lines.

MDhS has also been influenced by other texts. As Mark McClish has shown, almost 50 per cent of MDhS 7 has been appropriated from Kautilya's Arthashastra, the best known treatise of statecraft in early India.[103] Rammohun could not have known this as Kautilya's Arthashastra was not rediscovered until 1905, having been presumed lost for many centuries before that.[104] However, I take the view that it is worthwhile to consider the ideas contained in Kautilya's Arthashastra in some detail. The king in Kautilya's Arthashastra was an absolute ruler (whose powers encompassed law, governance, external relations with other territories, and war) and who invested in a close-knit structure of state officials at various levels of government (from his innermost circle to the village).[105] Though an absolute ruler, the king nevertheless sustained and exercised his political power by successfully negotiating with local as well as supra-regional landed powers and groups throughout his empire and even outside its territories.[106] The consequence of this was profound. To quote Olivelle, 'Even though the king was an absolute monarch, he was not a despot or tyrant.'[107] This is the main thrust of Rammohun's arguments on government too: that political power cannot be tyrannical, and must be shared. Borrowing from Kautilya's Arthashastra appeared to be an unintended consequence of his readings of the MDhS.

The MDhS conception of a government which integrated different local polities within the framework of a large administration was also influential as later DhS authors and commentators, such as Katyayana, Patanjali, and Apastamba, also followed this line of thinking. In this case, we can argue that since *Ancestral Property* and *Brief Remarks* cited both Katyayana and Apastamba, it is reasonable to assume that their author would have been familiar with their arguments.

That the DhS in fact proposed this specific view of governance has also been clarified through Indological research. In fact, Olivelle clarifies that the DhS tradition can even be read as a 'textualization of local practices'.[108] The noted legal scholar John Derrett also echoed a similar sentiment when he opined (albeit poetically):

> No [DhS] scholar, no matter if he were a great-grandfather, could expect his compositions to have any effect, to survive into several manuscript copies, unless he related the wisdom of ages in a contemporary guise. His name would add nothing to its value, which lay in its being accepted and transmitted as a true statement of transcendental verities. His work would be valued if it conformed to permanent values and agreed with life as it was lived.[109]

To the early Indian historian B.D. Chattopadhyay, the DhS emphasis on local practices is not incidental. Rather, it reveals a political theory which advocated the allocation of political power by large centralized state administrations to local communities.[110] MDhS even insisted that the state could not interfere in everyday governance but only appoint officials (*amatyan*) as overlookers.[111] However, this also led to the worry that official overseers ought not to exercise inordinate political power.[112] To counter this problem, MDhS chalked out an intricate plan whereby a system of checks and balances would be structured into the administration so that even official overseers could be held accountable for their actions.[113]

We recall that the appointment of qualified official overseers ('legislators') was also an important argument in *Brief Remarks*. In this context, consider that the MDhS (7.60) also suggested a specific typology of officials 'who are honest, intelligent, steadfast, and able to collect revenues properly, individuals who have been thoroughly investigated'.[114] Note that the 'individuals' were to be those 'whose ancestors were in royal service'

(MDhS 7.61).[115] Rammohun may have interpreted passages such as these to frame the theoretical context for his arguments concerning native employees who belonged to a community of scribal-elite. I argue that in the final analysis Rammohun was attempting to bring about a system in which EIC officials would be 'official overseers' and everyday governance could be managed by Indian native employees. However, *Brief Remarks* did not explain these points to Company officials.

While *Exposition* developed the argument on the role of Company officials, *Ancestral Property* tackled a more immediate problem: the case for considering the DhS as legitimate sources of scripture and legal literature. In the early 19th century, the DhS were not regarded as sources of law but widely assessed as inconsistent and contradictory. An even bigger problem was that the Company was familiar with British political and legal traditions but could not make much headway with texts which represented a very different system of thought. This context was not limited to the EIC in India but even the highest court of appeal in Britain, the Privy Council. For example, even 16 years after *Ancestral Property*, the Privy Council found it 'quite impossible' to rely on the interpretations of DhS 'founded upon authorities to which we have access only through translations and when the doctrines themselves and the reasons by which they are supported or impugned are drawn from religious tradition, ancient usages and more modern habits of the Hindus with which we cannot be familiar'.[116] The EIC also did not consider the DhS as scripture. This was problematic for Rammohun since the legitimacy of the DhS *was* based on their status as Hindu scripture.

In response to these problems, Rammohun focussed on the contradictions and inconsistencies of a text that Company men *did* consider as scripture—the Bible. He argued that EIC officials ought not to be 'surprised' with contradictions in DhS interpretation since Biblical interpretation too revealed many 'contradictions' (evidenced by multiple denominations in Christianity).[117] He also asserted, for example, the DhS emphasis on local practices had been mistakenly assessed as 'inconsistencies'. Further, this was not a DhS peculiarity since a careful perusal of common law would show that there were many legal differences between regions in Britain. The EIC also insisted on perceiving the DhS from a British legal standpoint than as a representative of a diverse scriptural tradition. This had led to a fundamental misunderstanding of the DhS.

Perhaps anticipating that this argument would be challenged, he opined that since British citizens did not experience any 'inconvenience' with different legal institutions in England and Scotland, they ought not to be inconvenienced with the plurality of legal practices in India. Finally, he asserted that Britain and India shared a 'reciprocal' political relationship and that one was dependent on the other.[118]

Rammohun's stress on the 'reciprocal relations' between Britain and India signalled the importance of his intervention as a native intellectual arguing for a DhS framework of law. It also underscored the simple but powerful idea that his political thought on accountable governance, though based on sources which officials in London did not know of, could nevertheless be explained in terms of legal and political principles which they adhered to in Britain. In this way, the DhS were explained to Company officials using terms, categories, and references which they were familiar with. Ultimately, it was not just the DhS but the way he explained them to his readers which defined his political thought.

***

Conclusion: Dharmashastras and Governmental Accountability

Rammohun's ideas of accountability and good governance was an inspired interpretation of the DhS. His arguments addressed two distinct readers—Company officials and contemporary Bengali society. For Company officials, he used terms such as 'constitution', 'executive', 'legislature', and 'common law' to explain his ideas. For Bengali society, he explained his ideas by employing Puranic myth.

Rammohun's ideas on governance also took the peculiar position of the EIC in India into account. He argued that while everyday supervision from London was quite impossible, accountability to the natives was far more achievable. He also warned of the danger of social revolution if the government was not accountable to its subjects. *Brief Remarks* introduced his ideas but the argument was only completed in *Ancestral Property*. The former referred to a history of governance which demonstrated the role of protest, dissent, and violence in political relations and stressed the importance of accountable forms of government while the latter showed that the basic legal principles which supported the legitimacy and practical relevance of the DhS in governance could be understood by Company officials. These ideas also appeared in petitions to the Supreme Court in Calcutta (*Memorial*) and King in Council in London (*Appeal*) on the freedom of the press in 1823. *Memorial* and the *Appeal* were significant because of their importance to his political project. He would not be able to criticize the lack of governmental accountability quite so freely with highly regulated press laws.

Rammohun's ideas were articulated to an administration which understood little of the customs and practices of its subjects. For example, *Brief Remarks* argued that the Company's interpretation of polygamy as a legitimate and legal practice showed how little the Company officials understood DhS law. The next chapter is concerned with a similar argument. Rammohun opined that the Company had mistakenly interpreted sati as a legitimate social practice. Unsurprisingly, the DhS and its ideas of government lay at the core of his understanding of sati. The focus on his sati writings demonstrates the applicability of his political thought in the most important of his projects of social reform.

Notes

1. Nag and Burman (eds), *EW* 2:92.
2. Patrick Olivelle, 'Explorations in Early History of the *Dharmaśāstras*', in *Between the Empires* (New York: Oxford University Press, 2006), 185.
3. Olivelle, Early History of the *Dharmaśāstras*, 185.
4. Patrick Olivelle (ed. and trans.), *Manu's Dharmaśāstra: A Critical Edition and translation of the Mānava Dharmaśāstra* (Oxford University Press: New York, 2005), 42–6.
5. Olivelle, Early History of the *Dharmaśāstras*, 185.
6. Brajadulal Chattopadhyay, *Studying Early India* (New Delhi: Oxford University Press, 2010), 110.
7. Olivelle (ed. and trans.), *Manu's Dharmaśāstra*, 38.
8. Donald R. Davis Jr. 'History of the Reception of the *Dharmaśāstra*', in *The Oxford History of Hinduism: A New History of Dharmaśāstra*, eds. Patrick Olivelle and Donald R. Davis Jr. (New York: Oxford University Press, 2018), 374.
9. Davis Jr, 'Reception of the *Dharmaśāstra*', 374.
10. Hatcher, 'Pandits at Work', 45–6.
11. Anantarama Vidyavagisaktr was a DhS scholar in Calcutta. Anantarama's defence of sati was written as a tract in Sanskrit. The tract criticized

Rammohun's 'half baked' ideas of Sati. Duncan Derrett opined that the work was a 'masterpiece' of scholarship (J. Duncan M. Derrett, 'Anantarama's Defence of Sati (c.1818–1820)', in *Bulletin of the Department of Post-Graduate Training and Research, Sanskrit College, Calcutta, 150th Anniversary Volume, 1824–1974*, ed. Bishnupada Bhattacharya [Calcutta: Calcutta Sanskrit College, 1979], 47; Hatcher, 'Pandits at Work', 51–4).

12. Ludo Rocher (ed. and trans.), *Jimutavahana's Dāyabhāga: The Hindu Law of Inheritance in Bengal* (New York: Oxford University Press, 2012), 39.

13. Rocher (ed. and trans.), *Jimutavahana's Dāyabhāga*, 7–18.

14. Rocher (ed. and trans.), *Jimutavahana's Dāyabhāga*.

15. Rocher (ed. and trans.), *Jimutavahana's Dāyabhāga*, 18.

16. Olivelle, *Manu's Dharmaśāstra*, 70.

17. Nag and Burman (eds), *EW* 1:9.

18. Nag and Burman (eds), *EW* 1:2.

19. Nag and Burman (eds), *EW* 1:4.

20. Ghose (ed.), *The English Works*, 375–6.

21. Rocher (ed. and trans.), *Jimutavahana's Dāyabhāga*, 17–36.

22. Nandini Bhattacharyya-Panda, *Appropriation and Invention of Tradition: The East India Company and Hindu Law in Early Colonial Bengal* (New Delhi: Oxford University Press, 2008), 252–3.

23. Bhattacharyya-Panda, *Appropriation and Invention of Tradition*, 252–3.

24. Bhattacharyya-Panda, *Appropriation and Invention of Tradition*, 243.

25. Ghose (ed.), *The English Works*, 383.

26. Ghose (ed.), *The English Works*, 379.

27. Ghose (ed.), *The English Works*, 375.

28. Ghose (ed.), *The English Works*, 380.

29. Ghose (ed.), *The English Works*, 383.

30. Ghose (ed.), *The English Works*, 384.

31. Ghose (ed.), *The English Works*, 379.

32. Quoted in Ludo Rocher, 'Hindu Law of Succession: From Shastras to Modern Law', in *Studies in Hindu Law and Dharmaśāstra*, ed. Donald R. Davis (New York: State University of New York Press, 2012), 184.

33. Ghose (ed.), *The English Works*, 384.

34. Rao, 'Purana as Brahminic Ideology', 87.

35. Ludo Rocher, *Puranas* (Harassowitz: Wiesbaden, 1986), 2–3.

36. Rocher, *Puranas*, 9.

37. Killingley, *Only True God*, 10.

38. Killingley, *Only True God*, 21.

39. Killingley, *Only True God*, 33.

40. H.H. Wilson, *Vishnu Purana* (Calcutta: John Murray, 1864), lxxii.

41. Rao, 'Purana as Brahminic Ideology', 93.

42. Rao, 'Purana as Brahminic Ideology', 94.
43. Ghose (ed.), *The English Works*, 376.
44. Ghose (ed.), *The English Works*, 376.
45. Rocher, *Puranas*, 2–3.
46. Wilson, *Vishnu Purana*, 320.
47. Wilson, *Vishnu Purana*, 321.
48. Wilson, *Vishnu Purana*, 320.
49. Wendy Doniger, "'Put a Bag over Her Head": Beheading Mythological Women', in *Off with Her Head! The Denial of Women's Identity in Myth, Religion and Culture*, ed. Howard Eilberg-Schwartz and Wendy Doniger (London: University of California Press, 1995), 16.
50. Doniger, 'Put a Bag over Her Head', 16.
51. Wilson, *Vishnu Purana*, 322.
52. Ghose (ed.), *The English Works*, 376.
53. Bayly, *Recovering Liberties*, 52.
54. A.K. Coomaraswamy, *Spiritual Authority and Temporal Power in the Indian Theory of Government* (New Haven: American Oriental Society, 1942) 6–7.
55. Coomaraswamy, *Spiritual Authority*, 50.
56. Coomaraswamy's ideas on Indian political thought and Kingship were accepted by contemporary scholars such as Lee Bowen and E.J. Thomas. Both considered *Spiritual Authority* to be a pioneering work on political theory (Lee Bowen, 'Review', *Speculum* 17, no. 3 [July 1942]: 418–20; E.J. Thomas, 'Review', *Bulletin of the School of Oriental and African Studies* 11, no. 2 (1944): 438–9).

    Historical works from the 1950s till the 1970s did not, however, respond to or critique the arguments of *Spiritual Authority*. This had a dismal effect on the visibility of the text in historical scholarship:

    1. Thomas R. Trautmann, 'CSSH Notes', *Comparative Studies in Society and History* 23, no. 3 (July 1981): 514–16. By the 1980s, scholars of early Indian kingship such as J.C. Heesterman 'did not know' of *Spiritual Authority*.

    2. William Jackson, 'Review', *Journal of South Asian Literature* 23, no. 1 (Winter–Spring 1988): 230–4. Heesterman's passing over of *Spiritual Authority* can be seen as an example of a new school of historical scholarship with different methodologies and concerns. These included scholars such as Ronald Inden, Romila Thapar, and Arjun Appadurai.

57. Coomaraswamy, *Spiritual Authority*, 2.
58. Coomaraswamy, *Spiritual Authority*, 3.
59. Coomaraswamy, *Spiritual Authority*, 16.
60. Coomaraswamy, *Spiritual Authority*, 84–7.

61. Ghose (ed.), *The English Works*, 376.

62. Ghose (ed.), *The English Works*, 376.

63. Wilson, *Vishnu Purana*, lix.

64. David Kopf, *The Brahmo Samaj and the Shaping of the Modern Indian Mind* (Princeton: Princeton University Press, 1979), 11; Bayly, *Recovering Liberties*, 51–4; Sarkar, 'Rammohun Roy and the Break with the Past', 13; Geraldine Forbes, *Women in Modern India* (Cambridge: Cambridge University Press, 1999), 15; Hugh Urban, *Tantra: Sex, Secrecy, Politics, and Power in the Study of Religion* (London: University of California Press, 2003), 79.

65. Wendy Doniger O' Flaherty, *Origins of Evil in Hindu Mythology* (Berkeley: University of California Press, 1976), 24.

66. Doniger O' Flaherty, *Origins of Evil*, 4.

67. Olivelle, *Manu's Dharmaśāstra*, 113.

68. Rocher, *Puranas*, 73.

69. A.K. Ramanujan, 'On Folk Mythologies and Folk *Puranas*', in *Purana Perennis: Reciprocity and Transformation in Hindu and Jaina texts*, ed. Wendy Doniger (New York: State University of New York Press, 1993), 120.

70. Quoted in Rocher, *Puranas*, 73.

71. Smarajit Chakraborti, *The Bengali Press, 1818–1868: A Study in the Growth of Public Opinion* (Calcutta: KL Firma Mukhopadhyay, 1976), 31.

72. Chakraborti, *Bengali Press*, 32.

73. Quoted in Salahuddin Ahmed, *Social Ideas and Social Change in Bengal, 1818–1835* (Leiden: EJ Brill,1965), 98.

74. Home, 'Supplementary Notes', 33.

75. Ghose (ed.), *The English Works*, 437.

76. Ghose (ed.), *The English Works*, 437.

77. Chakraborti, *Bengali Press*, 31.

78. Chakraborti, *Bengali Press*, 32.

79. Ahmed, *Social Ideas and Social Change in Bengal*, 106.

80. *Calcutta Journal*, April 24, 1822, RRPM, 299.

81. *Calcutta Journal*, April 24, 1822, RRPM, 299.

82. Ghose (ed.), *The English Works*, 442–3.

83. Ghose (ed.), *The English Works*, 445.

84. Ghose (ed.), *The English Works*, 459.

85. Ghose (ed.), *The English Works*, 446.

86. Ghose (ed.), *The English Works*, 439.

87. Ghose (ed.), *The English Works*, 394.

88. Ghose (ed.), *The English Works*, 418.

89. Ghose (ed.), *The English Works*, 421.

90. Ghose (ed.), *The English Works*, 434.
91. Ghose (ed.), *The English Works*, 394.
92. Ghose (ed.), *The English Works*, 394.
93. Ghose (ed.), *The English Works*, 395.
94. Ghose (ed.), *The English Works*, 402.
95. Ghose (ed.), *The English Works*, 446.
96. Ghose (ed.), *The English Works*, 389–90.
97. Patrick Olivelle, 'Early History of the *Dharmaśāstras*', 173.
98. Olivelle (trans.), *Manu's Dharmaśāstra*, 7.
99. Olivelle (trans.), *Manu's Dharmaśāstra*, 38.
100. Olivelle (trans.), *Manu's Dharmaśāstra*, 42.
101. Olivelle (trans.), *Manu's Dharmaśāstra*, 25.
102. Olivelle (trans.), *Manu's Dharmaśāstra*, 354.
103. Mark McClish, 'The Dependence of Manu's Seventh Chapter on Kauṭilya's *Arthaśāstra*', *Journal of the American Oriental Society* 134, no. 2 (April–June 2014): 243.
104. Patrick Olivelle (trans.), *King Governance and Law in Ancient India: Kauṭilīya Arthaśāstra* (New York: Oxford University Press, 2013), 1.
105. Olivelle (trans.), *Kauṭilīya Arthaśāstra*, 38
106. Olivelle (trans.), *Kauṭilīya Arthaśāstra*, 38.
107. Olivelle (trans.), *Kauṭilīya Arthashastra*, 39.
108. Olivelle, 'Early History of the *Dharmaśāstras*', 174.
109. John Derrett, *Dharmaśāstra and Juridical Literature* (Harassowitz: Wiesbaden, 1981), 3.
110. Chattopadhyay, *Studying Early India*, 135–52.
111. Chattopadhyay, *Studying Early India*, 140–1.
112. Olivelle, 'Early History of the *Dharmaśāstras*', 177.
113. Olivelle (trans.), *Manu's Dharmaśāstra*, 160.
114. Olivelle (trans.), *Manu's Dharmaśāstra*, 157.
115. Olivelle (trans.), *Manu's Dharmaśāstra*, 295.
116. Quoted in Ludo Rocher, 'Anglo-Hindu and Customary Law', in *Studies in Hindu Law and Dharmaśāstra*, ed. Donald Davis (New York: Anthem Press, 2014 [2012]), 634.
117. Ghose (ed.), *The English Works*, 390.
118. Ghose (ed.), *The English Works*, 396.

5 Against sati

S ati refers to the ancient Hindu practice of immolating widows on
the funeral pyres of their husbands.[1] Although references to sati
in India can be found in ancient and medieval indigenous sources,
the scriptural sanction for the practice is ambiguous and has been con-
tested throughout its history.[2]

From 1818 to 1831, Rammohun published essays, dialogues, petitions, and letters against the practice of sati in English and Bangla at
Calcutta and London. His writings expressed the view that modern
governments have a duty to protect the welfare of their subjects, an idea
which can be genealogically linked to his conception of accountable governance (developed in the previous chapter). In this chapter, I will argue
that his writings articulated his political thought on ethics and welfare.

Recent scholarship on the intellectual history of Bengal has not,
however, perceived Rammohun's writings on sati as part of his political
thought. This can be seen in the work of C.A. Bayly (whose conceptualization of Rammohun as a constitutional liberal did not include his ideas

on sati) and Andrew Sartori (who did not consider sati to be specific to Rammohun's classical liberalism).

Social historians of sati in Bengal (such as Geraldine Forbes, Ania Loomba, Kumkum Sagari, and Suresh Vaid) also do not consider his writings on sati to be a part of his political thought. This is primarily due to the limitations of the conceptual scope of their writings.[3] The best example of this school of writing is Lata Mani's study on sati—'Contentious Traditions: The Debate on Sati in Colonial India'.[4] The chapter engages with the framework, arguments, and implications of *Contentious Traditions*. For this reason, we briefly summarize its arguments here.

Lata Mani argued that the practice of sati led to an unequal debate on 'authentic Hindu tradition' amongst EIC officials and the native elite in Bengal. However, the Company was not motivated by concern for the widow's welfare but by fears of a revolution from its subjects; and even maintained official records ('colonial data') of the practice to gather evidence for this argument. Since native supporters and opponents of sati also constructed their arguments by referring to official records, their responses to sati were very similar to that of the Company's ('colonial discourse'). Mani asserts that Rammohun, much like his opponents and Company officials, was not concerned with 'the suffering widow' but the construction of an 'authentic Hindu tradition' based on Hindu scripture such as the DhS.[5] The assertion implies that he did not have a political thought of his own.[6] It is, however, based on only two writings—*Second Conference between an advocate and opponent of burning widows alive* (1820) and *Abstract of Arguments on Sati* (1830)—and as such is a very limited view of his work.[7]

I argue that Mani does not present an accurate representation of Rammohun's views on sati. As the previous chapter showed, he interpreted the DhS as texts of everyday ethical practice. Based on this methodological template, his sati writings interpreted the DhS as authoritative prescriptions of social conduct and governmental policy. He argued as follows: on social conduct, the DhS 'authorised' the immediate family and marital relations of the widow with a duty of care; and on government policy, decreed that the government had a duty to provide for the widow's welfare. Further, he addressed two separate groups of readers—the Bengali public on the one hand and Company officials on the other.

This chapter is divided into two sections: the first examines Rammohun's arguments for the Bengali public; and the second is concerned with his writings for EIC administrators. It will conclude that he was concerned with ethics, accountability, and governance throughout his writings on sati.

Domestic Abuse

Rammohun developed his critique of sati based on his observations of the everyday lives of women in Bengal. Historians do not, however, consider that his perspective and criticism of Bengali domesticity may have had any bearing on his ideas on sati.[8] For example, Geraldine Forbes argued that he understood very little of the personal lives of Bengali women in the early 19th century.[9]

A study of Rammohun's writings to the Bengali public, however, demonstrates a consistent argument that the contemporary prevalence of sati was the consequence of the normalization of domestic abuse in Bengali society. This argument was developed in two major tracts: *A Conference between an advocate and opponent of the practice of burning widows alive* (1818) and *Second Conference between an advocate and an opponent of burning widows alive* (1820). The term 'Conferences' is used here to denote both tracts. We note that his ideas on ethics have never been the focus of historical scholarship, and in this context re-interpret the *Conferences* to highlight this core feature of his work on sati.

Conferences collectively posed a challenge to the contemporary belief that the performance of sati guaranteed the widow, her husband, and their maternal and paternal relations a place in heaven by arguing that human beings were an end by themselves and not merely a means to an end (such as an afterlife in heaven). The main argument in both tracts was that the practice of sati violated the victims' rights. In this context, *Conferences* consistently presented the widow as a victim. This argument was articulated by carefully sketching out the unequal relations of power in the household and by highlighting a lack of empathy in Bengali society for the widow.

The first *Conference* (1818) introduced this argument through a debate between an 'advocate' and an 'opponent' of sati. Unsurprisingly, the 'opponent' of sati represented Rammohun's views.

In the first *Conference's* opening dialogue, the 'opponent' was told by the 'advocate': 'I am surprised that you endeavour to oppose the practice and Concremation and Postcremation of widows long observed in the country.' The use of terms such as 'Concremation' and 'Postcremation' highlighted Rammohun's familiarity with the scriptural vocabulary on sati. As his readers were informed in a footnote, 'Concremation' referred to the immolation of the widow alongside the body of her husband, and 'Postcremation' referred to sati committed after the husband's body had been cremated.[10]

The opening dialogue of the 'advocate' of sati also explained the specific points on which Rammohun wished to intervene. First, the assertion that he alone was criticizing the practice was a mistaken one. He argued instead that sati was widely criticized in Bengal. Second, the contention that sati was a historically established ritual would be a core point of debate in the tract. He scorned the argument that sati was legitimate because it had been 'long observed in the country' and argued that it was not a culturally specific ritual but a universally unethical practice, prohibited by 'every race of men'. Addressing the entire community of 'advocates', he argued that those who 'took delight' in sati were ultimately favouring a practice which the DhS opposed—suicide.[11] After declaring sati as suicide, the 'opponent' delegitimized all arguments which posed the practice as a part of Hindu tradition and instead asserted that it was prevalent due to the sadistic tendencies of the 'advocates' of the practice.

The first *Conference* now presented a series of terse dialogues on ethics between the 'opponent' and 'advocate'. At first, the 'advocate' did not engage with the 'opponent' but dismissed the notion of ethical practice as an example of a biased agenda which ignored the scriptural evidence of DhS texts, *Angira* and *Harita*.[12] When informed that these texts did not have the same authority as MDhS, the 'advocate' reluctantly conceded to the 'opponent' but still did not change his views on sati.[13] At this point, the 'opponent' defined the pro-sati stance as 'deliberate murder'.[14]

The perception of sati as 'deliberate murder' drew the attention of the reader from the rite to the victim. The 'opponent' argued that tying the sati victim to the funeral pyre of her husband and trapping her under heavy bamboos was legal evidence of coercion and the intent to kill.[15] Although the consistent references to the DhS have led to criticism that sati was conceptualized as the site of a religio-historical tradition, we find that in the first *Conference*, sati was seen as a contemporary unethical practice in Bengal. Rammohun consistently referred to the DhS to high-light the illegality of sati. For example, he noted that the DhS did not advocate tying down widows and placing heavy bamboos over them on the funeral pyre to prevent their escape.[16]

My argument that the DhS were conceptualized as texts of ethical practice is further strengthened by the confession of the 'advocate' that the practice of tying down widows had no scriptural sanction but was rooted in contemporary social anxieties such as fear of ridicule by 'oth-ers'. This signalled an important shift in the first *Conference*. A reference to the DhS had convinced the 'advocate' that sati was a contemporary practice being carried out to prevent societal gossip than a scripturally sanctioned ritual. The 'advocate', however, elevated societal 'gossip' to a 'sin'. The 'opponent' retorted that this conception of 'sin' and 'gossip' was deeply flawed since the social ridicule the 'advocate' feared came from those sections of society who advocated murder.[17]

The 'opponent' also called for a more domiciled and localized view of the argument for tying down widows. He noted that this practice was not 'prevalent throughout Hindustan' but a product of specifically Bengali social anxieties. The response of the 'advocate' only echoed the anxiety of the supporters of sati, that 'if women do not perform Concremation on the death of their husbands they might go astray; but when they burn themselves, that fear is done away'.[18]

The advocate's argument signified an important transition. From here onwards, the scriptural basis of sati was no longer an important subject of debate. Rather, the 'advocate' reframed his discussion by proposing a new theory of social control of women in Bengali households.[19] This theory was based on three propositions: first, he argued that wives were always subordinate to their husbands in Bengal; second, he asserted that husbands exercised a legitimate social control over their wives; and third, he opined that the consequence of not committing sati was that the wife (now widow) would rebel against contemporary norms and practices of control in the household and directly contribute to fostering an unwel-come and deeply unsettling social unrest. The 'advocate' concluded that since social stability was dependent on the husband being alive, his death would lead to social anarchy *unless sati was performed*.

Rammohun was very critical of the 'opponent's' theory. But, his criti-cism was not expressed in plain langauge. Rather, he took recourse to DhS interpretation to clarify his views on the matter. His interpretation focused on the urgent and contemporary need to pay attention to the welfare of the widow.[20] In the guise of the 'opponent' Rammohun argued that the ideas of the 'advocate' were a violation of social norms prescribed by the DhS. He noted that the 'advocate' had also conveniently ignored the DhS stipulation that the widow must be supported by her family relations (maternal and paternal). He was also of the view that the advocate's conception of social control was a misinterpretation of the idea of marriage. Instead, he argued that a careful reading of the DhS as well as a due regard to contemporary social realities would inevitably lead one to the conclusion that marriage ought not to be based on social control and subordination, but everyday ethical practices ('thoughts, words and actions').[21]

The first *Conference* thus articulated an argument for ethical practice by stressing the importance of everyday forms of conduct in the household.[22] Towards the end of the tract, this argument would be developed further to assert that the opponents of sati were in the majority while its advocates were a minority whose 'lack of empathy' for the sati was a product of, and amounted to, a regrettable lack of everyday ethical practice in Bengal.[23] The tract concluded that although sati was deeply detrimental to societal welfare, it was not seen as such because it had been normalized in Bengali society to the point that its 'advocates' did not perceive it as an inhuman act.[24] This conclusion had little to do with references to colonial discourse, data, and debates on tradition. Rather, it showed Rammohun as a distinctly independent political thinker.

Despite the originality of his views, the critical response to the first *Conference* was mixed. Some newspapers reviewed it very positively but considered it to be an extension of Mrityunjay Vidyalankar's opinions on sati rather an articulation of Rammohun's own ideas.[25] Others declared that the first *Conference* was a distinct argument. Buckingham's *Calcutta Journal* and *Calcutta Gazette* published 'Appreciative notices' which included the entire tract.[26] Buckingham was a close associate of Rammohun and would be deported in 1823 for his views against the government. The deportation from Bengal did not, however, stop Buckingham's writings against sati. His London journal, *Oriental Herald*, criticized the government's policy on sati and played an important role in mobilizing British public opinion against the practice.[27]

However, not all responses of the first *Conference* were positive and the argument of the tract also provoked harsh responses from advocates of sati. Chundrika Payno, a correspondent for the Bengali newspaper *Sambad Chandrika*, was scathing in his criticism of favourable reviews of Rammohun's tract in English-language newspapers.[28] Payno considered such reviews as misinformed and instead referred readers to *Dialogue between bidhaok and nissedhok* (1819) as the authentic DhS interpretation of sati. Payno's reference showed that Rammohun's tract had led to influential rebuttals.

Dialogue between bidhaok and nissedhok was an anonymous tract, structured much the same way as the first *Conference*, as a debate between an 'advocate' (*bidhaok*) and 'opponent' (*nissedhok*) of sati. The writer of the tract, Kasinath Tarkavagish, shared the perspective of the 'advocate' and the 'opponent' and held the same views as his counterpart in the first *Conference*.[29] This tract focussed on the question of whether sati was a legitimate Hindu ritual. This can be seen with the opening argument that sati was ordained by Hindu scripture and it is 'improper' to argue against it.[30]

Kasinath Tarkavagish's focus was the ritual of sati rather than its victim. *Dialogue between bidhaok and nissedhok* took on two of the most important arguments of the first *Conference*. First, it criticized and set aside Rammohun's interpretation of MDhS that widows should live after the death of their husbands, arguing that later DhS commentaries which recommended sati were better sources of information about the practice.[31] The argument that the tying of widows to the funeral pyre of her husband can be seen as evidence of intention to kill, an unforgivable sin in DhS law, was also dismissed.[32] Instead, the 'advocate' declared that all who supported sati 'are to reap glory and are not liable to sin.'[33]

Tarkavagish's argument is entirely consistent with the first *Conference*'s view that the advocates of sati ignored the victimization of the widow, avoided discussions on the ethical implications of the practice, and interpreted the DhS as authoritative prescriptions of ritual rather than ethical practices concerned with rights, duties, and obligations of society and state, as well as its implications on social welfare. This further explains Rammohun's deep interest in the DhS and the need to legitimize all his arguments with reference to a DhS context.

The contrast of *Dialogue between bidhaok and nissedhok* to the first *Conference* is most apparent in its explanation of sati. While Tarkavagish presented sati as a ritual and not 'a practice of burning widows', the first *Conference* referred to sati as 'the practice of burning of widows' than a ritual. Secondly, the discussions of everyday ethical practice in the household which featured prominently in the first *Conference* were absent in *Dialogue between bidhaok and nissedhok*. Finally, Tarkavagish denounced the first *Conference* by inverting its conclusion. While in the first *Conference*'s conclusion, the 'advocate' of sati had agreed with the 'opponent', Tarkavagish now presented a situation where the 'opponent' unequivocally agreed with the practice of sati and concluded that its scriptural authenticity was sound.[34]

Our discussion shows the degree to which Rammohun's emphasis on ethical practice and the interpretation of the DhS as a moral philosophy differed from his critics. This was also the primary reason why *Dialogue between bidhaok and nissedhok* prompted a detailed and systematic response in *Second Conference* (1820). This tract argued that *Dialogue*'s exclusive emphasis on scripture had led to a deeply disturbing absence of a focus on the sati victim.[35]

Much like the first *Conference*, *Second Conference* was also written as a debate between an 'advocate' and 'opponent' of sati and opined that the contemporary prevalence of sati was not due to an adherence to a DhS context but an unethical social stance towards the widow.[36] Rammohun argued that the ideas of the 'advocate' were based on the flawed assumption that women were socially dependent and cognitively deficient to men when in fact Bengali women had been deliberately handicapped since they were not educated.[37] The lack of education led to unequal relations of power in the household, laid the social foundations of domestic abuse, and ultimately resulted in sati.[38]

Second Conference traced the events leading up to sati by rooting the consequences of subordination, lack of education, and public visibility in a discussion of marriage. The *Conferences*' arguments were also discussed in other writings. *Second Defence of the Vedanta* (1820) opined that practices such as 'the acceptance of money under the guise of marriage' consequently led to the subordination of women after marriage.[39] In *Kavitakarer sahit vichar* (1820), he argued that women were ill-treated in everyday domestic life, although contemporary Bengali society worshipped feminine power (*devi shakti*) in household rituals.[40]

The focus on contemporary social practices before marriage is an important context to the arguments concerning domesticity in *Second Conference*. *Second Conference* highlighted the everyday abuse faced by women after marriage. After marriage, the new bride occupied the 'position of a menial servant' in the household and was expected to follow an exhaustive schedule of cooking and cleaning. She was treated badly by much of the family, including her 'father and mother-in-law, sister-in-law, brother-in-law, friends and connections'.[41] Rammohun's focus was clearly on large households. He argued that households comprising of large families only increased the burden of housework and scope of abuse.[42]

Rammohun argued that women were also mistreated by their husbands who engaged in 'criminal armours'.[43] This was not a general observation on social habits of men in Bengal but a specific reference to the practice of polygamy in Bengal by the Kulin Brahmins. Kulin practices were considered to be legitimate due to their high caste status.[44] This did not mean, however, that they were immune from criticism. As Salahuddin Ahmed observed, Kulin polygamy was widely criticized and reported in contemporary Bengali newspapers.[45] Kulin practices had also been strongly criticized and de-legitimized in *Second Defence of the Vedanta*.[46] *Second Conference* developed this argument further and argued that Kulin polygamy solidified and legitimized unequal power relations between the male and female members of the family and led to the subordination and abuse of women in the household.[47]

Second Conference's references to Kulin practices were not a brief detour from the main argument. Rather, it struck at the very heart of the 'advocate' ideas of sati. The 'advocate' had argued that sati was a *historical* practice rooted in Brahminical scripture but the stress of 'opponents' on the illegitimacy of the highest caste of Brahmins provided the context for Rammohun's argument that sati was a *contemporary* unethical social practice and a product of widely prevalent domestic abuse in Bengal. Two years later, in *Brief Remarks* too, Rammohun would continue to argue that contemporary social practice of insubordination of women in the household as well as the prevalence of polygamy ultimately led to sati.[48]

Second Conference also asserted that the EIC also held the same views as contemporary Bengali society. Company magistrates, for example, operated under the same assumption as Bengali men—that women were 'inferior', subordinate, and not capable of being socially independent. This had devastating consequences for Bengali women because the Company failed to intervene at crucial points in which a future sati could have been avoided. In this context, he opined that cases of marital separation were the most crucial points at which the EIC's intervention was required. However, marital separations, though common, were never permanent in Bengal since women were coerced back into the household by Company magistrates. After returning to the household, the abuse escalated to the point that the previously estranged wife was 'privately put to death' by her husband. If the husband died, family and relatives forced her to commit sati.[49] Rammohun pointed to failures in governance which had led to the abetment of domestic abuse and sati in Bengal. Durba Ghosh's research on the role of magistrates and judges to regulate domesticity in the Bengali household, with disastrous consequences for the victims, is important for us here.[50] Ghosh's research clearly shows that Rammohun was indeed referring to everyday instances of judicial abuse in early colonial Bengal.

Apart from Company magistrates, the *Conferences* also contained references for a broader audience.[51] Rammohun even appealed directly to the Marchioness of Hastings in *Second Conference* for an official intervention.[52] The appeal to the Marchioness instead of her husband, the Marquess of Hastings (and Governor General of Bengal), may have also been prompted by a lack of response to an earlier petition addressed to him. The contents of this failed petition and its follow-up letters and tracts reveal an important strand of Rammohun's writings on sati. This is the subject of the next section.

Misgovernance

Rammohun argued that the continuing prevalence of sati was an instance of misgovernance, urged the EIC's intervention, and outlined the duties and obligations of a government to its subjects. In August 1818, he petitioned Governor General Lord Hastings against the practice of sati. Hastings was widely perceived to be a reformer in Bengal since he had pushed through press reforms as part of a new Company policy towards newspapers as 'a useful instrument in promoting good government' earlier that year.[53]

Hastings' press reforms had an enormous impact on social reform in India since it led to the foundation of the first vernacular newspapers.[54] Rammohun himself made wide use of the vernacular press, editing the Bengali (and English) newspaper *Sambad Kaumadi* and the Persian weekly *Mirat al-Akhbar*.[55] *Kaumadi* was an important platform for his project against sati. Given this background, it is not surprising that the petition was addressed to Hastings.

Unfortunately, Hasting's ideas of reform did not extend to sati. In 1817, Hastings shelved a proposal to regulate the practice.[56] This would prove to be a disastrous step since 1818 recorded an unprecedented increase in the annual number of satis.[57] In this context, Rammohun's petition would have irked the Governor General since his chief argument was that sati was a form of misgovernance.

Rammohun's petition represents a parallel strand in his writings on sati. Consider, for example, the difference between the 1818 petition and the first *Conference*. Both appeared in 1818 but while the first *Conference* was primarily concerned with the social ethics of Bengali society, the petition was about the government's accountability. He argued that the government was obligated to protect the lives and property of its subjects. The practice of sati violated this obligation since it amounted to murder committed to possess the widow's property. He also traced the conception of obligations of government in Hindu law and argued that the DhS prohibited murder and *Dayabhaga* called upon the state to protect the property of the widow. Even in cases where sati was not committed in order to seize the widows' property, the practice itself amounted to suicide which was illegal in Hindu law.[58]

Although Rammohun had also described sati as suicide in the first *Conference*, the petition explained the implications of suicide differently. In the first *Conference*, suicide was seen as an undesirable social event while the petition perceived suicide as a failure of government to promote the welfare of the widow. The argument on misgovernance was further developed in his criticism of the official position that sati was a closely monitored practice which consisted of the widow immolating herself voluntarily. Instead, he cited eyewitness accounts of frequent cases where 'women after flying from the flames have been carried back by their relatives and burnt to death'.[59]

Rammohun was not exaggerating the failures of government regulations. By 1820, the EIC's criminal courts in Bengal (*Nizamat Adalat*) had also begun to notice the failures of the government to regulate sati.[60] Two years later, the government officially recognized that its existing policy was ineffective since it did not take native testimonies into account and passed a new order based on eyewitness testimonies of sati (citing instances very similar to those noted in the petition) and informed every police station in Bengal 'to use the utmost care and every effort to prevent the forbidden practices from taking place within the limits of the *thana* [station]'.[61]

In *Sambad Kaumadi*, Rammohun opined that while these regulations had been occasionally effective, police intervention was rare in the majority of cases.[62] The need of the hour, he stressed, was a uniform code of official responsibility throughout Bengal. The origins of this argument can be traced to his 1818 petition which explained his ideas by constructing a working principle of ethical governance guided by principles of welfare. He had argued that sati should be seen on par with banned practices such as female infanticide and human sacrifice, and appealed to the government that 'all these [practices] your petitioners humbly submit are murders according to every *Shastra* as well as the common sense of all nations'.[63]

The use of the phrase 'the common sense of all nations' drew attention to the contrast that the practice of sati posed to a government policy guided by ethical principles of welfare. This argument was further developed in Rammohun's pseudonymous tract in 1819. This tract distanced itself from Rammohun's writings by referring to sati by its ritualistic term 'Concremation' rather than 'the practice of burning widows alive', which was the case in *Conferences* and the 1818 petition. However, it also reiterated the basic argument that sati amounted to murder by presenting it as a practice which had led to the loss of 'thousands' of female lives and even referred to the 1818 petition to Hastings.[64] The pseudonymous tract appeared under the authorship of Hariharananda Bharati. This enabled Rammohun to adopt a persona of an ethical, informed Brahmin who argued that the government's confusion about the legal status of sati had led to more deaths in the meantime.[65]

In the guise of Hariharananda, Rammohun strongly asserted that Company administrators must recognize sati as incompatible with any system of ethics—Hindu or Christian—than a ritual specific to Hinduism. It also made a distinction between an ethical public calling for the banning of sati and the unethical project of the supporters of sati: 'I am at a loss to conceive how persons can reconcile themselves to the stigma of being accused of women murder without attempting to show the injustice of the charge they find themselves in.'[66] The psuedonimity also provided greater discursive space for bold opinions on government officials: 'I feel also surprise and regret that European gentlemen who boast about the humanity and morality of their religion should conduct themselves to persons who submit quietly to the imputation of murder with the same politeness and kindness that they would show to the most respectable persons.'[67]

Rammohun's 'surprise and regret' was not without context. The official attitude towards any form of legislation against sati can be seen in Governor General Lord Amherst's *Minute on Sati* (1827) which declared, 'I am not prepared to recommend an enactment prohibiting *Satis* altogether.'[68] Contributing to his frustration with Company policy were pre-constructed ideas of Indianness and sati. For example, in 1827, the Governor General's Council in Bengal wrote to the Court of Directors that sati should not be seen as murder or misgovernance but a highly localized mental state. 'In certain districts of Bengal,' they opined, 'the dispositions of the people are prone to violence.'[69]

Ultimately, in 1829, Governor General Lord William Bentinck and his council of advisors, supported by the Court of Directors, did intervene to pass a regulation abolishing sati. This was a marked change from Calcutta's and London's attitude towards institutional reform in India. That it was also influenced to some degree by Rammohun's writings on sati as misgovernance is evident since it also referred to the practice of sati as the 'burning alive of widows' and rejected the possibility of any religious sanction.[70]

This was, however, only a partial success for Rammohun since his project of representing an ethical public was discredited and questioned in contemporary newspapers. For example, Bhabanicharan Bandyopadhyay, the editor of the conservative Bengali newspaper *Samachar Chandrika* opined that Rammohun could not claim to represent the views of the entire Bengali community.[71]

Bhabanicharan Bandyopadhyay's views would have been taken seriously in Bengali society since *Samachar Chandrika* was a well-regarded newspaper with a large subscriber base.[72] Interestingly enough, Bandyopadhyay had honed his journalistic skills while helping with the editing of Rammohun's *Sambad Kaumadi*. He had been associated with the newspaper since its foundation but left after 13 editions owing to religious and ideological differences.[73] (He later claimed to have been the chief editor of *Sambad Kaumadi*, but this was hotly disputed by the then editor, Harihar Dutta).[74]

Bandyopadhyay was part of an orthodox Hindu community which opposed Rammohun's project of sati.[75] On 14 January 1830, he, along with important members of Bengali society—such as pandits of the Sanskrit college, Nimaychurun Siromoni and Huronath Tarkabhushan; and wealthy landlords, Gopi Mohun Deb, Radhakanta Deb, Maharaja Kalikisen Bahadur, Nilomoni De, Gokulnath Malik, Bhabanicharan Mitter, and Ramgopal Mitter—presented a petition against the abolition of sati to Bentinck.[76]

Even Ramchandra Vidyavagish, Rammohun's close ally, was a signatory to the petition.[77] What prompted *him* to take this decision is not altogether clear. According to Brajendranath Banerji, Vidyavagish had been coerced by his colleagues at Calcutta Government College where he had joined as faculty only three years ago when the incumbent, Kasinath Tarkapanchanan, had left for a more lucrative career at the *Zilla Aadalat*.[78] Tarkapanchanan had been a vicious critic of Rammohun's writings. As the new man on the job, Vidyavagish may have been anxious to secure the approval of his peers by following a course of action that would have been typical of his predecessor.

Vidyabagish's decision to sign the petition would have been a blow to Rammohun's project. So far, Rammohun's tracts, letters, and pseudonymous articles in newspapers had consistently argued that an ethical public could force the government into legislating against the practice. By signing the petition against the abolition of sati, on the other hand, it was as if Rammohun's close allies too were now claiming that he did not have the support of Bengali society but was an isolated figure in the debate on sati.

The petition's assessment of the regulation to abolish sati was also a direct criticism of Rammohun's writings on good governance. While Rammohun had argued that the abolition of sati would be an important step towards social welfare, the petition questioned the legitimacy of the government's regulation against sati and assessed it as 'not only an unjust and intolerant dictation in matters of conscience but is likely wholly to fail in procuring the end proposed'.[79]

Interestingly, the petition also contained a narrative of the attitude of successive governments towards sati.[80] The narrative of precedence went back 600 years, presented Company rule in Bengal as a representative of British political traditions from London, and included a number of important Company officials who had approved of sati (including the chairman of the Court of Directors, Nathaniel Smith; and Governors General Lord Clive, Warren Hastings, Lord Cornwallis, and Lord Moira). This narrative also strengthened the argument that the Company could not legislatively intervene in Indian social practices because it belonged to a very different system of laws. The authorities familiar with Indian law were referred to in detail. To this end, the petition contained the signatures of 120 Sanskrit pandits and 800 Bengali inhabitants. It even had a separate petition on the subject containing 346 signatories (including 28 pandits).[81]

Bentinck, however, did not agree with the petition's argument and opined that not only was abolishing sati in keeping with Hindu law but that the Company would always intervene to abolish those social practices which it deemed illegal.[82] His case for a uniform and consistent government policy towards sati consisted of three main arguments: first, the practice of sati was contrary to British and DhS prescriptions of law (thus the petition's argument about unfamiliar British institutions in India neglecting core ideas of Hindu religion and society did not apply); second, the focus of Hindu law was everyday ethical practice ('good conduct'); and third, abolishing sati was not an unprecedented measure since it was in accordance with a historical process of government commitment towards welfare. In this case, the government's call for abolishing sati was not an alien intervention into Indian social practices but a case of historical continuity.

The second and third points of Bentinck's reply were elaborated upon by Rammohun in *Abstract of arguments regarding the burning of widows* which appeared the same year. He argued that Hindu law had been deliberately misinterpreted by sati advocates to make the case for the illegality of government interventions and identified several examples of forgeries in Hindu laws which had been passed off as legitimate by his critics.[83] His point was that social rituals and laws required legitimation from the government and rechecking from qualified legal authorities in society since both had a responsibility to speak out against fakes. He also introduced a simple rule to judge the legitimacy of a legal precept in which a law was legitimate only when it reflected ethical social practice.

He was confident of the success of this rule and convinced that the Bengali public could pressurize the government into legislating against unethical social practices. In this context, he opined that the abolition had come about because sati contradicted contemporary ethical norms. He clearly thought of the abolition as the end of the sati debate and offered 'thanks to heaven' for 'rescuing the weaker sex from cruel murder under the cloak of religion'.[84] But Rammohun was wrong. The abolition of sati by the Governor General did not lead to the end of the sati debate.

On 6 February 1830, the petition writers who had earlier been dismissed by Bentinck founded the Dharma Sabha (with Bhabanicharan Bandyopadhyay as secretary) to overturn the regulation against sati by appealing to the Privy Council at London, recognizing a centre of sovereign power that was located far away from the EIC's government in India.[85] At the heart of their ideas on Company administration and law-making was the conviction that Company governance was outside the purview of everyday life in India since the government was far too distant from its subjects.

The Dharma Sabha was also very practical in its approach towards organizing a petition. A public appeal for a sum of 20,000 rupees was launched in *Samachar Chandrika* for financing their project; and Francis Bathie, a Supreme Court solicitor, was appointed as their representative.[86]

The appointment of Bathie did not go unnoticed in Calcutta and his suitability as a representative was criticized in *Sambad Kaumadi*.[87] Readers of the *Kaumadi* were told that the appointment was problematic because it did not make the government's decisions accountable to the Bengali public but a solicitor who only represented the interests of his clients, the Dharma Sabha. Nevertheless, with Bathie's help, the Dharma Sabha drafted a petition against the abolition of sati. The Sabha did not, however, publish their petition in Calcutta. This again attracted the criticism of *Sambad Kaumadi* which commented against its secrecy and announced Rammohun's intention of going to England to present a counter-petition against the Dharma Sabha.

Rammohun's *Anti-Suttee petition* was presented to the House of Lords and the Privy Council in July 1831. The petition claimed to represent the interests of the entire governed population of India. The emphasis on the governed population strengthened his argument that the abolition of sati was not his personal project but constituted a core aspect of the 'obligations' of the British government to Bengali society. The petition's main argument was concerned with the British government's accountability to an ethical public in India.[88]

Rammohun argued that legislating against sati was also a practical necessity for Britain since any official sanction to unethical practices could seriously undermine its political credibility in India. This argument was further developed in his final tract on sati—*Some remarks on the vindication of the resolution passed by government of Bengal in 1829 abolishing the practice of female sacrifice in India* (henceforth, *Remarks*).

Remarks was addressed to Company officials, specifically to an official anxiety that abolishing sati would result in political revolution against the EIC.[89] This early colonial anxiety had a lengthy history as successive Company administrations at London and Calcutta had refused to legislate against sati from 1787 to 1829 fearing a revolution from its subjects.[90] In this context, Rammohun argued that the natives of Bengal were happy with the abolition of sati and criticized EIC policy for being guided by the fear of revolution and loss of empire in India.[91]

In strong continuity with the 1818 petition, *Remarks* also outlined the possible policy of the British government on sati and argued that the government ought to frame policies which would enable official intervention to protect the welfare of its inhabitants from unethical social practices.[92] The consistency with which the same argument was made in two different cities, 13 years apart, shows that ideas of governance, ethics, and accountability were crucial to his sati writings.

Apart from Rammohun, the Court of Directors also petitioned the Privy Court against the Dharma Sabha.[93] The Court's arguments mirrored Rammohun's since they took the view that the practice was rooted in domestic cruelty towards the widow, that the abolition of sati would not lead to a revolution in Bengal, and that the state ought actively to intervene to prevent any further occurrences of the practice. This petition marked a major shift in Company policy—from a concern with an alleged political revolution to failures in governance. The Court also painted a deeply negative picture of the natives who supported sati and dismissed the view that the widow immolated herself voluntarily. They noted, 'In order to compel the widow in these cases to ascend the [funeral] pile, personal violence, intoxication, menace and persuasion was resorted to.'[94]

The endorsement by the Court of Directors to Rammohun's petition against the Dharma Sabha would have had an enormous impact on the councillors of the Privy Council. Amongst the councillors were former Governors General Marquess Wellesley and Lord Amherst and the former chairman of the Court of Directors, Charles Grant. Both Wellesley and Amherst had previously expressed an opinion against the practice of sati.

Rammohun was present during the Privy Council proceedings and his petition was presented to the Council for consideration.[95] The Council dismissed the Dharma Sabha's petition, decided not to revoke the regulation which had abolished sati, and echoed the Court of Directors' petition that the continuation of this practice would constitute a serious breach of good governance and social ethics. Further, the Council argued that the abolition of sati upheld ethical systems which were as much on par with the ideas of a 'Christian country' as it was with Hindu DhS law. This was a dismissal of the Dharma Sabha's argument that the EIC represented an alien system of ethics in India. This judgement was greeted with relief by Rammohun. In a letter to John Poynder, a member of the court of proprietors of the EIC who opposed sati, he wrote:

> Hearty congratulations on the protection afforded by the Privy Council to the female community in India. They have removed the odium from our character as a people. As we can no longer be guilty of female murder, we now deserve every improvement, temporal and spiritual.[96]

As the letter shows, Rammohun had interpreted the decision of the Privy Council as an effective declaration that an ethical Bengali public could henceforth legitimately hold the Company accountable for its decisions in Bengal. The Privy Council's decision demonstrated the success of both strands of his argument on social ethics and governance. First, Bengali society had been acknowledged as an ethical society; and second, the abolition of sati had been upheld in order to prevent misgovernance by the Company. Thus, Rammohun's project of pushing forward his political thought concerning governmental accountability to an ethical public had finally borne fruit after more than a decade of opposition.

***

Conclusion: Rammohun's Political Thought as a Response to sati

Rammohun's writings on sati articulated his political thought of social ethics and governmental accountability to a vast readership in Calcutta as well as in London. He had two distinct sets of readers—Bengali society and Company officials. To Bengali society, he focussed on everyday practices of domestic abuse in the household to show that sati was a product of the contemporary normalization of domestic abuse and subordination of women. To Company officials, he called for governmental intervention against the practice. As the previous chapter showed, the argument for government intervention to prevent unethical social practices was a core aspect of his political thought.[97]

Rammohun stressed that the continuing practice of sati in Bengal amounted to misgovernance and a violation of governmental 'obligations' to its subjects. In this context, note that the use of the term 'obligations' to subjects as a core feature of the 'principles of good government' can be found in his *Anti Suttee petition* of 1831.[98] His conception of the 'obligations' not only referred to the political and legal rights of its subjects, but also the requirement by the government to create the conditions by which such rights could be developed so that its subjects could build an ethical society.

Although the current historical scholarship argues that Rammohun did not call for government intervention in his early writings, this chapter has shown that this argument was consistently and consciously made over the 13 years of his involvement with sati (1818–31).[99] He stressed that government officials such as Company magistrates were complicit, for they refused to recognize the legality of marital separations and instead coerced women to return to the very households where they had been abused.

In this context, Rammohun expressed 'surprise' that the administrators knew so little of the laws and everyday lives of their subjects. He argued that the government's unfamiliarity with the legal traditions of

Bengal and its lack of engagement with the social contexts of its subjects had led to the murder of thousands.

This argument was validated in the Company's decision to abolish sati in 1829 and then upheld in the ruling of the Privy Courts in London in 1831 against conservative native opposition. Rammohun's writings in the post-abolition period (1830–31) highlight the emphasis on ethics and social welfare; and his responses to a system of governance which operated across vast distances.

The recognition of this context enables us to identify the importance of colonial governance on his political thought. In the final analysis, Rammohun's ideas of sati cannot be seen in isolation from the Company's methods of governing Bengal from the distant city of London.

As Chapter 1 showed, Rammohun interpreted the political stance of the EIC as the local representative of the British government in India. This chapter has explained how this argument was articulated through his sati writings which stressed that the Company at Calcutta as well as the British government in London had a duty to be accountable to the natives of India and intervene in matters concerning their welfare.

An important aspect of this argument, however, was Rammohun's conception of ethics—Hindu and Christian—and the ways in which he was able to create a common ethical framework which reconciled both systems of thought. His conception of Christian ethics and its relationship to his ideas of reform is the subject of the next chapter.

Notes

1. Ania Loomba, 'Dead Women Tell No Tales: Issues of Female Subjectivity, Subaltern Agency and Tradition in Colonial and Post-Colonial Writings on Widow Immolation in India', *History Workshop*, no. 36 (Autumn 1993): 210.
2. Arvind Sharma, 'The Scriptural Sanction for *Sati*', in *Sati: Historical and Phenomenological Essays*, ed. Arvind Sharma (Delhi: Motilal Banarsidass, 1996), 31–8.
3. Anand Yang, 'Who's Sati? Widow Burning in Early 19th Century India', *Journal of Women's History* 1, no. 2 (Fall 1989): 8.
4. Lata Mani, *Contentious Tradition: The Debate on Sati in Colonial India* (Berkeley: University of California Press, 1998).
5. Lata Mani, 'Contentious Traditions: The Debate on Sati in Colonial India', *Cultural Critique: The Nature and Content of Minority Discourse* 11, no. 7 (Autumn 1987): 121.

6. Mani, 'Contentious Traditions', 2–3.
7. Mani, 'Contentious Traditions', 49.
8. Forbes, *Women in Modern India*, 10.
9. Forbes, *Women in Modern India*, 11–15.
10. Ghose (ed.), *The English Works*, 323.
11. Ghose (ed.), *The English Works*, 323.
12. Ghose (ed.), *The English Works*, 324.
13. Ghose (ed.), *The English Works*, 325–6.
14. Ghose (ed.), *The English Works*, 329.
15. Ghose (ed.), *The English Works*, 329.
16. Ghose (ed.), *The English Works*, 330.
17. Ghose (ed.), *The English Works*, 330.
18. Ghose (ed.), *The English Works*, 330.
19. Ghose (ed.), *The English Works*, 331.
20. Hatcher, 'Pandits at Work', 54–9.
21. Ghose (ed.), *The English Works*, 331.
22. For an alternative view, see Dipesh Chakrabarty, *Provincializing Europe: Postcolonial Thought and Historical Difference* (Princeton: Princeton University Press, 2000), 121. Chakrabarty argued that Rammohun's ideas of welfare of women were prompted by a self-initiation into Western philosophy.
23. Chakrabarty, *Provincializing Europe*, 121.
24. Ghose (ed.), *The English Works*, 332.
25. Banerji, *Mrityunjay Vidyalankar*, 23. Mrityunjay offered an opinion on sati at the request of the chief justice of the Calcutta Supreme Court. He carefully went through multiple editions and manuscripts of Hindu scripture before concluding that sati was not absolutely necessary.
26. *Calcutta Journal*, 25 December 1818, and *Calcutta Gazette*, 24 December 1818, *RRPM*, 114.
27. Mani, 'Contentious Traditions', 23.
28. Chundrika Payno, 'A Letter in Justification of Suttees', *Calcutta Journal*, 25 June 1822, *RRPM*, 125.
29. Mani, 'Contentious Traditions', 55.
30. 'Tracts by Rammohun Roy, c. 1772–1833', Ms. Ind. 2014.1.5., Harvard University Library, Boston [henceforth, HUL], 1.
31. 'Tracts', HUL, 2–3.
32. 'Tracts', HUL, 2–3.
33. 'Tracts', HUL, 2–17.
34. 'Tracts', HUL, 17.
35. Ghose (ed.), *The English Works*, 337.
36. Ghose (ed.), *The English Works*, 359–60.
37. Ghose (ed.), *The English Works*, 360.

38. Ghose (ed.), *The English Works*, 361.
39. Ghose (ed.), *The English Works*, 120.
40. *BW,* 217.
41. Ghose (ed.), *The English Works*, 362.
42. Ghose (ed.), *The English Works*, 361.
43. Ghose (ed.), *The English Works*, 362.
44. S.N. Mukherjee, *Citizen Historian: Explorations in Historiography* (Delhi: Manohar Publishers, 1996), 45. Mukherjee shows that there is no clear evidence of when this practice began.
45. Ahmed, *Social Ideas in Bengal*, 34.
46. Ghose (ed.), *The English Works*, 121.
47. Ghose (ed.), *The English Works*, 362.
48. Nag and Burman (eds), *EW* 1:4.
49. Ghose (ed.), *The English Works*, 362.
50. Durba Ghosh, 'Household Crimes and the Domestic Order: Keeping the Peace in Colonial Calcutta, c.1770–1840', *Modern Asian Studies* 38, no. 3 (July 2004), 601.
51. Ghose (ed.), *The English Works*, 336
52. Ghose (ed.), *The English Works*, 336.
53. Ahmed, *Social Ideas in Bengal*, 85.
54. Ahmed, *Social Ideas in Bengal*, 88–93.
55. Ahmed, *Social Ideas in Bengal*, 121.
56. Mani, 'Contentious Traditions', 19.
57. Mani, 'Contentious Traditions', 21.
58. *Corr.,* 38–41.
59. *Corr.,* 38–41.
60. Nizamat Adalat to Magistrates of Zilla and City Courts in Bengal, 4 January 1815, *RRPM,* 109–10.
61. Government Order regarding Suttees, *Calcutta Journal,* 21 February 1822, *RRPM,* 122–3.
62. *Corr.,* 38–41.
63. *Corr.,* 38–41.
64. *Corr.,* 38–41.
65. *Corr.,* 38–41.
66. *Corr.,* 39.
67. *Corr.,* 40.
68. 'Lord Amherst's Minute on Suttee', 18 March 1827, *RRPM,* 129.
69. Governor General's Council to the Court of Directors, 10 April 1828, *RRPM,* 132.
70. Governor General's Council to the Court of Directors, 4 December 1829, *RRPM,* 154.

71. Brajendranath Banerji, *Bhabanicharan Bandyopadhyay* (Calcutta: Bangiya Sahitya Parisad, 1959), 22.

72. Banerji, *Bhabanicharan Bandyopadhyay*, 21.

73. Banerji, *Bhabanicharan Bandyopadhyay*, 21.

74. Banerji, *Bhabanicharan Bandyopadhyay*, 20.

75. Ahmed, *Social Ideas in Bengal*, 125.

76. *John Bull*, 19 January 1830, *RRPM*, 156.

77. Banerji, *Ramchandra Vidyavagish and Hariharananda Tirthaswamy*, 14.

78. Banerji, *Ramchandra Vidyavagish and Hariharananda Tirthaswamy*, 10.

79. *John Bull*, 19 January 1830, *RRPM*, 157.

80. *John Bull*, 19 January 1830, *RRPM*, 158.

81. *John Bull*, 19 January 1830, *RRPM*, 159.

82. *John Bull*, 19 January 1830, *RRPM*, 162–3.

83. Ghose (ed.), *The English Works*, 371.

84. Ghose (ed.) *The English Works*, 371.

85. *India Gazette*, 6 February 1830, *RRPM*, 163–5.

86. *John Bull*, 2 August 1830, *RRPM*, 174–7.

87. *John Bull*, 2 August 1830, *RRPM*, 171–2.

88. Ghose (ed.), *The English Works*, 479.

89. Rammohun Roy, 'Some remarks in the vindication of the Resolution passed by the Government of Bengal in 1829 abolishing the practice of female sacrifices in India', *RRPM*, 185–92.

90. Arvind Sharma, 'Introduction', in *Sati: Historical and Phenomenological Essays*, ed. Arvind Sharma (Delhi: Motilal Banarsidass, 1996), 1.

91. Roy, 'Some remarks', *RRPM*, 187.

92. Roy, 'Some remarks', *RRPM*, 187.

93. *In the matter of a petition to His Majesty in Council by certain Hindoo Inhabitants of Bengal, Bihar and Orissa against a regulation made and passed by the Governor General in Council of Fort William in Bengal on the 4th of December 1829 declaring the practice of Sati illegal and punishable by Criminal courts. A statement humbly submitted on the part of the Court of Directors of The East India Company to His Majesty in Council in support of the above-mentioned regulation* (London: J.L. Cox and Son, 1831).

94. *A Statement*, 6.

95. *Asiatic Journal*, August 1831, *RRPM*, 182–3.

96. *Corr.*, 728.

97. This is the argument of Chapter 3.

98. Ghose (ed.), *The English Works*, 479.

99. Ahmed, *Social Ideas in Bengal*, 64.

6 Ethics

Rammohun's conception of ethics was inspired by the four Gospels of the New Testament of the Bible.[1] In his view, the Gospels unequivocally supported the ideas that he held dear: a belief in one invisible god and the equality of all humankind.[2] He also went beyond their hermeneutic scope by attempting to integrate their ideas of equality, compassion, dignity, charity, and humility into the deep structure of his writings on Hindu scripture. This does not mean that he superimposed ideas of Christianity on Hindu scripture. Rather, he attempted to construct a meaningful dialogue between two systems of thought.

Rammohun's writings on the Gospels have been the subject of much scholarly scrutiny. Historians argue that his works were in response to interactions with Christian missionaries in Bengal, particularly the Baptist missionaries in Srerampore with whom he had developed a 'personal contact' since 1814.[3] Although the 'contact' began while *Vedanta Grantha* was being written, scholars do not perceive his writings on the

Gospels in the context of the rest of his work, but rather as a specific example of native engagement with Christianity.[4]

But to be fair to historians, Rammohun's writings on the Gospels were characterized by an exclusive focus on Christianity. His first text was a selection of Biblical passages, *The Precepts of Jesus: The Guide to Peace and Happiness* (1820). *Precepts of Jesus* was followed by *An Appeal to the Christian Public in Defence of the Precepts of Jesus* (1820), *Second Appeal to the Christian Public in Defence of the Precepts of Jesus* (1821), and *Final Appeal to the Christian Public in Defence of the Precepts of Jesus* (1823), as well as an intermittently published journal, *The Brahmunical Magazine* (1821–3) (which also appeared in Bangla as *Brahmin o misinari samvad*).

Rammohun's works were also the products of a complicated narrative of authorship. For instance, *Precepts of Jesus* was an anonymous publication and *Appeal to the Christian Public* was written as a third person intervention.[5] Rammohun only revealed his authorship in the *Second Appeal to the Christian Public* and *Final Appeal to the Christian Public*.[6] The *Brahmunical Magazine* was a pseudonymous publication and *The common basis of Hinduism and Christianity* was written under a fake name.[7]

While Rammohun's authorial choices render the task of finding a common thread of thought difficult, Dermot Killingley and R.S. Sugirtharajah have provided us with a framework within which one can appreciate the complexities in his writings. Both argue that it is beyond doubt that the Gospels were always interpreted as a case for ethical practice.[8] Nevertheless, both also consider Rammohun's intense engagement with the Gospels somewhat puzzling. Killingley is perplexed about why Rammohun wrote more on the Gospels than on the Vedanta.[9] Sugirtharajah stresses that the ethical interpretation of the Gospels was Rammohun's central concern but cannot explain why Christian ethics was crucial to a thinker who rejected all possibilities of Christian conversion in India.[10]

I will argue that much of the problems thrown up by current scholarship has to do with the conceptual limitations of their arguments. Killingley restricts the scope of Rammohun's interpretation of the Gospels to a textual comparative survey with Baptist and Unitarian thought in Britain and Calcutta.[11] Sugirtharajah locates the 'hermeneutical agenda' of Rammohun's writings in a 'global discourse' of Christian thought (but ignores the 'local' context). Torkel Brekke and Shyamlal Chatterjee restrict the scope of Rammohun's writings on the Gospels to intellectual engagements with the Baptists; and Raf Gelders and Willem Derde locate Rammohun's ideas of social reform in Bengal within the language of Protestant missionary conceptions of caste and social practice, opining that arguments against the Brahmins 'merely echoed' Protestant criticism of priests in Christian Europe.[12] These arguments ignore an important context in Rammohun's interpretations of the Gospels: that without exception, they also contained critiques of colonial domination and the unequal relations of power between EIC officials and natives. The lack of scholarly emphasis on such critiques has led to a narrow interpretation of his writings.

Rammohun's writing on the Gospels was a response to his project of accountable governance and social ethics. This chapter shows how the Gospels were interpreted as texts of ethical practices; highlights the methodological and conceptual similarities with his contemporaneous tracts on Hindu scripture and the foundation of the Brahmo Sabha; and concludes that the Gospels were integral to his thought.

The EIC

Rammohun opined that the Gospels were frequently referred by Christian missionaries as a celebration of the EIC's presence in Bengal.[13] He did have a point, for although the relationship between the Company and the missionaries was ambiguous and often fraught with conflict, the latter were clearly appreciative of the colonial context of trade in Bengal. One missionary in particular cited the Company's successful relations in Bengal as an important factor in his decision to opt for missionary work. In 1792, William Carey, a Baptist preacher in England opined that 'commerce shall serve the spread of the Gospel'.[14]

Carey eventually founded the Baptist Missionary Society (BMS) in Srerampore in 1800 (and also headed the Bangla department at the Fort William College).[15] He opined that missionaries and EIC officials had much in common—both endured hardship in Bengal and were members of institutions with well-defined goals and charters. Carey argued that if missionary work was analogous to that of the Company in Bengal, Baptist success was guaranteed. According to Brekke, Carey's views were not an exception, since all the Baptists celebrated the relationship between mercantilism, trade, and missionary activity.[16]

The Baptist celebration of colonial power in Bengal was consistently rejected in Rammohun's writings. The most developed form of this argument was in *Brahmunical Magazine* (1821–3) and was written under the pseudonym Shivaprasad Sharma. Under the guise of Sharma, Rammohun argued that the Baptists ought not to 'throw offensive reflections' upon Hindu practices but treat them with 'respect'.[17]

Rammohun strongly asserted that an *inevitable* consequence of the political presence of the EIC in Bengal was that the Gospels *too* were perceived by the natives as a representative of violent political change and social disorder; and suggested that the missionaries instead preach in 'countries not conquered by the English'.[18] He elaborated on this theme by arguing that the Company was based in London and that the Gospels were rooted in social and cultural practices located in Europe. This argument also served to highlight the reasonableness of his idea that the Gospels ought to be interpreted as a general argument for ethics than a religious doctrine.

Rammohun then focused on the methods by which the Gospels were currently being propagated in Bengal. He opined that the missionaries had purposefully ignored the social environment and omitted to consider the opinions of the natives. His argument was also based on a contemporary context. As Killingley noted, all Christian missionaries in the early 19th century 'regarded themselves as bringing enlightenment to a benighted world and tended to ignore indigenous traditions'.[19]

Rammohun then sketched out the political context of this argument. He estimated that Bengal had been a British territory for approximately 50 years.[20] During the first three decades, the natives had been given to believe that their religious activities would be free from British interference. However, in the last 20 years, the missionaries had violated this belief by attempting to convert the natives, Hindus as well as Muslims, into Christianity.[21] In other words, the progressive dissemination of the Bible was linked with the establishment of the Company as a sovereign power.[22]

Rammohun explained this argument by drawing attention to two phases of Company rule. Phase one referred to the years between the acquisition of the dewani and the Permanent Settlement (1765–93) while phase two harked back to the period following the Act of 1813. The phases were demarcated to highlight the importance of a specific policy. The first featured a policy of non-intervention in religious affairs of the natives while the second referred to an overly aggressive intervention of the missionaries. He argued that missionary activity was undesirable since it led to social instability and conflict in Bengali society. On the other hand, the EIC's earlier policy of non-intervention had not led to any such social consequences. In his opinion, the EIC ought to favour the case for non-intervention as the mainstay of its religious policy in India.[23]

Rammohun's argument concerning the EIC's religious policy has been validated by recent research on the history of religion by Penelope Carson.[24] Carson argues that the religious policy of the EIC can indeed be divided into distinct phases.[25] The first phase (1640–1793) represented a lengthy period of non-interference in religious affairs of the natives of India.[26] In the second phase (1794–1813), the Company in London faced severe criticism from the British public and circulated elaborate plans to allow missionaries to visit India. However, Lord Cornwallis warned against such manoeuvres and his successor, John Shore, even wrote to the Court of Directors that 'the clergy in Bengal were not respectable'.[27] This stalemate between Calcutta and London reached its climax in 1812, the year before the renewal of the Company's charter.

The year 1813 marked the beginning of the third phase. By this time, the Company found itself under even greater pressure to promote Christianity. The Houses of Parliament received more than 908 petitions containing more than half a million signatures from the British public and missionaries. Objectors to the Company's policy of non-interference typically argued that the Company's religious policy amounted to bad governance.[28] Ultimately, the Company made an official commitment to contribute towards 'the religious improvement of its subjects' in India.[29] That Rammohun was clearly aware of this context can be seen from the fact that the *Precepts of Jesus* was also published in London and *Second Appeal to the Christian public* and *Final Appeal to the Christian public* were addressed to the British public.

The theme of bad governance was also an important strand in Rammohun's arguments. He singled out the four Gospels (from the text of the Bible) and argued that they were primarily texts of ethics and law. This argument however brought him into debate and conflict with the Baptist missionaries in Bengal. The next section explores this in greater detail.

The Baptists

Rammohun had interacted with the Anglicans, Baptists, and Unitarians since c.1814.[30] His close association with various Christian denominations, however, created problems for him in Bengali society where Christianity was looked upon with a degree of suspicion. Worse still, the Baptists had also touted him as a potential convert in 1815–16.[31] So, it is not altogether surprising that his first published work on the Gospels, *Precepts of Jesus*, was an anonymous publication. As an anonymous author, he was able to divert attention away from public suspicion of his Christian connections and argue that everyday social ethics constituted the essence of the teachings of Christ.

Rammohun opined that his interpretation of the Gospels was most reasonable since only 'a very small portion' of the actual words of Jesus remained accessible to contemporary readers.[32] He was not only pointing out problems with the *content* of the Gospels but also the *context* in which they were being interpreted by Christian missionaries in Bengal. He argued that the missionaries 'taught Biblical instruction' to potential converts as if they were 'brought up in a Christian country with dogmatical notions imbibed from their infancy'.[33] Unfortunately, the missionaries did not pay close attention to this context and their ignorance had cost them dear. The Baptists suffered from the continuous social hostility towards their ideas. The BMS's Joshua Marshman has even left us an eyewitness account of the grave impact of native hostility on a fellow missionary, John Thomas. Thomas became so 'frantic with joy' with a case of native conversion that it 'destroyed the balance of his mind'. Thomas eventually had to be physically confined where he 'raved'. Unfortunately, Thomas was not the only casualty of a hostile Bengali society; William Carey's wife had also 'lost her mind' by this time.[34]

The Baptists' hardships did not pay off as Carey had initially expected. New converts were often confused about Baptist practices.

For example, the natives often confused Baptism with the Hindu practice of ritualistic immersion in water to 'wash away sins'.[35] In this context, *Precepts of Jesus* presented three cases of confused and ultimately flawed conversions.

The first case concerned a former convert from the Muslim community in Bengal, Inayat Khan. Khan, 'a man of respectable family', who had initially converted to Christianity but later 'speedily returned to Muhammadanism pleading that he had been unable to reconcile his understanding to certain dogmas preached to him' by the missionaries.[36] The second case concerned an elite convert, Jawad Sabat. Sabat was 'an Arab traveller, translator and scholar' who had been in Srerampore from 1807 to 1813. Sabat had been sent by the senior chaplain of Madras to the Baptists as a Munshi to assist in the translation of the Bible. However, he inaugurated 'a furious controversy' in Bengali society by publishing 'an obnoxious tract' on the Prophet Muhammad. In response, Governor General Lord Minto restricted the areas in Calcutta where the Baptists could preach.[37]

Rammohun opined that Sabat was 'a grossly unprincipled Arab' but 'eminently learned' and noted that the latter had expressed his disillusionment with Christianity by printing 'several hundred copies of a treatise in Arabic' against the missionaries. While both Sabat and Inayat Khan were Muslims, the third case concerned the Hindu population in Bengal. He recounted witnessing an incident in 1819 in which the Bishop of Calcutta had been heckled over an alleged breach of promise by recent Hindu converts. On hearing their threats against Christianity, he concluded that the converts were 'unprincipled'. Thus, he opined that the missionaries themselves misunderstood the motivations of the natives.[38]

The three cases form the contextual background against which Rammohun declared the suitability of his interpretation of the Gospels as a general argument for ethics. He declared that this interpretation would not lead to the sort of confusions which Inayat Khan and Sabat had experienced; neither would it give any scope to 'unprincipled' native converts to take advantage of the Bible. Further, unlike the missionaries, he claimed to have interpreted the Gospels in the context of their suitability to the specific social and religious dynamics in India where 'nearly three-fifths of the inhabitants are

Hindus and two-fifths Mussalmans'.[39] He stressed that *his* interpretation correctly assessed Indian social conditions, while the Christian missionaries' did not.

To Rammohun, Hinduism and Islam represented 'gross idolatry' and 'belief in one god' respectively.[40] For instance, on comparing the three cases of conversion referred to earlier, we recall that Inayat Khan and Sabat were Muslims and reconverted to Islam from Christianity since neither were able to 'reconcile the dogmas' preached by the missionaries and were confused about how the concept of the Trinity could possibly relate to 'the belief in one invisible god'.[41] For Khan and Sabat, the missionary interpretation of the Bible was problematic since it led to irreconcilable doctrinal implications. Rammohun noted that the case of the Hindu converts was different from Sabat and Khan. This is because contemporary Hindu doctrines of multiple gods or idols were perfectly compatible with missionary ideas of trinity.[42] The Hindu converts' protest against their conversion was not therefore a consequence of doctrinal confusion but a regrettable lack of 'principles' or ethics. For Rammohun, this case highlighted the urgent need for a general ethical discourse in contemporary Hindu society.

Rammohun's point was that the Gospels could contribute to a discourse of social ethics in contemporary Bengali society if it was seen as 'moral doctrines' concerned with everyday ethical practices.[43] He sketched out an interpretation of the Gospels which was concerned with social welfare and argued that religion was a doctrine which emphasized the relations of equality among members of society against all forms of illegitimate regulation and control.[44]

Rammohun's interpretation of religion in *Precepts of Jesus* is also consistent with his first known text, *Tuhfat* (c.1803). Both highlighted the connection between the belief in one god and ethical practices of individual members of society; rejected rituals, miracles, and superstitious practices in religion; stressed the crucial importance of ethics in contemporary society; and cited ecclesiastical authorities as the chief instigators of social conflict.[45]

Precepts of Jesus also justified Rammohun's project of social reform of religious, domestic, and political practices in Bengal. It showed that he was not simply articulating his perception of an ideal society but rather arguing that the current instability of social and political relations only necessitated social reform. In *Final Appeal to the Christian public*, the Bible was even interpreted as 'the source for civil law'.[46]

***

Rammohun's writings on the Gospels were not preachy monologues directed at the Bengali public but dramatic controversies in the form of debates with William Carey, William Ward, and Joshua Marshman, members of the Baptist Missionary Society (BMS).[47] The BMS were based at Srerampore, a Danish colony, and claimed the protection of the Danish Crown. The EIC had limited control over their activities and were unable to regulate their printing press (which by publishing more than 220,000 volumes of translations or selected tracts of the Bible in 40 oriental languages served as the main vehicle for the dissemination of their ideas from 1801 to 1831). The printing press was Carey's brain-child. His conception of printing was not however restricted to 'religious publications' but also encompassed 'Indian classics, grammars, vocabularies, dictionaries, maps', and journals of political and social events.[48] The BMS was nothing short of a formidable publishing house.

Although some biographers (such as Sophia Collet) opined that Rammohun did not expect the Baptists to respond angrily to his writings, recent scholarship has largely shown these views to be incorrect. Killingley argues that since *Precepts of Jesus* purposefully rejected core Baptist doctrines such as the doctrine of trinity and belief in Biblical miracles, it follows that he *intended* to provoke a response from the Baptists.[49]

Rammohun's criticism had the desired effect. The Baptists 'viciously attacked' *Precepts of Jesus* (and his response to the Baptist 'attack' was the context in which *Appeal to the Christian public, Second Appeal to the Christian public, Final Appeal to the Christian public*, and *Brahmunical Magazine* were written). Joshua Marshman was at the frontline of the Baptist response.[50] Marshman even identified Rammohun as the author of *Precepts of Jesus* and perceived his ideas to be that of a 'heathen' Hindu than a Unitarian Christian.[51]

Unfortunately, historians do not consider the reasons why Rammohun chose to be anonymous. I argue that he debated anonymously with the Baptist missionaries so that the latter could legitimize his perspective as that of a Hindu and remove all doubt of the author as being a potential Christian convert. Once his own position as a Hindu was clear, Rammohun clarified his authorship and proceeded to introduce changes in the debate by shifting its focus from a discussion on Christian theology to his own political project of introducing a general discourse of social ethics in Bengal.

Precepts of Jesus is the earliest example of Rammohun's treatment of the Gospels as a text of social ethics for Hindu and Muslim Bengali society. He argued that references to god in the Gospels could be reconceptualized as a sovereign who governed his subjects by providing for a peaceful society through a legal system which promoted ethical practice.[52] In this interpretation, the Gospels became an argument for accountability, ethics, and good government, 'a simple code and well fitted to regulate the conduct of the human race in the discharge of their various duties to god, to themselves and to society'.[53] A closer look at Rammohun's language shows references to governmental vocabulary such as codes and regulations. So, Christianity was referred to as an ecclesiastical doctrine and legal tradition.

Precepts of Jesus was also an argument for the governance of the self through ethical social practices and a case for a system of law based on such practices. The 'principal strength' of Christianity in this context was 'a due estimation of the law'.[54] Everyday ethical practices constituted the core ideas of law in Abrahamic systems of thought and that Jesus himself formalized contemporary ethical practices into a systematic framework of law by borrowing from a specific epistemology of law and social practice.[55] By focusing on Christ as a lawmaker and promoter of ethical practice, Rammohun could contradict the missionary interpretation of the Bible as a text of miracles.[56]

Rammohun systematically rejected missionary interpretation in *Appeal to the Christian public, Second Appeal to the Christian public*, and *Final Appeal to the Christian public* to support his own point of view. He argued that the emphasis on Biblical miracles diverted attention from the ethical ('moral') content of the Gospels and instead proposed a 'separation' between 'moral' practices of the Bible and 'other matters' such as rites and rituals. 'Moral' referred to a general case for ethics in society. As he clarified, 'The sense in which the word moral is used is quite general and applied equally to our conduct in religious and civil matters.'[57]

Rammohun explained Biblical miracles as narrative tools of legitimization by which Christ could claim the 'authority of the teacher'.[58] He also warned of the dangerous consequences of debates over the nature of Christ's miracles by arguing that they had historically led to wars and conflicts over differing interpretations of the Bible and severely hampered the political and social stability of the regions under the sway of Christianity.[59]

Rammohun now pitched his interpretation as a 'harmonious system' which championed 'truth, charity and liberality' and urged that 'man should do unto others as he should wish to be done by'.[60] He also attempted to sand-paper away the influence of any contemporary Christian denomination on his thought. For instance, *Precepts of Jesus* proposed an argument for 'common sense' and 'the laws of reason' independently of any contemporary influences.[61]

Rammohun was not being entirely truthful in *Precepts of Jesus* for he was certainly inspired by the Unitarians (and had even 'allied' with the Unitarian school of thought in Calcutta by then).[62] Killingley notes that his association with the Unitarians is not surprising since his ideas of the Bible were very similar to their interpretation.[63] (For example, the Unitarians also stressed on ethical practices as a form of worshipping one invisible god.)[64] So, even by arguing from within a Unitarian tradition, he could confidently assert his view that Jesus stressed on social ethics; and that being ethical was 'sufficient to secure the peace and happiness of mankind at large'.[65]

To promote a wider dissemination of his ideas, Rammohun enlisted two Baptist missionaries, William Adam and William Yates, to help him translate the New Testament into Bangla.[66] Under Rammohun's influence, William Adam even converted to Unitarianism. The Baptists were furious with this development and denounced Rammohun in *The Friend of India* (their English language journal) as well as *Samachar Darpan* (their Bangla newspaper). Adam was singled out for scorn as his former Baptist colleagues now publicly referred to him as 'the second fallen Adam'.[67]

Rammohun also had to contend with the views of Dr. R. Tytler, a British medical surgeon and member of the Asiatic Society of Bengal. On 3 May 1823, Tytler published angry denouncements of Rammohun's views on Unitarianism in the *Bengal Hurkaru*.[68]

Rammohun responded via a fake name—Ram Doss—and humorously proposed to attack his own ideas.[69] He claimed (tongue-firmly-in-cheek) that Tytler and he were both 'sincere worshippers', since Hinduism and Christianity have 'a common basis'.[70] He even invited Tytler to consider the similarities between Rama (the mythological hero of the epic Ramayana) and Jesus. Both appeared in sacred scripture, both apparently performed miracles, and both could lay claim to a large number of worshippers in contemporary times.[71] So, how different were they from one another? If Jesus could be born into a human family and still be considered a god, then why couldn't the same case be made for Rama? He asserted that Trinitarians had much in common with polytheistic Hinduism but the Unitarians could not as they never much bothered about the human traits of Jesus.[72]

Upon discovering the truth of Ram Doss's authorship, an enraged Tytler published an even harsher letter, demanding an in-person open debate 'with the renegade Rammohun Roy'.[73] 'I am ready to meet you at any time!' he declared grandly.[74] Rammohun, a seasoned controversialist, in turn challenged Tytler to several newspaper debates on Unitarianism. After 20 days of an angry (and awkward) correspondence, Tytler abruptly left Calcutta for England.[75]

Rammohun was not, however, intimidated by either Tytler or the Baptist missionaries and continued experimenting with his ideas on Christianity. But the question is: why did he not declare any religious affiliation in *Precepts of Jesus*? The answer, I argue, lies in his scepticism of missionary attempts to preach the Gospels in non-Western societies and his anxiety that Bengali society should not be informed that he was inspired by Unitarian thought.

In 1821, he published his views on the subject in *Padri o shishya samvad* (*A Padre and his disciples*), a short dialogical Bangla satire. This tract was structured around a conversation between a European Missionary who preached Trinitarianism and three confused disciples. Interestingly, the tract was set in China and all three disciples were indigenous Chinese men. They were not named but only referred to as the 'first', 'second', and 'third' disciple (*shishya*).

The padre began by asking the three disciples if there was one god or many. The first replied that there were three gods, the second opined that there were but two gods, and the third claimed that there was no god at all. The padre was perplexed with these responses and demanded an explanation. On being told their opinions were based on his teachings, he angrily declared them to be heretics (*pasandas*). The disciples, in turn, blamed the padre for his 'strange' ideas.[76] The padre then asked each man what he thought about the question of god.

The first disciple replied that he believed that there were three gods because the padre had told him of three divinities in Christianity: god, his son Jesus, and the holy ghost. The padre responded that the first disciple was ignorant since the three divinities ultimately merged into one. But the disciple was not convinced and argued that the three divinities could not merge into one just as the number 3 can never be equal to the number 1. Caught on the backfoot, the padre could only opine that the subject was mystical and profound. The disciple did not find the topic to be profound but contradictory and illogical. The padre, however, continued to insist that the topic was so profound that it could not be explained. At this point, the second disciple laughingly interjected by opining, 'You have come here to teach us this religion from 10,000 miles—and we don't understand why.' The padre admonished him for 'gross ignorance'.[77] 'The Kali age has arrived in China' he announced; and then asked the second disciple how he had worked out that there were two gods.

The second disciple opined that he had always known that there were many gods but the padre had reduced it to just two. The padre swiftly discarded this argument and instead declared that the disciple's reasoning was flawed. The disciple partly agreed and even admitted that the padre had never mentioned anything about two gods. Nevertheless, he continued to insist that it was the only inference that he could draw. On being questioned further, he recalled that the padre had indeed mentioned that there were three separate Christian divinities—god the father, his son Jesus, and the holy ghost. However, the second disciple thought there were only two gods because Jesus had died more than 1,800 years ago in a village in the Western lands (*poschim desh*).[78] On hearing this, the padre angrily declared the entire conversation as a waste of time.

The padre had not, however, finished with his enquiries. He now turned to the third disciple and declared him to be the biggest heretic of them all. 'How can you say that there is no god?' he demanded. The third disciple confessed that he had not understood the padre's teachings very well. 'I am not a pandit,' he offered by way of explanation. The only detail he had been able to comprehend was that there was one god and he had given Christianity its name. The padre was confused with this response. 'Of course, it is true,' he exclaimed, 'but I am surprised with your answer that there is no god.'[79]

The third disciple explained his response in some detail by picking up an object from the ground. 'This object exists here,' he told the padre, 'but, if I place it elsewhere, then it will no longer be present here.' 'Yes,' said the padre impatiently, 'but how can this example be suitable here?' The third disciple explained that his reasoning was probably difficult to understand because he was not as 'refined' in thought as people from the Western lands. Nevertheless, he agreed to explain his point again by reminding the padre of what he had taught, that there was but one god in Christianity and while Jesus was the true god, he had been crucified 1,800 years ago. 'So, what answer will I have apart from saying that there is no god?' the disciple asked.[80]

The padre warned all three disciples that if they continued to question the tenets of Christianity, they will suffer through life, while dying, and even after death. The disciples were surprised with this assessment. 'You have taught us a religion that we don't understand,' they told him. And then came the parting shot: 'Just because we don't understand your religion, you think that we will perish in hell.'[81]

Padri o shishya samvad also contained references which Rammohun's Bangla audience would have found familiar: the second disciple argued that he was not a pandit, and the padre declared that China was in the Kali age, a mythical era of demise and destruction in the Hindu cosmological calendar. The title also reflected the preferences of the intended audience: Christian missionaries were traditionally called padre in Indian society.[82] While the original Bangla version contained no references to Unitarian thought, a later English translation (produced in 1823) cautiously introduced the idea as the padre now identified a distinct Socinian influence in the responses he received and referred to it as evidence of 'the Devil's work in China.'[83] The English translation's title also underwent a slight change. It was now titled *A Dialogue between a missionary and three Chinese converts* (as opposed to 'disciples').

Rammohun stressed that the problem was not with Christian texts but European Trinitarian missionaries who seemed to have forgotten that their cultural context and that of their audience differed. The original Bangla version introduced this argument towards the end of the tract by highlighting the confusion felt by the three Chinese disciples with Trinitarian discourse and their annoyance on being told that they were destined for hell.[84] The English translation added to this line of thought. Here, all three men rebuked the padre in turn and opined that he did not seem to know enough about Chinese society and thought.[85]

As Rammohun would argue in *Precepts of Jesus*, the doctrine of Trinitarianism could be confusing since it represented *one* god as *three* divine beings. If the 'absurdity' of Hinduism consisted of its rituals and beliefs in multiple manifestations of one god (*ek brahman*), the ideas of Trinitarianism only consolidated such 'absurdity' with a fresh set of rituals and practices.[86] In a letter to Henry Ware in 1824, Rammohun argued that 'sincere conversion to Trinitarian Christianity was morally impossible'.[87] On the other hand, Unitarian thought would be far more comprehensible to the Hindus since it was based on sound reasoning.[88] Unitarianism, he argued, was 'a true religion' and notable for its compassionate view of the social world.[89]

However, Rammohun was not interested in promoting Unitarianism in India. As he would later admit, 'I have not done anything to deserve being called the promoter of the cause', and went on to confess that all Unitarian doctrines that he believed in were for 'my own salvation and my own peace'.[90] Neither was he interested in the question of conversion to Christianity. 'Under the existing circumstances,' he wrote, 'there is no human possibility of converting Hindus into any sect of Christianity.'[91] Instead, he had interpreted the Gospels because he was inspired by their emphasis on social ethics.[92]

In *Precepts of Jesus*, Rammohun discovered that the Gospels contained detailed prescriptions on ethical conduct. This was a perspective that he valued highly. His readings into Hindu scripture had not revealed any discussion on prescriptive ethics.[93] He now decided to work within two different systems of thought and integrate his findings from the *Precepts of Jesus* into Hindu scripture. His critic, Joshua Marshman, was aware of the Gospels' importance to his project. Marshman read *Precepts of Jesus* alongside Rammohun's interpretations of Hindu scripture and concluded that he was attempting to relate Christianity to Hinduism. To Marshman, Rammohun's interpretation of the Gospels was problematic *precisely because* he refused to write from within an exclusively Christian tradition.[94]

Rammohun, in turn, (wrongly) criticized Marshman for having failed to acknowledge the Bible's status in Bengal as a representative of British cultural practices.[95] Nevertheless, he may have realized that a straightforward reference to *Precepts of Jesus* would evoke societal controversy and so referred to the DhS and a known scriptural authority, Vyasa, to establish the legitimacy of his views on prescriptive ethical practice. He proceeded to introduce arguments concerning ethics through a discussion of the idea of worship in Hindu scripture.

Hindu Scripture

Rammohun had very definite views on worship in Hindu scripture and expressed these with increasing fervour through the 1820s. He disagreed with current views of worship (such as those espoused by his critic Subrahmanya Shastri) and instead asserted that everyday ethical practices in one's own household, family, and society were the only legitimate form of worship.[96]

Subrahmanya Shastri was a resident of the Madras Presidency but had taken it upon himself to educate the Bengalis on the meaning and purpose of worship in Hindu scripture. According to him, the purpose of worship was to gain religious knowledge (*brahmogyan*). And religious knowledge could not be gained by just about anyone, but only those who read the Vedas, DhS, and executed the everyday duties of a Brahminical householder (which included five obligatory fire sacrifices and public rituals). Only a thorough mastery of these texts and duties would enable one to gain some perspective into the absolute knowledge of the universe (*brahma vidya*).[97]

Although Shastri carefully expounded the duties of each caste according to DhS prescriptions, the full weight of his interpretation was only applicable to well-off Brahmin men who could read the Vedas and conduct expensive rituals. He also did not have much of an opinion of Bengali Brahmins and considered them to be amongst those who did not read the Vedas. He even warned them that they could never attain salvation if they did not perform their duties. In fact, such Brahmins might as well be non-Brahmins, he scoffed.[98]

Rammohun responded to Shastri in *An apology for the pursuit of final beatitude independently of Brahmunical observances* in Sanskrit, Bangla, Hindi, and English in 1820. He admitted that Shastri ('a diligent observer of Brahminical tenets') had a point since the Vedas indeed prescribed certain rules to any Brahmin who wished to seek religious knowledge.[99] He also agreed that the Brahmins of Bengal were 'generally deficient' in their studies on Hindu scripture.[100] He himself had made a similar assessment of the state of Brahmanical learning in Bengal in his Bangla tract *Gayatrir artha* (The Meaning of the Gayatri, 1818).[101]

But Rammohun was not in complete agreement with Shastri. The Vedas and DhS only created a conducive environment by which religious knowledge could be acquired, he argued. Neither was indispensable for gaining such knowledge.[102] Significantly, he referred to Vyasa and Shankara to make this argument by opining that the latter had originally raised the question of whether an individual could gain religious knowledge without the regulations of caste, rites, or rituals, perhaps unaware that the former had already offered a solution in the affirmative by citing evidence from the Vedas.[103]

Rammohun now pronounced his complete agreement with Vyasa. He also opined that the Vedas did not have an exclusive preserve on the question of what constituted religious knowledge since the Puranas and the Gita could impart religious knowledge just as well.[104] As far as he was concerned, Shastri had ignored an important point: that scripture, rites, and rituals were but a means by which one could reflect on the Supreme Being every day. 'What should we say more?' he demanded by the way of conclusion.[105] Unfortunately, there was a lot 'more' that he could have clarified. For example, if the performance of rites and rituals did not guarantee religious knowledge, then what did? Also, did his ideas simply appeal to those who were inspired by or interested in the Vedas?

Rammohun's readers would not have had to wait very long for the answers. Just two years later, in 1823, he published a more detailed argument in *Humble suggestions to his countrymen who believe in one god*, alongside a Bangla version, *Prarthnapatra* (*A Humble Request*).[106] He began by opining that the Vedas had firmly established the view that the universe had been created by a single god who could not be perceived through language, thought, or sight but only reflected upon; and then went on to propose that the right method of worship to such a god was through everyday ethical conduct in society.[107]

Rammohun also had a simple rule by which his readers could figure what counted as ethical conduct. His English and Bangla versions varied slightly in this regard. The former only stressed that every individual should treat others as they would wish to be treated and consider their disappointments and unhappiness as their own.[108] The latter elaborated on the theme by opining that if such an individual meets anyone else who practices good conduct (*nishta acharan*), they ought to maintain cordial relations with them even if they do not read sacred scriptures, for such people are on the path of understanding the Supreme Being.[109] In spite of the slight variations, it is clear that Rammohun was essentially restating (and interpreting) a dictum which he had highlighted in the *Precepts of Jesus*: 'Do unto others what you would be done by.'[110]

Rammohun also broadened the scope of his ideas. He pleaded with his readers to be considerate to alternative methods of devotion and identified with the 'religious sentiments' of medieval thinkers who had not read the Vedas (such as Kabir, Nanak, and Dadu) by considering them 'brethren'. He also made a case for religious music and argued that salvation could be acquired by instrumental melodies and harmony and appealed for the compassionate (*daya*) treatment of Christian missionaries.[111] He was particularly interested in those Christian denominations that believed in one invisible god. 'We should feel no reluctance to co-operate with them in religious matters,' he insisted.[112] In the case of the Trinitarians, he introduced an argument which had also appeared during this time in his public spat with Tytler: readers were invited to carefully consider the similarities between Rama and Jesus than employ 'harsh and abusive language' towards the missionaries.[113] His arguments promoted the idea of a peaceful, caring, affectionate, and stable society where religious conflict and social discord were to be avoided through temperate and ethical behaviour.

In 1825, Rammohun published *Translation of a Sunscrit tract on different modes of worship* in Sanskrit and English under a pseudonym, Shivaprasad Sharma. He did not begin with an elaborate discussion of his ideas but a query raised by a certain Ramadhan Sarma. Sarma was confused that while some DhS recommended worship 'by the means of idols', others contained 'passages dissuading from such worship'.[114]

In this context, he enquired into the right method of worship according to Hindu scripture.

Clearly, Rammohun's interpretation of worship would travel through the discursive terrain of the DhS and revisit the question of worshipping idols. Beginning with Sarma's query also gave the impression that his ideas had generated some degree of curiosity in Bengali society. He responded that Vyasa had proposed a solution to the problem by suggesting that the worship of idols was simply a means to an end and not an end by itself. In time, the worshipper would realize that the Supreme Being was invisible, compassionate, and resided 'in the heart of all beings'.[115] Consequently, worship would also be reconceptualized as a discourse of ethics, charity, friendship, and compassion to reflect this interpretation.[116] Note that this argument was earlier made in *Precepts of Jesus*: 'Did not Jesus declare that acts of charity and beneficence toward fellow-creatures will be accepted as the manifestation of love towards god and be the sufficient cause of eternal life?'[117] It is possible that he began the tract with a DhS context and references to Vyasa to camouflage the influence of Christian ethics on his ideas of worship.

Rammohun had been able to present a persuasive argument for the reconceptualization of the meaning of worship in Hindu society. But his argument was fragile; for the orthodox Bengali Brahmin community had a monopoly on the interpretation of religious knowledge and frequently challenged and dismissed his views on scripture. If he wanted his ideas to be taken seriously, he would have to challenge their authority. And this is exactly what he did.

Rammohun had already made some headway in this direction by publishing a critical interpretation of the Gayatri Mantra, one of the most well-known mantras of the time, in *Gayatrir artha* (1818), in Bangla.[118] He complained that although the Brahmins could recite the mantra, they were yet unaware that it was 'the essence and embodiment of the Supreme Being'.[119] Chiding his (Brahmin) contemporaries, he instead directed them to 'understand the meaning of the *mantra* before you recite it'.[120] The Gayatri Mantra's 'true meaning', he asserted, lay in its advocacy of self-knowledge through mindfulness, reflection, and meditation.[121] He did not, however, admonish his contemporaries but those who had taught them, alleging that the teachers of Brahminical learning in Bengal were lazy, ignorant, and selfish and mainly responsible for misdirecting their students.[122]

Rammohun revisited this argument in 1827 when he published *Gayatra paramposanavidhanam* (On Gayatri and worship) in Bangla. But this time, he took the purport of his arguments further. He argued that the Brahmins did not have any privileged access to *Gayatri*, since non-Brahmins also had a right (*adhikar*) to recite the mantra.[123] Interestingly, he also translated the tract in English as *Divine Worship by Means of Gayatri* (1827).[124] The English as well as the Bangla versions offered this interpretation of the Gayatri Mantra.

According to Rammohun, Gayatri made a case for a personal connect between individuals and the Supreme Being (and, by extension, dissuaded the role of any mediators). The Supreme Being, he argued, 'governed' the material world through the consciousness of the individuals.[125] By this he meant that the Supreme Being had the same control over the universe as the individual had over his body. A realization of this analogy in the individual would lead to the 'consciousness of the divine' or 'Om Tat Sat'.

Rammohun interpreted 'Om Tat Sat' as 'the three terms [which] collectively imply that the object (everyday life) when contemplated through *Om* (the divine) described what was existing'.[126] 'Described as what was existing' is a rather vague phrase, but when contextualized with his intended readership ('public') and political project (reform of contemporary socio-religious practices), the argument becomes clearer. 'Om Tat Sat' literally meant that the worship of the Supreme Being was only possible through ethical practices.

In 1829, Rammohun summarized his ideas in a short dialogical tract, *The Universal Religion: Religious Instructions founded on Sacred Authorities*. It was also published in Bangla as *Anusthan* (1829). 'Sacred authorities' referred to the texts of Hindu scripture. The English version contained an appendix in Sanskrit which quoted selected passages from MDhS, Gita, Mahanirvana Tantra, Vedanta, Brihadaranyaka Upanishad, Mundaka Upanishad, and Katha Upanishad.[127] The Bangla version did not contain an appendix but declared in the very first line that Rammohun's idea of worship was in accordance with the Upanishads.[128]

According to Rammohun, a careful perusal of Hindu scripture showed that all worship was to be directed to the 'adoration' of a single, formless, invisible Supreme Being—'the author and governor of the universe.'[129] He also took pains to stress on the universality of his arguments. Every religion in the world acknowledged the presence of a Being who had imparted consciousness, language, intellect, nature, and time to the material world, he asserted. In this sense, he was not hostile to any religion or creed but only wished for societal harmony through worship of the Supreme Being. He insisted on the establishment of certain societal rules in the interests of community welfare, warning that those who didn't follow any rules ultimately cause severe societal disruptions. Besides, Hindu scripture also upheld the norm of following societal rules, he added.[130]

Rammohun's intellectual debt to the Gospels was evident when he once again restated the dictum of 'Do unto others' by opining that one must act to 'secure one's good' but 'in such a manner as not only to prevent our own or other's ill but to secure our own or other's good'. He also opined that places of worship were 'preferable' as long as they were open to all and located at a convenient site whenever people were able to meet.[131] His ideas on a place of worship were influenced by Unitarian services in Calcutta, a point which we will explore further in the next section.

A Place of Worship

Unitarian places of worship made a deep impression on Rammohun. He was so inspired by churches and chapels that he founded a Unitarian mission (under the charge of William Adam) and attended its services along with his son, Radhaprasad. His presence generated much societal controversy as contemporaries first speculated if he had converted to Christianity and then wondered why he specifically chose to attend Unitarian services instead of those by more established Christian denominations.[132] In 1823 he published a short pseudonymous tract under the name of his associate Chandrasekhar Deb, *Answer of a Hindoo to the Question 'Why do you frequent a Unitarian place of worship instead of the numerously attended established churches?'*, to respond to such queries.[133]

Rammohun insisted that Unitarianism did not contradict his faith in Hinduism but emphasized on a view of worship that he agreed with. Unitarian services reminded him of the existence of a 'single, invisible, omnipotent divinity'. Repeated visits to a Unitarian place of worship could clarify his interpretations of Hindu scripture as a discourse of ethical practice.[134] He was deeply critical of the role of religious authorities in overseeing and legitimizing rites and rituals, and on comparing Hindu religious authorities with Christian missionaries, found them much the same:

> I already feel weary of the doctrine of 'Man-God' or 'God-man' frequently inculcated by the Brahmins in pursuance of their corrupt traditions: the same doctrine of Man-God though preached by another body of priests, better dressed, better provided for and eminently elevated by the virtue of conquest cannot effectually tend to excite my anxiety or curiosity to listen to it.[135]

Rammohun's 'weariness' with Christian missionaries and his critique of the divinity of Christ highlighted another context—the social position of the Brahmin in Bengal. His writings stressed that the right to supervise and conduct rituals translated to the exercise of disproportionate power which eventually led to unethical practices in society.

Rammohun attempted to reach out to a wider membership by appealing to the American and English churches to subscribe to the Unitarian Mission. His plan was that the mission would be part of a global discourse on Unitarian thought.[136] Dwarkanath Tagore and William Adam even attempted to reach out to British and Bengali residents in Calcutta and suggested that its name be amended to *British Indian Unitarian Association*.[137] Unfortunately, the mission did not receive very favourable press. The conservative newspaper *John Bull* mocked at Rammohun's aspirations and considered the mission to be a vanity project of a few rich men in Calcutta. The 'orthodox faiths have little to fear', the newspaper opined.[138] These words proved to be prophetic as the residents of Calcutta did not take to the Unitarian Mission and its ideas of religion.[139] The mission had failed in its purpose.

However, Rammohun was not willing to let go of the idea of a congregation and a place of worship where prayers could be held, devotional songs could be sung from hymn books written specifically for the purpose, and a congregation could be informed about the value and virtue of ethical practice as a form of religious worship. He decided to found the Brahmo Sabha, a Hindu mission based on his interpretation of Hindu scripture and shorn of a Christian discursive genealogy. Its members, drawn from his own Atmiya Sabha associates, engaged in a participatory form of worship, sang from Brahmo hymns, read from Brahmo prayer books, and discussed the importance of ethics in Brahmo meetings.

No one is quite sure about the Brahmo Sabha's precise origins. Popular Brahmo lore has two versions of the story. In the first version, Chandrasekhar Deb and Tarachand Charkrabarty expressed their dissatisfaction of having to pray at a Unitarian Mission to Rammohun who took this to heart and founded the Brahmo Sabha. In another version, William Adam himself gave Rammohun the idea of founding a new society, along Hindu lines of thought.[140] Adam was of the opinion that Rammohun's ideas diverged significantly from Unitarian philosophy but could contribute to an important public discussion on ethical practice in Bengal.[141]

Whichever is the correct version of the tale, the fact is that the Brahmo Sabha came into being in 1828.[142] The Sabha provided a space where members of any caste or class could gather, pray, and plan. Meetings were held every Saturday.[143] There was an element of ceremony in its proceedings. Two Telugu Brahmins were employed to read from the Vedas and recite their verses out loud.[144] Utsavananda Vidyavagish, formerly of the Atmiya Sabha, read out from the Upanishads in Sanskrit. Ramchandra Vidyavagish, a close associate (and the brother of Rammohun's friend and teacher, Hariharananda Bharati) translated the Sanskrit recitations into Bangla.[145]

Rammohun also composed hymns, which were sung by Vishnu Chakravarty, a well-known vocalist of the time, with a musical accompaniment by Ghulam Abbas. The use of music, hymns, and songs divided opinion in contemporary Bengali society. Some found the music to be appropriate, thematically significant, and aesthetically powerful while others insisted that it was distasteful.[146] Rammohun took a sharp view of any criticism of the Sabha's use of music. When the *Calcutta Gazette* published a disparaging report on the supposed performance of dance in the Brahmo meetings, he insisted that dance was not a part of the proceedings while singing was perfectly acceptable since it had also been prescribed by the DhS as a form of worship.[147]

Rammohun was probably touchy about disparaging reports about the *Sabha* because his hymns were expressions of his own thought on god and worship.[148] He had completed his major prose writings on religion and ethics by this time and now intended to provide a different sort of platform for his ideas. His hymns were concerned with ethics and the worship of a formless divinity, and published in *Brahmasangeet* (Brahmo Songs, 1828). He also published *Brahmopasana* (Brahmo Practice, 1828), a companion prose text wherein he argued that good behaviour was epistemically indispensable to the worship of the Supreme Being (*parameshwar*). The Supreme Being, he opined, had created all human beings; and that one must always respect the divine by being good. Rammohun's texts for the Brahmo Sabha conceptualized ethical conduct as a form of worship. He implored to the Brahmos to treat others as they themselves would prefer to be treated.[149] His engagement with religion and scripture was geared towards the creation of a certain typology of individual—humble, unworldly, and reflective.

Rammohun hoped that the Brahmo Sabha would ultimately contribute towards building an ethical public sphere in India. Just four years later, in 1832, he finalized an argument detailing the ways in which an ethical public in India could hold the EIC accountable for its government far more effectively than political authorities in London, and published it as *Exposition*.

***

Conclusion

The intellectual genealogy of Rammohun's ethics can be traced to his writings on missionary activities in Bengal. He was deeply critical of the methods by which the missionaries preached the Gospels and particularly concerned with their celebration of colonial power and attempts to preach their doctrines by criticizing Hinduism and Islam in favour of Christianity. Such methods, he warned, must be avoided for they led to social instability and confusion. Instead, the Gospels required to be radically reinterpreted as ethical doctrines if Christianity was to play a positive role in Bengali society.

Rammohun also wrote lengthy texts, tracts, and articles in the Bangla and English-language newspapers to argue that the missionaries had misinterpreted the Gospels. In *Precepts of Jesus* (1820), he asserted that Christ's importance lay in his emphasis on prescriptive ethics. It marked a turning point. As he later wrote to John Digby, 'the doctrines of Christ' were far more suited for arguments concerning ethical practice than any other religion that he was aware of.[150] In *Second defence of the Vedanta* (1816), he had even argued that Hindu scripture did not have much information on prescriptive ethics.[151] Consequently, the ideas of ethics in the Gospels featured prominently in his reinterpretation of the meaning and purpose of worship in Hindu scripture.

Rammohun always advocated for the existence of a single, invisible, and formless god. He was very appreciative of Christian denominations that agreed with this perspective (such as the Unitarians). He was so inspired by Unitarian places of worship that he invested in a Unitarian mission and attended its services with his family. When the Unitarian mission failed, he blended his own unique interpretation of Christian ethics and Hindu scripture in the institution of the Brahmo Sabha. The role of the Brahmo Sabha was to be able to contribute to the existence of an ethical public that would be invested in religious knowledge and social reform. It was this conception of an ethical public that led him to declare with such confidence in *Exposition* that the natives of India were politically aware and ethically capable of holding the government of the EIC accountable for its actions.

Notes

1. R.S. Sugirtharajah, *The Bible and Asia: From the Pre-Christian Era to the Postcolonial Age* (Cambridge, MA: Harvard University Press, 2013), 85.
2. Nag and Burman (eds), *EW* 4:85.
3. Torkel Brekke, 'Baptism and Bible in Bengal', *History of Religions*, 45 (2006), 213–33; Shyamlal Chatterjee, 'Rammohun Roy and the Baptists of Serampore: Moralism vs. Faith', *Religious Studies*, 20 (1984), 669–80.
4. Chatterjee, 'Baptists of Serampore', 669.
5. Dermot Killingley, *Rammohun Roy in Hindu and Christian Tradition: The Teape Lectures* (Newcastle upon Tyne: Grevatt & Grevatt, 1993), 117.
6. Killingley, *Rammohun Roy*, 118–19.
7. Killingley, *Rammohun Roy*, 123.
8. Killingley, *Rammohun Roy*, 129; Sugirtharajah, *Bible and Asia*, 87; Chatterjee, 'Baptists of Serampore', 669.
9. Killingley, *Rammohun Roy*, 141.
10. Sugirtharajah, *Bible and Asia*, 87.

11. Killingley, *Rammohun Roy*, 141.
12. Raf Gelders and Willem Derde, 'Mantras of Anti-Brahmanism: Colonial Experience of Indian Intellectuals', *Economic and Political Weekly*, no. 38 (2003), 4611–17.
13. Nag and Burman (eds), *EW* 2:171.
14. As quoted in Brekke, 'Bible in Bengal', 215.
15. Siddiq Khan, 'William Carey and the Serampore Books: 1800–1834', *International Library Review*, 11 (1961): 197–280.
16. Brekke, 'Bible in Bengal', 215.
17. Nag and Burman (eds), *EW* 2:171.
18. Nag and Burman (eds), *EW* 2:137.
19. Killingley, *Rammohun Roy*, 108.
20. Nag and Burman (eds), *EW* 2:137.
21. Nag and Burman (eds), *EW* 2:137.
22. Penelope Carson, *East India Company and Religion, 1698–1858* (Woodbridge: Boydell and Brewer, 2012), 2.
23. Nag and Burman (eds), *EW* 2:137.
24. Carson, *East India Company and Religion*, 2.
25. Carson, *East India Company and Religion*, 2–3.
26. Carson, *East India Company and Religion*, 21.
27. Khan, 'William Carey', 210.
28. Carson, *East India Company and Religion*, 3.
29. Carson, *East India Company and Religion*, 2.
30. Brekke, 'Bible in Bengal', 230.
31. Brekke, 'Bible in Bengal', 228.
32. Ghose (ed.), *The English Works*, 555.
33. Ghose (ed.), *The English Works*, 557.
34. Brekke, 'Bible in Bengal', 217.
35. Brekke, 'Bible in Bengal', 217.
36. Ghose (ed.), *The English Works*, 557.
37. Khan, 'William Carey', 226.
38. Ghose (ed.), *The English Works*, 557.
39. Ghose (ed.), *The English Works*, 560.
40. Ghose (ed.), *The English Works*, 560.
41. Ghose (ed.), *The English Works*, 557.
42. Ghose (ed.), *The English Works*, 484.
43. Ghose (ed.), *The English Works*, 483.
44. Ghose (ed.), *The English Works*, 550.
45. *Tuhfat*, 8.
46. Ghose (ed.), *The English Works*, 550.

47. Killingley, *Rammohun Roy*, 107.
48. Khan, 'William Carey', 229.
49. Killingley, *Rammohun Roy*, 141.
50. Killingley, *Rammohun Roy*, 107.
51. Killingley, *Rammohun Roy*, 107.
52. Ghose (ed.), *The English Works*, 555.
53. Ghose (ed.), *The English Works*, 547.
54. Ghose (ed.), *The English Works*, 483.
55. Ghose (ed.), *The English Works*, 550.
56. Chatterjee, 'Baptists of Srerampore', 669.
57. Ghose (ed.), *The English Works*, 560.
58. Ghose (ed.), *The English Works*, 555.
59. Ghose (ed.), *The English Works*, 556.
60. Ghose, (ed.), *The English Works*, 547–8.
61. Ghose (ed.), *The English Works*, 484.
62. Killingley, *Rammohun Roy*, 129–38.
63. Killingley, *Rammohun Roy*, 132.
64. Sugirtharajah, *Bible and Asia*, 87.
65. Ghose (ed.), *The English Works*, 550–2.
66. Nag and Burman (eds), *EW* 4:52.
67. Sastri, 'Rammohun Roy: The Story of His Life', 15.
68. Sastri, 'Rammohun Roy: The Story of His Life', 16.
69. Sastri, 'Rammohun Roy: The Story of His Life', 16.
70. Nag and Burman (eds), *EW* 4:56.
71. Nag and Burman (eds), *EW* 4:58.
72. Nag and Burman (eds), *EW* 4:58.
73. Nag and Burman (eds), *EW* 4:60.
74. Nag and Burman (eds), *EW* 4:60.
75. Nag and Burman (eds), *EW* 4:74.
76. *BW*, 262.
77. *BW*, 262.
78. *BW*, 263.
79. *BW*, 263.
80. *BW*, 263.
81. *BW*, 263.
82. John Stevenson, *Dialogues between certain Brahmans, Marattas, and others and a Christian on the Hindoe and Christian Religions* (London: James Nisbet, 1829), 69.
83. *BW*, 263.
84. *BW*, 263.

85. *BW*, 263.
86. Nag and Burman (eds), *EW* 5:97.
87. Nag and Burman (eds), *EW* 4:49.
88. Nag and Burman (eds), *EW* 4:49.
89. Nag and Burman (eds), *EW* 4:50.
90. Nag and Burman (eds), *EW* 4:84.
91. Nag and Burman (eds), *EW* 4:45.
92. Ghose (ed.), *The English Works*, 675.
93. Nag and Burman (eds), *EW* 2:100.
94. Nag and Burman (eds), *EW* 2:171.
95. Nag and Burman, (eds), *EW* 2:140.
96. Nag and Burman (eds), *EW* 2:117.
97. *BW*, 230.
98. *BW*, 230.
99. Nag and Burman (eds), *EW* 2:123.
100. Nag and Burman (eds), *EW* 2:123.
101. *BW*, 176.
102. Nag and Burman (eds), *EW* 2:123.
103. Nag and Burman (eds), *EW* 2:124.
104. Nag and Burman (eds), *EW* 2:124.
105. Nag and Burman (eds), *EW* 2:125.
106. Although neither version was published under his name, his authorship would not have been in doubt as it was a clear development of his earlier work and employed similar language and phraseology.
107. Nag and Burman (eds), *EW* 2:200.
108. Nag and Burman (eds), *EW* 2:200.
109. *BW*, 260.
110. Nag and Burman (eds), *EW* 2:200.
111. *BW*, 260.
112. Nag and Burman (eds), *EW* 2:201.
113. Nag and Burman (eds), *EW* 2:201.
114. Nag and Burman (eds), *EW* 2:197.
115. Nag and Burman (eds), *EW* 2:197.
116. Nag and Burman (eds), *EW* 2:197.
117. Nag and Burman (eds), *EW* 5:8.
118. Killingley, *Only True God*, 19–21; 30–45.
119. *BW*, 177.
120. *BW*, 177.
121. *BW*, 176–7.
122. *BW*, 176–7.

123. *BW*, 341.
124. Nag and Burman (eds), *EW* 2:75.
125. Nag and Burman (eds), *EW* 2:76.
126. Nag and Burman (eds), *EW* 2:77.
127. Nag and Burman (eds), *EW* 2:132–4.
128. *BW*, 353.
129. Nag and Burman (eds), *EW* 2:129.
130. Nag and Burman (eds), *EW* 2:132.
131. Nag and Burman (eds), *EW* 2:131.
132. Nag and Burman (eds), *EW* 2:192–3.
133. Nag and Burman (eds), *EW* 2:192–3.
134. Nag and Burman (eds), *EW* 2:192–3.
135. Nag and Burman (eds), *EW* 2:193.
136. *Bengal Hurkaru*, 3 January 1828, *RRPM*, 78.
137. *Bengal Hurkaru*, 3 January 1828, *RRPM*, 79.
138. *John Bull*, 3 January 1828, *RRPM*, 80
139. Home, 'Supplementary Notes', 44.
140. Sastri, 'Rammohun Roy: The Story of His Life', 17.
141. Killingley, *Rammohun Roy*, 145–6.
142. Sastri, 'Rammohun Roy: The Story of His Life', 17.
143. Banerji, *Rammohun Roy*, 56–7.
144. Sastri, 'Rammohun Roy: The Story of His Life', 17.
145. Banerji, *Rammohun Roy*, 56.
146. Chattopadhyay, *JB*, 157.
147. Shastri, *History of the Brahmo Samaj*, vol. 1, 77.
148. Banerji, *Rammohun Roy*, 56.
149. *BW*, 342.
150. Nag and Burman (eds), *EW* 4:95.
151. Nag and Burman (eds), *EW* 2:100.

Conclusion

The Political Thought of Rammohun Roy

Rammohun Roy (1772/4(?)–1833) found an interest in many rich and varied fields: administration, governance, statecraft, law, religion, translation, society, and culture. But through the diversity and extent of his interests, he pursued one unifying thread. That thread amounted to a political thought which encompassed three distinct but related themes: 1) the importance of ethics in Bengali society; 2) the restructuring and relocation of the Company's administration from the distant and invisible government in London to Calcutta; and 3) the ethical and legal obligation of the Company to be accountable to its subjects. The three themes highlight an internal coherence in his writings and a hitherto undiscovered conceptual neatness in his political thought. The most developed form of this argument was *Exposition*, published in London in 1832.

Exposition was primarily concerned with the EIC's revenue and the judicial administration in Bengal. But it was not merely a source on agrarian and institutional history; it also contained detailed suggestions on how an 'isolated commercial body' which primarily ruled by 'the exertion of superior force' could transition into a government concerned with the welfare of its inhabitants.[1] I surmise that suggestions such as these were influenced by Rammohun's prior association with the EIC.

Rammohun had been associated with the EIC's district administration in the revenue department. From 1804 to 1814, he was formally employed as a dewan, Faujdar (native court official), and (acting) Sheristedar (Chief native court official) but also worked in an informal capacity as a Munshi (language teacher). His period of association coincided with a very distinct phase of Company rule in Bengal. During this period, the working relationship between Company officials and native employees was fluid and informal. This does not, however, mean that native employees did not have an important role in Company administration. EIC officials depended on their native employees to read official documents (as well as native petitions in Persian), pay revenue receipts (*challan*), record witness statements, and even took their advice on matters pertaining to Company regulations. The role of the native employee in governance was championed in *Exposition*.

Rammohun was also a member of an intergenerational scribal elite, educated in Persian.[2] The scribal elite were mostly Hindu and upper-caste, coming from families who had been educated in madrasas for generations. All madrasas in Bengal followed a syllabi consisting of geometry, astronomy, measurement, Perso-Arabic political thought, and Persian poetry and literature. An education in the madrasas also led to the scribal elite actively participating in a Persian public sphere that extended to all former dominions of the Mughal Empire.[3]

In this context, *Exposition* not only championed the role of the native employee but also identified with a scribal elite community educated in madrasas in Bengal, 'a system of education which has hitherto existed among the respectable classes' in India.[4] The fact that Rammohun acknowledged the importance of a madrasa education in a text written in English in London for a British readership shows that Perso-Arabic thought remained an important context in his writings.

The influence of early modern thought on Rammohun's writings has hitherto been an under-studied area of research in historical scholarship. In recent years, Partha Chatterjee's *Black Hole of the Empire* has emerged as a pioneering new voice in this area.[5] Following Chatterjee, this book draws out its influence. I have argued that *Tuhfat* was influenced by *akhlaq* philosophy, specifically the best-known text of the genre, *Akhlaq-i Nasiri*. I have also shown that *Akhlaq-i Nasiri* was a familiar text in early-19th-century Bengal known to Company officials and native intellectuals.

Tuhfat and *Akhlaq-i Nasiri* also share certain discursive similarities. *Akhlaq-i Nasiri* is primarily a text of ethics and though a Persian text, referred to an extensive Arabic vocabulary. This is on account of its use of syllogisms, for which Arabic is better suited than Persian. *Tuhfat* primarily articulated an argument about ethics and ethical practice. Though a Persian text, *Tuhfat* also referred heavily to Arabic words on account of its syllogistic structure. Rammohun also demonstrated a concern with its accessibility for readers. For instance, he referred to Persian poetry to explain complicated syllogistic arguments.

Tuhfat examined the role of religion in contemporary Bengali society. Its ideas concerning religious practices, critique of ecclesiastical authorities (*mujtahids*), ethical practice, the human soul, and conceptual categories such as 'nature' and 'habit' also feature in many subsequent writings. Historians have, however, considered *Tuhfat* to be an isolated text, with little or no influence on later writings. One reason for this could be that it was not referred to in any other work.

Rammohun's writings on Hindu scripture were also written in a different style from *Tuhfat* and appealed to a different audience. While the latter was written for a Persian-educated native elite, the former was addressed to a Bengali 'public' (*sarvvasadharan lok*). While some historians are sceptical of the role of the Bengali public in his writings, this book has drawn on recent research on the history of the book to show that the Bengali public sphere was characterized by traditions of orality, manuscript culture, and print, which reinforced and consolidated each other. The popularity of a tract/text did not depend upon the print literacy of its intended readership, but rather the ability of the author to be 'oral-literate', that is, successfully incorporate and appeal to oral traditions (such as that of reading aloud, for example) in order to make his/her writings more accessible.[6]

Rammohun was 'oral-literate'. The majority of his English and Bangla writings were humorous, informal, dramatic, ironical, sarcastic, consistent, and short. This would have made them easy to narrate and read aloud. He also used shorter sentences and smaller words than his contemporaries (such as Mrityunjay Vidyalankar), ensuring a greater clarity of prose. He published in the popular press and distributed his works for free, enabling a greater circulation of his works. We have seen that throughout his career, he prioritized the publication of free tracts from the popular press over more prestigious projects from the elite presses in Calcutta. His works on Hindu scripture were widely reprinted in Calcutta during his lifetime. After his death, his writings were priced and published by private publishers who clearly perceived a market for them.

Rammohun's translation and interpretation of Hindu scripture was always in the context of his project of ethics and social reform. He frequently departed from the texts of Hindu scripture to include his own observations on social practice. Interpreting religious scripture as ethics was a vital part of his project. For example, his translations of the Upanishads (1816–19) argued that early Indian writings prohibited female infanticide and polygamy. Similarly, his writings on the Vedanta criticized Brahminical power and reinterpreted religious practices as ethical practices; and in *Gayathri* (1828), he boldly interpreted worship as a case for everyday ethical conduct.

A consistent concern with ethics and an ethical society can also be seen in Rammohun's tracts on sati (1818–31) which interpreted the practice as fundamentally unethical and illegal. He interpreted early Indian legal texts, the DhS, to stress that these texts did not, in fact, advocate the practice. He may have referred to the DhS because it was referred to widely by native intellectuals in Calcutta as the methodological template by which different world views could be advocated and new social contexts explored.[7] It is unsurprising, therefore, that Rammohun referred to these texts to highlight *his* arguments about social practices, ethics, and accountability.

The DhS were also interpreted in writings on property law (1822–30). Rammohun criticized the Company for misunderstanding indigenous legal systems and not engaging with Bengali society. He argued that the Company's interpretation of the DhS was faulty. In *Brief Remarks* and

Ancestral Property, he warned Company officials that polities in India had previously collapsed when they did not govern well. Rammohun's arguments were not without context. As Nandini Bhattacharyya-Panda has shown, the Company's interpretation of property law in Bengal was indeed problematic. The Company deliberately imposed a definition of legality on texts such as the Dayabhaga, thereby altering its arguments and scope.

Rammohun's tracts on property law and sati show that EIC officials were an important part of his intended readership. He even employed a range of categories and concepts to familiarize his readers with the subject matter of his arguments. The adoption of terms such as 'constitution', 'Common Law', 'executive', and 'legislature' was also an implicit acknowledgement that the Company in India represented political traditions rooted in Britain. His political thought was expressed in constitutional idioms in recognition of the colonial context in India.

Rammohun argued that the EIC was 'obligated' to introduce reforms in their methods of governance and was accountable to Bengali society for its laws, its officials, and its judges. He stressed that an ethical 'public' was capable of holding the Company accountable for its government. To articulate this point to the Bengali public, his writings on Hindu scripture consistently reinterpreted religious practices as a case for ethical practices. His writings in newspapers such as the *Sambad Kaumadi* and *Mirat al-Akhbar* clearly articulated his project of governmental accountability to the public. For example, he protested strongly against restrictions on the freedom of the press in 1823 by arguing that newspapers and journals were important platforms of critique. Newspapers reported not only on the success but also on the failure of government policies and were therefore critical channels of communication between the administrators and the governed.

Rammohun's writings on religion and politics were part of a single project. His works on Hindu scripture and *Tuhfat* articulated an argument for ethical practice. In his interpretation of the DhS, he argued that the Company was legally obligated to be accountable to its subjects in Bengal. His numerous interventions on sati made a strong case for this. In 1832, when the Privy Courts at London upheld the decision of the Company to abolish sati, Rammohun opined that the EIC could henceforth be held accountable to an ethical Bengali public.[8] He noted that not only did the Privy Council's decision vindicate his political thought but it also set a precedent, which he intended to follow up.

Unfortunately, Rammohun never got the chance to follow up on the precedent set by the Privy Council. He was exhausted and ill as so many years of campaigning, writing, and lobbying had begun to take a toll on him.[9] To make matters worse, he was also in grave financial difficulties. His considerable fortune had vanished overnight when his banking agents, Messrs. Mackintosh & Co., declared bankrupcy in 1833.[10] He approached the Court of Directors of the EIC for a loan but was declined.[11] As his medical condition worsened, he was advised to move out of London.

In September 1833, Rammohun arrived at Stapleton Grove near Bristol.[12] Initially, his health seemed to improve as he visited a nearby chapel, received visitors, and animatedly discussed Hindu philosophy and Christian theology with them.[13] However, this state of affairs was not to be as he developed a fever on the 19th of September and took to his bed. Within a week, he slipped into a coma and died.[14] The end was sudden, and it came before he had the chance to consolidate his ideas concerning ethics, politics, and government into a single text. *Exposition* had been a step in this direction, but it required a follow-up. That never came.

In the two centuries that have since passed, Rammohun's works have continued to be read, critiqued, quoted, celebrated, and denounced. He is widely considered to be a highly original political thinker, but nevertheless contradictory and inconsistent. In this book, I have argued that Rammohun articulated a political thought which was concerned with making a distant and invisible EIC headquartered at London accountable to an ethical Bengali public. This argument consistently runs through the body of his work and is simultaneously the essence and the conceptual frame of his writings.

Notes

1. *Exposition*, 51.
2. Collet, *Rammohun Roy*, 496. Ram Comul Sen, for example, was a Baidya educated in Persian.
3. Chatterjee, *Cultures of History*, 219.
4. Nag and Burman (eds), *EW* 2:68.
5. Chatterjee, *Black Hole*, 139.

6. The term 'oral-literate' was coined by V. Narayan Rao. Cited in Orsini, 'Introduction', *History of the Book*, xiv.

7. Hatcher, 'Pandits at work', 45–6.

8. *Corr.*, 728.

9. Home, 'Supplementary Notes', 67.

10. Nag and Burman (eds), *EW* 4:129.

11. Home, 'Supplementary Notes', 65.

12. Mary Carpenter, *Last days of Rammohun Roy in England* (Calcutta: Saraswat Library, 1915), 147.

13. Carpenter, *Last days of Rammohun Roy*, 155.

14. Carpenter, *Last days of Rammohun Roy*, 163–8.

Appendix

Table A.1 Rammohun Roy's works in Bangla and Other Languages (Sanskrit, Hindi, Arabic, and Persian) and Their Publication History in Calcutta, c.1803–1905

Year	Works in Bangla and other languages (Sanskrit, Hindi, Arabic, and Persian) c. 1803–29	Publishing History of Rammohun's Works in Bangla and Other Languages (Sanskrit, Hindi, Arabic, and Persian), c. 1834–1905
1803 (?) 1804	*Tuhfat-ul- Muwahidin* [A gift to the believers of one god] (Introduction in Arabic and main text in Persian)	1. Reprint by Rammohun's son, Ramaprasad Roy (Calcutta, 1859). 2. Reprint by Bhai Baldev Narayan (Patna, 1898). 3. English translation by Obaidullah el-Obaid undertaken for the Adi Brahmo Samaj (Calcutta, 1884). 4. English Translation by J.C. Ghose (Calcutta, 1906).

Year	Works in Bangla and other languages (Sanskrit, Hindi, Arabic, and Persian) c. 1803–29	Publishing History of Rammohun's Works in Bangla and Other Languages (Sanskrit, Hindi, Arabic, and Persian), c. 1834–1905
		5. Bangla translation from Obaid's translation by Jyotirananda Das. Commissioned by Sadharan Brahmo Samaj (Calcutta, 1949).
		6. Unpublished but printed by V. Rai (Calcutta, 1918).
1815	*Vedanta Grantha* (in Bangla)	
1816	*Vedantasar* (in Bangla) Publishers: Ganga Kishore Lulu Ji Print run: 1,000 copies distributed evenly between the publishers.	
1816	Isho Upanishad (in Bangla) Publishers: Ganga Kishore Lulu Ji Print run: 1,000 copies distributed evenly between the publishers.	1. Reprint (Calcutta, 1852). Price: 6 annas
		2. Reprint (Calcutta, [year not known]) Price: 4 rupees
		3. Reprint (Calcutta, 1839). Price: 4 annas
		4. Abstract of the Introduction to Rammohun Roy's Bangla Translation of the Isho Upanishad, Tattvabodhini Sabha Press (Calcutta, 1843).
1816	*Utsavanander sahit vichar* (in Sanskrit but using Bangla instead of Nagari alphabet)	Not reprinted in any of Rammohun's Collected Bengali works in the 19th century. Presumed lost until 1918.
1817	Katha Upanishad (in Bangla) Publisher: Lulu Ji Print run: 500 copies	Reprint (Calcutta, 1840). Price: 3 annas
1817	Mundaka Upanishad (in Bangla) Publisher: Lulu Ji Print run: 500 copies	

(Cont'd)

Table A.1 (*Cont'd*)

Year	Works in Bangla and other languages (Sanskrit, Hindi, Arabic, and Persian) c. 1803–29	Publishing History of Rammohun's Works in Bangla and Other Languages (Sanskrit, Hindi, Arabic, and Persian), c. 1834–1905
1817	Second Defence of Hindu Theism (in Bangla) Publisher: Lulu Ji Print run: 500 copies	
1817	Brihadanyanka Upanishad (in Bangla)	
1817	Bhattacharyer sahit vichar Also appeared in English as Second Defence of the Monotheistical System of the Vedas in 1817	Abstract of Rammohun's debate with a Bhattacharya, Tattvabodhini Sabha Press (Calcutta, 1844).
1818	Sahamaran bishoye pravartak o nivartaker samvad (in Bangla) Publisher: Huru Roy Print run: 500 copies Also appeared in English as Translation of a Conference between an advocate for and an opponent of Burning Widows Alive from the original Bungla in 1818.	
1818	Gayatrir artha [The Meaning of the Gayatri] (in Bangla) Publisher: Lulu Ji Print run: 500 copies	
1818	Mandukya Upanishad (in Bangla) Publisher: Lulu Ji Print run: 500 copies	Abstract of Rammohun Roy's introduction to the Bangla translation of the Mandukya Upanishad, Tattvabodhini Sabha Press (Calcutta, 1844).
1818	Debate with Ramgopal Suromana (in Bangla) Publisher: Lulu ji Print run: 500 copies	

Year	Works in Bangla and other languages (Sanskrit, Hindi, Arabic, and Persian) c. 1803–29	Publishing History of Rammohun's Works in Bangla and Other Languages (Sanskrit, Hindi, Arabic, and Persian), c. 1834–1905
1818	*Goswamir sahit vichar* [Debate with Goswami] (in Bangla)	Abstract of Rammohun's Controversy with a Goswami Tattvabodhini Sabha Press (Calcutta, 1844).
1819	*Sahamaran bishoye pravartak o nivartaker dwitiyo samvad* (in Bangla) Publisher: Baptist Mission Press Print Run: 500 copies Also appeared in English as *A Second Conference between an Advocate for and an Opponent of Burning Widows Alive*	
1819	Brihadaranyaka Upanishad (in Bangla)	
1819	*Atmanatmaviveka* [Translation of a work by Shankara] (in Bangla)	
1819	Brihadanyanka Upanishad (in Bangla)	
1820	*Subrahmanya Shastri'r sahit vichar* [Debate with Subrahmanya Shastri] (in Bangla, Hindi, and Sanskrit, and a Bangla transliteration of Sanskrit) Publisher: Baptist Mission Press Print run: 500 copies of each language translation. Appeared in English as *Apology for the pursuit of final beatitude independently of Brahmunical observances*	

(Cont'd)

Table A.1   (*Cont'd*)

Year	Works in Bangla and other languages (Sanskrit, Hindi, Arabic, and Persian) c. 1803–29	Publishing History of Rammohun's Works in Bangla and Other Languages (Sanskrit, Hindi, Arabic, and Persian), c. 1834–1905
1820	*Kavitakarer sahit vichar* [Debate with Kavitakar] (in Bangla)	
1820	*Brahma pautalik samvad* [Dialogue between a Theist and an Idolater] (in Bangla) Written under a pseudonym—Brajamohun Majumdar	Reprint (Calcutta, 1846). Price: 4 annas. Still attributed to Brajamohun Majumdar
1821	*Brahman o missionary samvad,* Nos. 1,2,3 [Brahmunical Magazine] (in Bangla)	
1821	*Padri o shishya samvad* [A Padre and His Disciples] (in Bangla)	
1823	*Chari proshner uttar* [*Reply to Four Questions*] (in Bangla)	Reprint (Calcutta, 1848). Price: 8 annas
1823	*Pathyapradan* [*Medicine for the sick offered by one who laments his inability to perform righteousness*] (in Bangla)	
1823	*Gurupaduka* [*Reply to a pseudonymous polemic*] (in Bangla)	
1824	*Prarthnapatra* [*Prayer Letter*] (in Bangla) Also Appeared in English as *Humble Suggestions to his countrymen who believe in One God* in 1824.	
1826	*Brahmanishtha grihastha lakshan* [*On characteristics of Brahmo Householders*] (in Bangla)	Reprint Tattvabodhini Sabha Press (Calcutta, 1853). Print run: 500 copies Price: 6 annas

Year	Works in Bangla and other languages (Sanskrit, Hindi, Arabic, and Persian) c. 1803–29	Publishing History of Rammohun's Works in Bangla and Other Languages (Sanskrit, Hindi, Arabic, and Persian), c. 1834–1905
1826	*Kayashther sahit madyapan vishayak vichar* [*Shastric disputation with a Kayastha on drinking wine*] (in Bangla)	
1827	*Gayatra paramposanavidhanam* [*On Gayatri and worship*] (in Bangla)	
1827	*Vajrasuchi* [translation of a Mahayana Buddhist text, *Prathama-nirnaya* elaborating on the meaning of *Brahmana*] (in Sanskrit and Bangla)	
1828	*Brahmasangeet* [*Brahmo songs*] (in Bangla)	1. Reprint (Calcutta, 1835). Price: 4 annas 2. Reprint (Calcutta, 1844). Price: 6 paise 3. Reprint Tattvabodhini Sabha Press Print run: 500 copies. Price 4 annas. (Calcutta, 1853). Note: Rev. J. Long remarked that the 1853 reprints were 'much used' in Bangla society at the time.
1828	*Brahmopasana* [*Brahmo observances*] (in Bangla)	Reprint (Calcutta, 1889).
1829	*Sahamaran Vishayak* [*On sati*] (in Bangla)	
1829	*Anusthan* [*Catechism of divine worship*] (in Bangla)	

(Cont'd)

Table A.1 (*Cont'd*)

Year	Compilations of Rammohun's Bengali works after his death in 1833	Publishing History of the Compilations of Rammohun's Bengali works after his death in 1833
1834	*Gaudiya Vyakaan* [*A textbook of Bangla Grammar*] (in Bangla) (posthumous) Publisher: Calcutta School Book Society. Number of Copies: 1930 Price: 8 Annas [Prepared for the press by Rammohun's son, Radhaprasad Roy]	Reprint (Calcutta, 1845). Price: 5 annas. Note: Four editions followed, with the last one in 1856. All published by the Calcutta School Book Society.
1839	*Bangla Works of Rammohun Roy* Publisher: privately printed by one of Rammohun's collaborators and member of the *Brahmo Samaj*, Anandamohun Bannerjee. *The Calcutta Courier* reported on 6 January 1840 that the copies were distributed for free to the Bangla public.	Reprint Tattvabodhini Sabha Press (Calcutta, 1872).
1840–1848	*Bangla works of Rammohun Roy Pancho-Upanishad* [*Five Upanishads of Rammohun Roy: Isho, Cena, Mundaka, Mandukya, Katha*] Selections from the several books of the *Vedanta* by Raja Rammohun Roy Published by Debendranath Tagore for *Tattvabodhini Sabha*, Calcutta. Also serialised in the monthly *Tattvabodhini Patrika*, ed. Akshay Kumar Dutta in Calcutta	

Year	Compilations of Rammohun's Bengali works after his death in 1833	Publishing History of the Compilations of Rammohun's Bengali works after his death in 1833
1873–1880	*Raja Rammohun Roy Pronit Granthavali* [*Bangla and Sanskrit works of Rammohun Roy*] Compiled and Published by Raj Narain Bose and Anandachandra Vedantavagis Printed: Adi Brahmo Samaj, Calcutta.	
1905	*Raja Rammohun Ray-er Sanskrit o Bangla Rachnavali* [*Raja Rammohun Roy's Collected Bangla works*] Printed: Panini Press, Allahabad and Calcutta	

Note: The Bangla tiles of Rammohun's works and their reprints were not given in the catalogues of James Long and the Calcutta School Book Society. Thus, Bengali titles unfortunately could not be provided throughout. Publishing information has been provided wherever available.

Sources:

1. Rev. J. Long, *Returns Relating to Native Printing presses and publications in Bengal: A Return of the names and writings of 515 persons connected with Bengali literature, either as authors or translations of printed works chiefly during the last fifty years and a catalogue of Bengali newspapers and periodicals which have issued from the press from the year 1818 to 1855 submitted to Government* (Calcutta, 1855). Henceforth, Returns
   a. List of Books and pamphlets issued in Calcutta in 1853-4, 8-20.
   b. Register of Bengali authors, editors and translators, 41-62.

2. *The First Report of the Calcutta School Book Society [CSBS] read at the first annual General Meetings of the subscribers, held at the Town Hall of Calcutta, July 4, 1818, with an appendix, a list of contributions received and the accounts of the institutions for the year 1817–1818* (Calcutta, 1818). Henceforth *First Report.*

3. *The Seventh Report of the Calcutta School Book Society's Proceedings, Eighth and Ninth years, 1826–27 with an appendix, the accounts of the institution, Read the 5th March, 1828* (Calcutta, 1828), 4. Rammohun Requested by CSBS to write a Bengali grammar book in Bengali for native students. Henceforth *Seventh Report.*

4. *The Ninth Report of the Calcutta School Book Proceedings, thirteenth and fourteenth years, 1830–1 with an appendix, the accounts of the institution, Read February 1832.* (Calcutta, 1832), 9. Rammohun's Bengali grammar delayed, astronomy book delayed over circumstances which the CSBS "cannot control". Henceforth *Ninth Report*.

5. *The Tenth Report of the Calcutta School Book Society's proceedings. Fifteen and Sixteenth years, 1832-22, with an appendix, the accounts of the Institution, Read 21ˢᵗ March, 1834* (Calcutta, 1834). Henceforth *Tenth Report*.

   a. *Tenth Report*, 1–22.

   b. Appendix No. 1: List of Books Issued from the CSBS depository 1ˢᵗ Jan 1832-31ˢᵗ Dec. 1833, 23–26.

   c. Appendix, No. 2: Depository List, 27–31.

6. *The Father of Modern India, Commemoration Volume of the Rammohun Roy Centenary Celebrations*, ed. Satis Chandra Chakravarty (Calcutta, 1935).

A. Catalogue of an Exhibition of Rammohun's relics and writings, 29–41.

   a. Rammohun Roy's writings newly discovered, exhibit nos. 30, 31, 32, 30A, 31A, 32A, 33, 34.

   b. Rammohun Roy's Publications, first editions, exhibit nos. 35, 35A, 36, 37, 38, 39, 40.

   c. Rammohun Roy's Publications, later editions, exhibit nos. 50, 51, 52, 53, 54, 55, 56.

   d. Abstracts or Collections, made by others, of Rammohun Roy's writings, exhibit nos. 77, 78, 79, 80, 81, 82.

   e. Collected works of Rammohun Roy, exhibit Nos. 83, 84, 85, 86.

B. Appendix E: A list of the principal publications and other writings of Raja Rammohun Roy in Persian, Bengali, English, Sanskrit and Hindi in chronological order, 133–147.

7. *The Golden Book of Rammohun Roy: Published on the occasion of the 225ᵗʰ Birth Anniversary of Raja Rammohun Roy*, ed. Saroj Mohan Mitra (Calcutta, 1997).

   a. Appendix E: A list of the principal publications and other writings of Raja Rammohun Roy in Persian, Bengali, English, Sanskrit and Hindi in chronological order, 562–574.

8. Rev. J. Long, *Catalogue of the Vernacular Literature Committee's Library* (Calcutta, 1855). Henceforth, *Vernacular Catalogue*.

Table A.2 Rammohun Roy's works in English and Their Publication History in Calcutta

Year	Works in English, c. 1816–1831	Publishing History of works in English, c. 1816–1906
1816	*Translation of the Abridgement of the Vedanta* Publisher: Times Press Print run: 500 copies	
1816	*Translation of the Isho Upanishad* Publisher: Hindustani Press Print run: 500 copies	Reprint. Tattvabodhini Sabha Press (Calcutta, 1844).
1816	*Translation of the Cena Upanishad* Publisher: Hindustani Press Print run: 500 copies	
1817	*A Defence of Hindu Theism in reply to an Advocate for Idolatry at Madras* Publisher: Times Press Print run: 500 copies	Reprint. Tattvabodhini Sabha Press (Calcutta, 1844).
1817	*A Second Defence of the Monotheistical System of the Vedas in reply to an apology for the present state of Hindu worship* Publisher: Mr. Johnson Print run: 500 copies	
1818	*Translation of a Conference between an advocate for and an opponent of Burning Widows Alive from the original Bungla* Publisher: Baptist Mission press Print run: 1000 copies	
1819	*Translation of Mundaka Upanishad* Publisher: Times Press Print run: 500 copies	
1819	*Translation of Katha Upanishad* Publisher: Times Press Print run: 500 copies	

(Cont'd)

Table A.2 (*Cont'd*)

Year	Works in English, c. 1816–1831	Publishing History of works in English, c. 1816–1906
1820	*An apology for the pursuit of final beatitude independently of Brahmunical observances in Sanskrit, Bengali, Hindi and English* Publisher: Baptist Mission Press Print run: 500 copies	Reprint. Tattvabodhini Sabha Press (Calcutta, 1844).
1820	*A Second Conference between an advocate for and an opponent of Burning Widows Alive* Publisher: Baptist Mission press Print run: 500 copies	1. Bengali Translation by Rakhaldas Haldar in 1844 2. Reprint. (Calcutta, 1859).
1820	*The Precepts of Jesus: Extracted from the Books of the New Testament ascribed to the four Evangelists* Publisher: Baptist Mission Press Print run: 500 copies	
1820	*An Appeal to the Christian public in defence of the Precepts of Jesus by a Friend of Truth* Publisher: Baptist Mission Press Print run: 500 copies	
	Reply to the observations of the Editor of the Friend of India on the above appeal Publisher: Mirror Press Print run: 500 copies	
1821	*Brahmunical Magazine* Nos. 1,2,3	
1822	*Brief Remarks Regarding Modern Encroachments on the Ancient Rights of Females according to the Hindu law of Inheritance* Publisher: Unitarian Press, Calcutta	Reprint (Calcutta, 1853).

Year	Works in English, c. 1816–1831	Publishing History of works in English, c. 1816–1906
1823	*The Brahmunical Magazine*, no. 4	Second Edition Unitarian Press (Calcutta, 1823).
1823	*Humble Suggestions to His Countrymen who believe in One God*	
1823	*A Vindication of the Incarnation of the Deity as the common basis on Hinduism and Christianity against the attacks of R. Tytler*	
1823	*Petitions against the Press Regulations Memorial to the Supreme Court Appeal to the King in Council*	
1823	*A letter on English Education Lord Amherst, Governor General in Council*	
1823	*Final Precepts of Jesus*	
1823	*Dialogue between a Missionary and Three Chinese Converts*	
1824	*A letter to Rev. Henry Ware on Prospects of Christianity in India*	
1825	*Translation of a Sanskrit Tract on Different Modes of Worship*	
1826	*Bengali Grammar in the English Language* Publisher: Unitarian Press Price: Rupee 1	1. Reprint (Calcutta, 1845). Price 5 annas 2. Reprint *Tattvabodhini Patrika* (Monthly Journal of the *Adi Brahmo Samaj*) (Calcutta, 1933).

(*Cont'd*)

Table A.2 (*Cont'd*)

Year	Works in English, c. 1816–1831	Publishing History of works in English, c. 1816–1906
1827	*A Translation of a Sanskrit Tract, inculcating the Divine Worship esteemed by those who believe in the revelation of the Vedas as the most appropriate to the nature of the Supreme Being*	1. New Edition in English *Brahmunical Magazine*, 1,2,3,4 (Calcutta, 1827). 2. Reprint Tattvabodhini Sabha Press, (Calcutta, 1844).
1828	*Answer of a Hindoo to the question of "Why do you frequent a Unitarian place of worship instead of numerously attended established Churches?"*	
1828	*Petition to the Government against Regulation III of 1828 for the Resumption of Lakhiraj Lands.*	
1829	*The Universal Religion: Religious Instructions founded on sacred authorities.*	
1830	*Abstract of the arguments regarding the Burning of Widows considered as a religious rite.*	
1830	*Essays on the Rights of Hindus over Ancestral Property according to the Law of Bengal.*	
1830	*Letters on the Hindu Right of Inheritance.*	
1830	*Address to Lord William Bentinck Governor General of India upon the passing of the Act for the Abolition of Sati.*	
1831	*Petition to the House of Commons to the Memorial of the advocates of Sati.* [written in response to the petition of the Dharma Sabha]	

Year	Compilations of Rammohun Roy's works in English undertaken after his death in 1833	Publication History of the compilation of Rammohun Roy's works in Bengali undertaken after his death in 1833
1840–1848	*English Works of Rammohun Roy* Compiled by Debendranath Tagore for Tattvabodhini Sabha	
1840–1848	*Translations of Rammohun's Upanishads* Compiled by Debendranath Tagore for Tattvabodhini Sabha	Reprint Tattvabodhini Sabha Press (Calcutta, 1872).
1885	*The English Works of Raja Rammohun Roy*, edited with an Introduction by Jogendra Chunder Ghose, volume I.	
1887	*The English Works of Raja Rammohun Roy*, edited with an Introduction by Jogendra Chunder Ghose, volume II.	
1901	*The English Works of Rammohun Roy*, edited by Jogendra Chandra Ghosh, published by Srikanta Roy.	
1906	*The English Works of Rammohun Roy and an English Translation of the Tuhfat*, edited by Jogendra Chandra Ghosh.	

Notes:
Unpublished
Rammohun was commissioned by the CSBS to write a textbook on Geography in 1817. Appeared as unpublished in:

- o *Second Report*, Appendix no 18, Synopsis of the various works of their several editions, 97.
- o *Fourth Report*, Appendix v, 36.
- o *Fifth Report*, Appendix vii, 36.

Uncredited
Rammohun helped with the publication of Ferguson's Hindu astronomy. Originally commissioned by the CSBS in 1817, the project ran into problems because of lack of technical information about translation of specific Sanskrit words into English.

In 1820, Rammohun was asked by the CSBS to help with the work, which he agreed. Finally published in 1834 after years of delays. Rammohun's contribution was not acknowledged.

+ Tenth Report of the CSBS (Calcutta, 1830) Appendix, No. 2, Depository List, 27–31.

Sources: Compiled and prepared by the author from the following:

1. *Second Report*
   a. Synopsis of the various works and their several editions published by and for the Calcutta School Book Society, during the first two years of its establishment; with the works for which it is under engagements, 97.
   b. No. II, Memorandum of the indigenous works which have appeared from the native presses, drawn up for the Calcutta School Book Society Committee by the Corresponding Secretary, 47.
2. *The Golden Book of Rammohun Roy*, ed. Saroj Mohan Mitra, Calcutta, 1997, 562–574.
3. Rev. J. Long, *Returns Relating to Native Printing presses and publications in Bengal* (Calcutta, 1855).
   a. List of Books and pamphlets issued in Calcutta in 1853–4 or the Bengal year 1260, 8–20.
   b. Register of Bengali Authors, editors, translators, 41–62.

Table A.3 'Popular' Bangla Tracts Published in 1820 Identified by the Calcutta School Book Society

Serial Number	"Popular" Bangla tracts published in 1820 identified by the Calcutta School Book Society	Author	Publisher
1	*Description of Krishna and the gods of the Hindus with an account of Jesus Christ and Muhammad* [Karuna Nidhan Bilas]	Kali Shankar Ghoshal	Lulu Ji
2	*Account of the Ten Incarnations of Krishna* [Das Avatar Kotha]	Not known	Not known
3	*Amours of Krishna* [Podancho Duto]	Not known	Not known
4	*Legends of Krishna by a blind man* [Bilbo Mangal]	Not known	Not known
5	*Praises of Krishna* [Narada Sambad]	Not known	De Souza
6	*Account of Krishna* [Jaya Deva]	Not known	Not known
7	*Account of Kali* [Chandi]	Not known	Not known
8	*Account of Durga and other gods* [Anuda Mangal]	Not known	Ganga Kishore Bhattacharya
9	*Praises of Shiva* [Mahima Staba]	Not known	Lulu Ji
10	*Praises of Ganga and Ganges River* [Ganga Taringini]	Not known	Ganga Kishore Bhattacharya
11	*Geeta Govinda by Jaideva* [Geeta Govinda] Price: Rupee 1	Translator not mentioned	Biswanath De

(Cont'd)

Table A.3 (*Cont'd*)

Serial Number	"Popular" Bangla tracts published in 1820 identified by the Calcutta School Book Society	Author	Publisher
12	Praises of Chaitanya [*Narotoma Bilas*][1]	Not known	Not known
13	*Account of Chaitanya* [Chaitanya Charitra]	Not known	Not known
14	*The amours of a Prince and Princess* [Bidya Sundar]	Not known	Biswanath De
15	*On the choice of women* [Rosho Manjari]	Not known	Biswanath De
16	*On the choice of women* [Roti Manjari]	Not known	Biswanath De
17	*On the choice of women* [Adiros]	Not known	Biswanath De
18	*On the choice of women* [Rosho Podhiti]	Not known	De Souza
19	*On the choice of women* [Shringar Tilok]	Not known	Not known
20	*On the choice of women* [Kama Shastra]	Not known	Not known
21	*On the choice of women* [Roti Kula]	Not known	Not known
22	*On the choice of women* [Roti Bilas]	Not known	Not known
23	*Rules for acquisition and preservation of wealth* [Lakshmi Charitra]	Not known	Ganga Kishore Bhattacharya

[1] The translations of the Sanskrit pandits notwithstanding, this text is not concerned with Chaitanya but with Narottam Thakur, a close follower. I thank the anonymous referee for alerting me to this point. A further reference can be found in: Amiya P. Sen, *Chaitanya: A Life and Legacy* (Delhi: Oxford University Press, 2019), 167.

Serial Number	"Popular" Bangla tracts published in 1820 identified by the Calcutta School Book Society	Author	Publisher
24	*Twenty Five tales of Betal (companion to the mythical King Vikramaditya)* [Betal Panchabingsoti]	Not known	Ganga Kishore Bhattacharya
25	*Thirty two thrones* [Batris Singhasan]	Mrityunjay Vidyalankar	Serampore Press
26	*Tales of a Parrot* [Toti Itihas]	Not known	Not known
27	**Translation of the Vedanta**	Rammohun Roy	Ganga Kishore Bhattacharya- 500 copies Lulu ji- 500 Copies
28	*The Bhagvad Gita*	Translator not known	Not known
29	**Translation of Isho Upanishad**	Rammohun Roy	Ganga Kishore Bhattacharya- 500 copies Lulu ji- 500 Copies
30	**Translation of Cena Upanishad**	Rammohun Roy	Ganga Kishore Bhattacharya- 500 copies Lulu ji- 500 Copies
31	**Translation of Katha Upanishad**	Rammohun Roy	Lulu ji-500 Copies
32	**Translation of Mandukya Upanishad**	Rammohun Roy	Lulu ji-500 Copies

(Cont'd)

Table A.3   (*Cont'd*)

Serial Number	"Popular" Bangla tracts published in 1820 identified by the Calcutta School Book Society	Author	Publisher
33	*Translation of Mundaka Upanishad*	Rammohun Roy	Lulu ji-500 Copies
34	*Vedanta Chandrika* (in defence of Hindu Idolatry against the observations of Rammohun Roy), Price: Rupee 1	Mrityunjay Vidyalankar	Not known
35	*Reply to the Treatise of Mrityunjay Vidyalankar or the second defence of Hindu Theism*	Rammohun Roy	Lulu ji-500 Copies
36	*Reply to Ram Gopal Suromona* [*Reply to a Goswamin*]	Rammohun Roy	Lulu ji-500 Copies
37	*Reply to the Observations of Shoba Shastri*[2]	Rammohun Roy	Baptist Mission Press -500 Copies
38	*Dialogue between a True believer and an Idolator* [**Brahma Pautalik Sambad**]	Birjomohun Majumdar [pseudonym of Rammohun Roy]	Not known
39	*Translation of the Gayathri*	Rammohun Roy	Lulu ji-500 Copies
40	*Method for gaining true knowledge of God* [Probodh Chadrodayo]	Not known	Not known
41	*Apology for the pursuit of final beatitude independent of Brahmunical observances*	Rammohun Roy	Baptist Mission Press 500 copies
42	*The Precepts of Jesus*	Rammohun Roy	Baptist Mission Press 500 copies

---

[2] "Shobha Shastri" is none other than Subrahmanya Shastri, a critic of Rammohun's translations of Hindu scripture.

Serial Number	"Popular" Bangla tracts published in 1820 identified by the Calcutta School Book Society	Author	Publisher
43	*Verses in Censure of earthly enjoyments* [Shanti- sotok]	Not known	Not known
44	*On the common actions and ceremonies of life* [Title is in English]	Not known	Ganga Kishore Bhattacharya
45	*Moral Sayings* [Chanakya-Sloka]	Not known	Ganga Kishore Bhattacharya
46	*Gift to the Guru* [Guru Dakshina]	Hurochandra Gopal	Serampore Press
47	*The trials of Men* [Purush Porikha]	Tarkalankar Roy	Serampore Press
48	*Hitopadesa*	Mrityunjay Vidyalankar	Serampore Press
49	*On the burning of Widows* [Sahamaran]	Kalachandra Basu	Not known
50	**On the burning of widows** **[Sahamaran Sambad]**	Rammohun Roy	Hurro Roy 1000 copies
51	**Second Conference on the burning of widows** **[Sahamaran Bishoye Ditito Sambad]**	Rammohun Roy	Baptist Mission Press 500 copies
52	*History of Raja Krishna Chanda Ray* [Krishna Chandra Charitra]	Not known	Not known
53	*Vocabulary of Umuru Singh, arranged alphabetically and translated from Sanskrit* [Umuru Singh Obidhan]	Pitambar Mukherkee	Biswanath De
54	*Bengali Grammar* [Vyakaran]	Muthur Mohun Dutt	Serampore Press
55	English Grammar [Inglish Darpan]	Ram Chandra	Not Known

(Cont'd)

Table A.3   *(Cont'd)*

Serial Number	"Popular" Bangla tracts published in 1820 identified by the Calcutta School Book Society	Author	Publisher
56	*English Grammar* [Inglish Darpan]	Ganga Kishore Bhattacharya	Ferris and Co.
57	*On ceremonial impurities with rules for mourning* [Asoch Babostha, Asoch Panchali]	Not known	Lulu Ji
58	*Book on Medicine* [Ashodho Grantha]	Ram Comul Sen	Hindustani Press
59	*On Astrology* [Prankrishna Muhadadi]	Gopi Nath Bhattacharya	Biswanath De
60	*On Astrology* [Jyotish Shastra]	Ram Chandra	Lulu ji
61	*Description of Dreams* [Swapnapotol]	Ram Chandra	Lulu ji
62	*Astrological almanac* [Ancha Pustak]	Ram Chandra	Biswanath De
63	*Annual Almanacs* [Ponjika]	Not known	Not known
64	*On Poetry* [Rag mala]	Not known	Not known
65	*Rules for Music* [Sangit Tarangini]	Not known	Ganga Kishore Bhattacharya

Notes: The table has been transcribed from the original document produced by the Calcutta School Book Society.

All writings in bold are by Rammohun Roy. We find that 14 of the 65 tracts are attributable to him. One tract is a pseudonymous publication. He is the most visibly productive author in the popular press at the time. Since 33 of the tracts do not have authors and translators mentioned, we can also conclude that anonymity was widely practised in the publication of tracts. All translations are by the Calcutta School Book society. The tracts 15-22 have identical titles because they were deliberately not translated by the society at the behest of the Sanskrit *Pandits* employed by them. This is because they constituted low print cultures.

The list shows that Rammohun was published by publishers of low print cultures as well. This shows the populist bent of the writings. By not restricting the publications to the exclusively elite presses (such as the Baptist Mission press), Rammohun was making a point about the accessibility of his work.

Sources:

1. *Second Report*
   a. Synopsis of the various works and their several editions published by and for the Calcutta School Book Society, during the first two years of its establishment; with the works for which it is under engagements, 97.
   b. No. II, Memorandum of the indigenous works which have appeared from the native presses, drawn up for the Calcutta School Book Society Committee by the Corresponding Secretary, 47.
2. *The Golden Book of Rammohun Roy: Published on the occasion of the 225th Birth Anniversary of Raja Rammohun Roy*, ed. Saroj Mohan Mitra (Calcutta 1997), 562–74.

Select Bibliography

Manuscript Sources

Oriental and India Office Collections (OIOC), British Library, London

Bengal Criminal-Judicial Consultations (1814–33)
Bengal Military Consultations (1809–14)
Bengal Military Proceedings (1811–12)
Bengal Political Consultations (1811–12)
Bengal Revenue Proceedings (1793–15)
Board's Collections (1815–35)
General and Draft Dispatches to India (1800–33)

District Records, Registers, and Official Reports

Bengal District Records, Dinajpur: Letters Received, c.1787–1788, Volumes 1–2. Edited by Walter Firminger. Calcutta: Bengal Record Room, 1924.
Bengal District Records: Midnapur: Letters Received, c.1763–1774, Volumes 1–4. Edited by Walter Firminger. Calcutta: Bengal Record Room, 1926.

Bengal District Records, Rangpur: Letters Issued and Received, c.1779–1787, Volumes 1–6. Edited by Walter Firminger. Calcutta: Bengal Record Room, 1914.

Circular Orders of the Sudder Board of Revenue at the Presidency of Fort William from the year 1788 to the end of August 1837. Edited by William Peters. Calcutta: Printed on the orders of the Bengal Board of Revenue, 1838.

Doss, Ramchunder. *A general register of the Hon'ble East India Company's civil servants of the Bengal establishment from 1790 to 1842, comprising the dates of their respective appointments, furloughs, retirements, deaths, etc., etc., alphabetically arranged.* Calcutta: Baptist Mission Press, 1844.

General regulations, for the conduct of the collectors, in the Revenue Department. Passed by the Right Honorable the Governor General in Council, on the 8th June, 1787. Calcutta: Honourable Company's Press, 1787.

Primitiae Orientales, Containing the Theses in the Oriental Languages Pronounced at the Public Disputations in 1803–1804 by Students of the College of Fort William in Bengal, with Translations. Calcutta: College of Fort William, 1803.

Regulations of the Government of the Presidency of Fort William in Bengal, 1793–1834, Volumes 1–10. Calcutta, 1834.

Report from the Select committee on the affairs of the East India Company: with minutes of evidence in six parts, and an appendix and index to each. London: Ordered by the House of Commons to be printed, 1832.

Statement humbly submitted, on the part of the Court of Directors of the East-India Company to His Majesty in Council. London: J.L. Cox and Son, 1831.

The fifth report from the Select Committee on the Affairs of the East India Company. London: Ordered by the House of Commons to be printed, 1812.

West Bengal District Records, New Series, Murshidababad Nizamat: Letters Received, 1773–1856. Edited by Dutta J. Gupta and Sisir Kumar Bose, Volumes 1–2. Calcutta: Office of the Superintendent of Census Operations, West Bengal & Sikkim, 1964.

English Translations of Sanskrit and Persian Texts

Jimutavahana's Dāyabhāga: The Hindu Law of Inheritance in Bengal. Edited by Ludo Rocher. Translated by Normal Brown. New York: Oxford University Press, 2001.

The Early Upaniṣads: Annotated Text and Translation. Translated by Patrick Olivelle. New York: Oxford University Press, 1998.

Manu's Code of Law: A Critical Edition and Translation of the Mānava-Dharmaśāstra. Translated and edited by Patrick Olivelle, with editorial assistance from Suman Olivelle. New York: Oxford University Press, 2005.

King, Governance, and Law in Ancient India: Kauṭilya's Arthaśāstra. Translated and edited by Patrick Olivelle. New York: Oxford University Press, 2013.

Ṭūsī, Naṣīr al-Dīn Muḥammad ibn Muḥammad. *The Nasirean Ethics.* Translated by G.W. Wickens. London: Allen & Unwin, 1964.

Books, Articles, and Reviews

Aidt, Toke S., and Franck Raphaël. 'Democratization under the threat of Revolution: Evidence from the Great Reform Act of 1832.' *Econometrica* 83, no. 2 (March 2015): 505–47.

Alam, Javed. *India: Living with Modernity.* Delhi: Oxford University Press, 1999.

Alam, Muzaffar. 'The Pursuit of Persian: Language in Mughal Politics.' *Modern Asian Studies* 32, no. 2 (May 1998): 317–49.

———. *The Languages of Political Islam: India, 1200–1800.* London: University of Chicago Press, 2004.

Alam, Muzaffar, and Sanjay Subrahmanyam. *Writing in the Mughal World: Studies on Culture and Politics.* New York: Columbia University Press, 2011.

Alavi, Seema. 'Medical Culture in Transition: The Mughal Gentleman and the Native Doctor in Early-Colonial India.' *Modern Asian Studies* 42, no. 5 (September 2008): 853–97.

Anand, Mulk Raj. *A Writeup of Raja Ram Mohan Roy about Burning of Widows Alive.* Delhi: B.R. Publishing Corporation, 1989.

Armitage, David. 'Making the Empire British in Scotland, 1542–1701.' *Past and Present*, no. 155 (May 1997): 34–63.

———. *Foundations of Modern International Thought.* Cambridge: Cambridge University Press, 2013.

Bagchi, Amiya. 'Transition from Indian to British Systems of Banking (1800–1850).' *Modern Asian Studies* 19, no. 3 (April 1984): 501–19.

Bagchi, Barnita. 'Connected and Entangled Histories: Writing Histories in the Indian Context.' *International Journal of the History of Education* 50, no. 6 (August 2014): 813–21.

Bagchi, Nirmalya. *Rammohan Charcha Itihashe Banchana O Bahela* [Rammohun Roy: History and Context]. Calcutta: Subarnarekha, 1995.

Bandyopadhyay, Sanghamitra, and Elliot Green. 'On the Relationship between Fertility and Wealth: Evidence from Widow Suicides (*Satis*) in Early-Colonial India.' *Economics Letters* 120, no. 2 (August 2013): 302–4.

Banerji, Brajendranath. *Bhabanicharan Bandopadhyay* [in Bangla]. Calcutta: Bangiya Sahitya Parisad, 1959.

———. 'A Chapter in the Personal History of Raja Rammohun Roy'. *Calcutta Review* (1931): 156–79.

———. *Fort William Colleger Pandit* [Pandits of Fort William College]. Calcutta: Bangiya Sahitya Parisad, 1942.

———. *Fort William Colleger Pandit* [Pandits of Fort William College], 5th edition. Calcutta: Bangiya Sahitya Parisad, 1959.

———. *Mrityunjay Vidyalankar* [in Bangla]. Calcutta: Bangiya Sahitya Parisad, 1943.

———. *Rajah Rammohun Roy's Mission to England*. Calcutta: N.M. Raychowdhury & Co.,1926.

———. *Ramchandra Vidyavagish and Hariharananda Tirthaswamy* [in Bangla]. Calcutta: Bangiya Sahitya Parisad, 1942.

———. *Rammohun Roy* [in Bangla]. Calcutta: Bangiya Sahitya Parisad, 1942.

———. 'Rammohun Roy: From New and Unpublished Sources'. *Calcutta Review* (1934): 60–74.

Bannerjee, Pompa. *Burning Women: Widows, Witches and Early Modern European Travellers in India*. London: Springer, 2003.

Bannerjee, Sumantha. 'City of the Dreadful Night: Crime and Punishment in Colonial Calcutta'. *Economic and Political Weekly* 38, no. 21 (May 2003): 2045–55.

Bannerji, Himani. *Inventing Subjects: Studies in Hegemony, Patriarchy and Colonialism*. New Delhi: Anthem, 2001.

Bayly, C.A. *The Birth of the Modern World*. Oxford: Oxford University Press, 2004.

———. *Indian Society and the Making of the British Empire*. Cambridge: Cambridge University Press, 1988.

———. 'Rammohun Roy and the Advent of Constitutional Liberalism in India, 1800–30'. *Modern Intellectual History* 4, no. 1 (April 2007): 25–41.

———. *Recovering Liberties: Indian Thought in the Age of Liberalism and Empire*. Cambridge: Cambridge University Press, 2012.

Bhandarkar, D.R. *Some Aspects of Ancient Hindu Polity*. Benares: Benares Hindu University, 1929.

Bhattacharya, Bishnupada, ed. *Bulletin of the Department of Post-Graduate Training and Research, Sanskrit College: 150th Anniversiy Volume, 1824–1974*. Calcutta: Sanskrit College, 1979.

Bhattacharya, Tithi. *The Sentinels of Culture: Class, Education and the Colonial Intellectual in Bengal, c.1848–85*. Delhi: Oxford University Press, 2005.

Bhattacharyya-Panda, Nandini. *Appropriation and Invention of Tradition: The East India Company and Hindu Law in Early Colonial Bengal*. Delhi: Oxford University Press, 2008.

Biswas, Dilip, ed. *Rammohun Smaran* [In Deference to Rammohun]. Calcutta: Papyrus, 1960.

———. *Rammohun Samiksha* [A Survey of Rammohun's Writings]. Calcutta: Saraswat Library, 1983.

Bloch, Maurice. *Ritual, History and Power: Selected Papers in Anthropology.* London: Athlone, 1989.

Bose, Nemai Sadhan. *Indian Awakening and Bengal.* Calcutta: Firma K.L. Mukhapadhyay, 1976.

Bowen, John. 'The East India Company's Education of its Own Servants'. *The Journal of the Royal Society of Great Britain and Ireland*, no. 3/4 (October 1955): 105–23.

Bowen, Huw. *The Business of Empire: The East India Company and Imperial Britain, 1756–1833.* Cambridge: Cambridge University Press, 2006.

Bowring, John. *Autobiographical Recollections of Sir John Bowring.* London: Henry S. King, 1877.

Bradley-Birt, F.B. *Young Men of Bengal.* Calcutta: S.K. Lahiri and Co., 1955.

Bray, John. 'Krishnakant Basu, Rammohun Ray and Early-Nineteenth Century Contacts in Bhutan and Tibet'. *Tibet Journal Special Issue* 34, no. 3 (2009): 1–28.

Brekke, Torkel. 'Baptism and Bible in Bengal'. *History of Religions* 45 (2006): 213–33.

Buchan, Bruce. 'The East India Company: The Evolution of a Territorial Strategy and the Changing Role of Directors, 1749–1800'. *Business and Economic History* 23, no. 1 (Fall 1994): 52–61.

Bushby, H.J. *Widow-burning: A Narrative.* London: Longman, Brown, Green, and Longmans, 1855.

Carey, William. *Grammar and the Bengali Language.* Srerampore: Baptist Missionary Press, 1818.

Carman, John. 'Translations of the Protestant Bible in India: An Unfinished Dialogue?' *Journal of Hindu–Christian Studies* 4, no. 3 (1991): 11–20.

Carpenter, Mary. *The Last Days in England of Rajah Rammohun Roy.* Calcutta: Rammohun Library and Free Reading Room, 1915 [1866].

Carson, Penelope. *The East India Company and Religion, 1698–1858.* Woodbridge: Boydell and Brewer, 2012.

Chakrabarti, Kunal. 'Cult Religion: The *Purāṇas* and the Making of a Cultural Territory in Bengal'. *Studies in History* 5, no. 1 (April 2018): 1–16.

———. *Religious Process: The Purāṇas and the Making of a Regional Tradition.* New Delhi: Oxford University Press, 2018.

Chakrabarti, Smarajit. *The Bengali press, 1818–1868: A Study in the Growth of Public Ppinion.* Calcutta: Firma K.L. Mukhopadhyay, 1976.

Chakrabarty, Dipesh. *Provincializing Europe: Postcolonial Thought and Historical Difference.* Princeton, New Jersey: Princeton University Press, 2000.

Chanda, Mrinal K. *History of the English Press in Bengal, 1780–1857*, Volume 1. Calcutta: K.P. Bagchi & Co., 1987.

Chatterjee, Kumkum. *The Cultures of History in Early Modern India: Persianization and Mughal Culture in Bengal*. New Delhi: Oxford University Press, 2009.

———. 'The King of Controversy: History and Nation Making in Late Colonial India'. *American Historical Review* 10, no. 5 (December 2005): 1454–75.

———. *Merchants, Politics, and Society in Early Modern India: Bihar, 1733– 1820*. Leiden: E.J. Brill, 1996.

———. 'The Persianization of *Itihasa*: Performance Narratives and Mughal Political Culture in Eighteenth Century Bengal'. *Journal of Asian Studies* 67, no. 2 (May 2008): 513–43.

———. 'Scribal Elites in Sultanate and Mughal Bengal'. *Indian Economic and Social History Review* 47, no. 4 (October 2010): 445–72.

Chatterjee, Partha. *The Nation and Its Fragments: Colonial and Postcolonial Histories*. Princeton, New Jersey: Princeton University Press, 1993.

———. *The Black Hole of Empire: History of a Global Practice of Power*. Princeton, New Jersey: Princeton University Press, 2012.

Chatterjee, Shyamlal. 'Rammohun Roy and the Baptists of Srerampore: Moralism versus Faith'. *Religious Studies* 20, no. 4 (December 1984): 669–80.

Chattopadhyay, Dilip Kumar. *Dynamics of Social Change in Bengal: 1817–1851*. Calcutta: Punthi Pustak, 1990.

Chattopadhyay, Nagendranath. *Mahatma Raja Rammohun Roy Jibancharit* [Life Story of Mahatma Rammohun Roy]. Calcutta: Sadharan Brahmo Samaj, 1912 [1881].

Chattopadhay, Swathi. 'Blurring Boundaries: The Limits of "White Town" in Colonial Calcutta'. *Journal of the Society of Architectural Historians* 59, no. 2 (June 2000): 154–79.

Chattopadhayaya, Brajadulal. *Studying Early India: Archeology, Texts and Historical Issues*. Delhi: Orient Blackswan, 2003.

Chattopadhyaya, Gautam, ed. *Awakening in Bengal in Early Nineteenth Century: Selected Documents*. Calcutta: Progressive Publishers, 1965.

Chaudhari, Rosinka. 'The Politics of Naming: Derozio in Two Formative Moments of Literary and Political Discourse, Calcutta, 1825–31'. *Modern Asian Studies* 44, no. 4 (July 2010).

Chittabrata, Palit. *New Viewpoints on Nineteenth Century Bengal*. Calcutta: Progressive Publishers, 2006.

Clark, T.W. 'Languages in Calcutta, 1760–1840'. *Bulletin of the School of Oriental and African Studies* 18, no. 3 (October 1956): 453–74.

Cockayne, George. *Complete Baronetage*, Volumes 1–2. Exeter: William Pollar, and Co., 1902.

Cohn, Bernard. *Colonialism and Its Forms of Knowledge: The British in India*. Princeton, New Jersey: Princeton University Press, 1996.

Colebrooke, H.T. *Two Treatises on the Hindu Law of Inheritance*. Cambridge: Cambridge University Press, 2013 [1810].

Collet, Sophia Dobson. *The Life and Letters of Raja Rammohan Roy*, 3rd edition. Edited by Dilip Kumar Biswas and Prabhat Chandra Ganguli. Calcutta: Sadharan Brahmo Samaj, 1962 [1900].

Colley, Linda. *The Ordeal of Elizabeth Marsh: A Woman in World History*. New York: Anchor, 2007.

Coomaraswamy, A.K. *Spirtual Authority and Temporal Power in the Indian Theory of Government*. New Haven, Connecticut: The American Oriental Society, 1942.

Dalal, Ghulam Abbas. *Ethics in Persian Poetry: With Special Reference to Timurid Period*. New Delhi: Abhinav Publications, 1995.

Das, Sisir Kumar. *Sahibs and Munshis: An Account of the College of Fort William*. New Delhi: Orion Publications, 1978.

Dasgupta, B.N. *Rajah Rammohun Roy: The Last Phase*. New Delhi: Uppal Publishing House, 1982.

Dasgupta, Jyotirmay. 'Notes on Rammohun Roy at Rangpur'. *Modern Review*, no. 3 (1928): 274–8.

Datta, Vishwanath. *Sati: A Historical, Social and Philosophical Enquiry into the Hindu Rite of Widow Burning*. New Delhi: Manohar, 1988.

Davidson, C.J.C. *Tara the Suttee: An Indian Drama in Five Acts with Copious Notes, Explanatory, Original and Selected*. London: Published by the author, 1851.

Davidson, Donald. *Subjective, Intersubjective, Objective*. Oxford: Oxford University Press, 2001.

Derrett, John D. *Essays in Classical and Modern Hindu Law*, Volume 1. Leiden: E. J. Brill, 1976.

———. *Dharmaśāstra and Juridical Literature*. Wiesbaden: Harassowitz, 1981.

Desai, A.R. *Social Background of Indian Nationalism*. Calcutta: Popular Prakashan, 1948.

Dharwadker, Vinay. 'English in India and Indian Literature in English: The Early History, c. 1579–1834'. *Comparative Literature Studies* 39, no. 2 (2002): 93–119.

Dimmit, Corneilia, and J.A.B. Buitenen, eds. and trans. *Classical Hindu Mythology: A Reader in the Classical Puranas*. Philadelphia: Temple University Press, 1978.

Dodson, Michael. *Orientalism, Empire and National Culture, c. 1770–1880*. New York: Cambridge University Press, 2007.

Doniger O' Flaherty, Wendy. *Origins of Evil in Hindu Mythology*. Berkeley: University of California Press, 1976.

Doniger, Wendy, ed. *Purana Perennis: Reciprocity and Transformation in Hindu and Jaina Texts*. New York: State University of New York Press, 1993.

———. "'Put a Bag over Her Head": Beheading Mythological Women'. In *Off with Her Head! The Denial of Women's Identity in Myth, Religion and Culture*, edited by Eilberg Howard Schwartz and Wendy Doniger. London: University of California Press, 1995.

Dumézil, Georges. *An Essay on Two Indo-European Representations of Sovereignty*. New York: Zone Books, 1988.

Dutt, Rajani P. *India Today*. London: Victor Gollancz, 1940.

Farina, Mir. *The Social Space of Language Vernacular Culture in British Colonial Punjab*. Berkeley: University of California Press, 2010.

Fisch, Jörg. *Cheap Lives and Dear Limbs: The British Transformation of the Bengal Criminal Law, 1769–1817*. Wiesbaden: Franz Steiner, 1983.

Fisher, Michael H. 'The Imperial Coronation of 1819: Awadh, the British and the Mughals'. *Modern Asian Studies* 19, no. 2 (April 1985): 239–77.

Forbes, Geraldine. *Women in Modern India*. Cambridge: Cambridge University Press, 1999.

Forooqui, Amar. 'Governance, Corporate Interest and Colonialism: The Case of the East India Company'. *Social Scientist* 35, no. 9/10 (September–October 2007): 44–51.

Foster, William. 'James Mill in Leadenhall Steet, 1819–1836'. *Scottish Historical Journal* 10, no. 38 (January 1913): 162–73.

Gaukroger, Steven. *Francis Bacon and the Transformation of Early-Modern Philosophy*. New York: Cambridge University Press, 2001.

Gelders, Raf, and Willem Derde. 'Mantras of Anti-Brahmanism: Colonial Experience of Indian Intellectuals'. *Economic and Political Weekly* 38, no. 43 (October 2003): 4611–17.

Ghani, Kashshaf. 'Vestige of a Dying tradition: *Tuhfat ul-Muwahhidin* in Nineteenth Century Bengal'. *Studia Iranica* 44, no. 1 (2015): 55–81.

Ghose, Benoy, ed. *Selections from English Periodicals of 19th Century Bengal, c. 1815–33*. Calcutta: Papyrus, 1978.

Ghosh, Anindita. *Power in Print, Popular Publishing and the Politics of Language and Culture in a Colonial Society, 1780–1870*. New Delhi: Oxford University Press, 2006.

Ghosh, Durba. 'Household Crimes and the Domestic Order: Keeping the Peace in Colonial Calcutta, c. 1770–1840'. *Modern Asian Studies* 38, no. 3 (July 2004): 599–623.

Ghoshal, Atmaram. *Freedom of Speech and Expression in the Constitution of India.* Calcutta: Rabindra Bharati University Press, 2000.

Gladwin, Francis. *Compendium of ethics, translated from the Persian of Sheikh Sady of Shiraz.* Calcutta: Stuart and Cooper, 1788.

———. *The Persian Moonshee.* Calcutta: J. Debrett, 1795.

Goswami, Manu. *Producing India: From Colonial Economy to National Space.* Chicago: University of Chicago Press, 2004.

Guha, Ramchandra, ed., *Makers of Modern India.* Delhi: Penguin India, 2010.

———. *Rammohan Roy: The First Indian Liberal.* Delhi: Penguin Random House India, 2018.

Halbfass, Wilhelm. *India and Europe: An Essay in Philosophical Understanding.* Delhi: Motilal Banarasidass, 1990.

Harington, J.H. *An Elementary Analysis of the Laws and Regulations Enacted by the Governor-General and Council at Fort William in Bengal, for the Civil Government of the British Territories under That Presidency.* London: Honourable Company's Press, 1821.

Hasan, Nurul S. 'The Mughal Background of Raja Rammohun Roy's Thought'. In *Rammohun Roy and the New Learning*, edited by B.P. Barua, 24–42. Hyderabad: Orient Longman, 1988.

Hatcher, Brian A. *Idioms of Improvement: Vidyasagar and Cultural Encounter in Bengal.* Delhi: Oxford University Press, 1996.

———. *Bourgeois Hinduism, or Faith of the Modern Vedantists: Rare Discourses from Early Colonial Bengal.* New York: Oxford University Press, 2008.

———. 'Pandits at Work: The Modern Shastric Imaginary in Early Colonial Bengal'. In *Trans-Colonial Modernities in South Asia*, edited by Michael S. Dodson and Brian A. Hatcher, 57–79. London: Routledge, 2012.

Hoppit, Julian. 'Introduction'. In *Parliaments, Nations and Identities in Britain and Ireland, 1660–1850*, edited by Julian Hoppit, 1–14. Manchester: Manchester University Press, 2003.

Hunter, W.W. *Bengal MS Records: A Selected List of 14,136 Letters in the Board of Revenue, Calcutta*, Volumes 1–4. London: W.H. Allen, 1894.

Inden, Ronald B. *Text and Practice: Essays on South Asian History.* New Delhi: Oxford University Press, 2006.

Irvine, William. 'The Baillie Collection of Arabic and Persian MSS'. *The Journal of Royal Asiatic Society of Great Britain and Ireland* 37, no. 3 (July 1905): 560–5.

Islam, Sirajul. *The Permanent Settlement in Bengal: A Study of Its Operation.* Dacca: Bangla Academy, 1979.

Joshi, V.C., ed. *Rammohun Roy and the Process of Modernization in India.* Delhi: Vikas Publishing House, 1975.

Kaviraj, Sudipta. 'Laughter and Subjectivity: The Self-Ironical Tradition in Bengali Literature'. *Modern Asian Studies* 34, no. 2 (April 2000): 379–406.

———. 'Modernity and Politics in India'. *Daedalus* 129, no. 1 (Winter 2000): 137–62.

Khan, Sadiq. 'William Carey and the Srerampore Books: 1800–1834'. *International Library Review* 11, no. 3 (January 1961): 197–280.

Killingley, Dermot. 'Rammohun Roy on the *Vedānta Sūtras*'. *Religion* 11, no. 2 (April 1981): 151–69.

———. *The Only True God: Bengali and Sanskrit Works on Religion by Rammohun Roy, Selected and Translated*. Newcastle upon Tyne: Grevatt & Grevatt, 1982.

———. *Rammohun Roy in Hindu and Christian Tradition: The Teape Lectures*. Newcastle upon Tyne: Grevatt & Grevatt, 1993.

Kinra, Rajeev. *Writing Self, Writing Empire: Chandar Bhan Brahman and the Cultural World of the Indo Persian State Secretary*. Oakland: University of California Press, 2015.

Kolff, D.H.A. 'The End of the *Ancien Regime*: Colonial War in India, c. 1798–1818'. In *Imperialism and War: Essays on Colonialism and War in Asia and Africa*, edited by H.L Wesseling and J.A. De Moor, 22–49. Leiden: E.J. Brill, 1989.

Kopf, David. *British Orientalism and the Bengal Renaissance: The Dynamics of Indian Modernisation, 1773–1835*. Berkeley: University of California Press, 1969.

———. *The Brahmo Samaj and the Shaping of the Indian Mind*. Princeton, New Jersey: Princeton University Press, 1979.

Lehmann, Fredrick. 'The Eighteenth Century Transition in India: Responses of Some Bihar Intellectuals'. PhD diss., University of Wisconsin, 1967.

Lobban, Michael. 'Blackstone and the Science of Law'. *The Historical Journal* 30, no. 2 (June 1987): 311–35.

Loomba, Ania. 'Dead Women Tell No Tales: Issues of Female Subjectivity, Subaltern Agency and Tradition in Colonial and Postcolonial Writings on Widow Immolation'. *History Workshop* 36, no. 1 (Autumn 1993): 209–27.

Majeed, Javed. *Ungoverned Imaginings: James Mill's the History of British India and Orientalism*. New York: Oxford University Press, 2001.

Majumdar, J.K., ed. *Rajah Rammohun Roy and the Last Moghuls: A Selection of Documents*. Calcutta: Art Press, 1939.

———. *Raja Rammohun Roy and Progressive Movements in India: A Selection of Records, 1775–1845*. Calcutta: Art Press, 1941.

Majumdar, R.C. *On Rammohan Roy*. Calcutta: Asiatic Society, 1972.

Mani, Lata. 'Contentious Traditions: The debate on Sati in Colonial India.' *Cultural Critique: The Nature and Content of Minority Discourse*, no. 7 (Autumn 1987): 119–156.

———. *Contentious Traditions: The Debate on Sati in Colonial India*. Berkeley: University of California Press, 1998.

Marshall, P.J. 'Indian Officials in the East India Company in Eighteenth Century Bengal.' *Bengal Past and Present* 84 (1967): 95–120.

———. *Bengal: The British Bridgehead: Eastern India 1740–1828*. Cambridge: Cambridge University Press, 1987.

———. 'British Society under the East India Company.' *Modern Asian Studies* 31, no. 1 (February 1997): 89–108.

Matilal, Bimal Krishna, ed. *Moral Dilemmas in the Mahābhārata*. Simla: Indian Institute for Advanced Study, 1989.

McClish, Mark. 'The Dependence of Manu's Seventh Chapter on Kauṭilya's Arthaśāstra.' *Journal of the American Oriental Society* 144, no. 2 (April–June 2014): 241–62.

McLane, John R. *Land and Local Kingship in Eighteenth-Century Bengal*. Cambridge: Cambridge University Press, 1993.

Mehta, Uday Singh. *Liberalism and Empire: A Study in Nineteenth-Century British Liberal Thought*. London: University of Chicago Press, 1999.

Metcalf, Thomas R. *Ideologies of the Raj*. Cambridge: Cambridge University Press, 1995.

Mishra, Bankey Bihari. *The Central Administration of the East India Company, 1773–1834*. Bombay: University of Manchester Press, 1959.

Mitra, Saroj, ed. *The Golden Book of Rammohun Roy*. Calcutta: Rammohun Library & Free Reading Room, 1997.

Mohanty, J.N. 'Dharma, Imperatives and Tradition: Towards an Indian Theory of Moral Action.' In *Indian Ethics: Classical Traditions and Contemporary Traditions*, Volume 1, edited by Purushottama Bilmoria, Prabhu Joseph, and Renuka Sharma, 57–78. Hampshire: Ashgate, 2007.

Moore, Adrienne. *Rammohun Roy and America*. Calcutta: Satis Chandra Chakravarty, 1942.

Mukherjee, Amitabha. *Reform and Regeneration in Bengal (1774–1823)*. Calcutta: Rabindra Bharati University Press, 1968.

Mukherjee, S.N., and Edmund Leach, eds. *Elites in South Asia*. Cambridge: Cambridge University Press, 1970.

———. *Citizen Historian: Explorations in Historiography*. Delhi: Manohar, Publishers, 1996.

Mukhopadhyay, Amal Kumar. *The Bengali Intellectual Tradition: From Rammohun Roy to Dhirendranath Sen*. Calcutta: K.P. Bagchi & Company, 2015 [1979].

Mukhopadhyay, Anindita. *Behind the Mask: The Cultural Definition of the Legal Subject in Colonial Bengal, 1775–1911.* New Delhi: Oxford University Press, 2006.

Mukhopadhyay, Satish Kumar. *The Career of Rajah Rai Durlabham Mahindra, Rai Durlabh, Diwan of Bengal, 1710–70.* Bagda: C. Mukherjee, 1974.

Myers, John Brown. *William Carey: The Shoemaker Who Became 'the Father and Founder of Modern Missions'.* London: S.W. Partridge & Co., 1887.

Nandy, Ashis. *Bonfire of Creeds: The Essential Ashis Nandy.* New Delhi: Oxford University Press, 2004.

Nandy, Krishna Kanta. *Life and Times of Cantoo Babu, the Banian of Warren Hastings,* Volume 1. Calcutta: Allied, 1978.

Olivelle, Patrick, and Donald R. Davis, eds. *The Oxford History of Hinduism: A New History of Dharmaśāstra.* New York: Oxford University Press, 2018.

———, ed. *Gṛhastya: The Householder in Ancient Indian Religious Culture.* New York: Oxford University Press, 2019.

Orsini, Francesca, ed. *The History of the Book in South Asia.* London: Ashgate, 2013.

Parry, Jonathan. *The Politics of Patriotism: English Liberalism, National Identity and Europe, 1830–1866.* Cambridge: Cambridge University Press, 2006.

Peers, Douglas M. 'Between Mars and Mammon: The East India Company and Efforts to Reform its Army'. *Modern Asian Studies* 33, no. 2 (June 1990): 385–401.

Pennington, Brian K. 'Constructing Colonial Dharma: A Chronicle of Emergent Hinduism, 1830–1831'. *Journal of the American Academy of Religion* 69, no. 3 (September 2001): 577–603.

Pernau, Margrit, and Yunus Jaffery. *Information and the Public Sphere: Persian Newsletters from Mughal Delhi.* New Delhi: Oxford University Press, 2009.

The Persian Reader, or, Select Extracts from Various Persian Writers. Calcutta: Calcutta School Book Society, 1825.

Phillips, John A., and Charles Wetherell. 'The Great Reform Bill of 1832 and the Rise of Partisanship'. *Journal of Modern History* 63, no. 4 (December 1991): 621–46.

Phiroze, Vasunia. *The Classics and Colonial India.* Oxford: Oxford University Press, 2013.

Pocock, J.G.A. *Political Thought and History: Essays on Theory and Method.* Cambridge: Cambridge University Press, 2009.

Poddar, Arabinda. *Renaissance in Bengal: Search for Identity.* Simla: Indian Institute for Advanced Study, 1977.

Potts, Daniel. *British Baptist Missionaries in India, 1793–1837: The History of Serampore and Its Missions.* Cambridge: Cambridge University Press, 1967.

Price, Pamela. *Kingship and Political Practice in Colonial India*. Cambridge: Cambridge University Press, 1996.

Ramsbotham, R.B. *Studies in the Revenue Administraion of Bengal, 1769–1787*. London: Oxford University Press, 1926.

Rattray, Robert Haldane. *The Exile: A Poem*. London: British Library Historical Print Editions, 2011 [1837].

Ray, Ajit. *The Religious Ideas of Rammohun Roy*. New Delhi: Kanak Publications, 1976.

Rocher, Ludo. *The Purāṇas*. Wiesbaden: Harassowitz, 1986.

Rocher, Rosane. *Orientalism, Poetry, and the Millennium. The Checkered Life of Nathaniel Brassey Halhed, 1751–1830*. Delhi: Motilal Banarsidass, 1983.

———. 'The Career of Rādhākānta Tarkavāgīśa, an Eighteenth-Century Pandit in British Employ'. *Journal of the American Oriental Society* 109, no. 4 (December 1989): 627–33.

———. 'Sanskrit for Civil Servants 1806–1818'. *Journal of the American Oriental Society* 122, no. 2 (April–June 2002): 381–90.

Rocher, Rosane, and Ludo Rocher. *The Making of Western Indology: Henry Thomas Colebrooke and the East India Company*. London: Routledge, 2012.

Roselli, John. *Lord William Bentinck: The Making of a Liberal Imperialist, 1774–1839*. London: Sussex University Press, 1974.

Roy, Atul Chandra. *The Career of Mir Jafar Khan (1757–65)*. Calcutta: Das Gupta Publishers, 1953.

Roy, B.B. *Socioeconomic Impact of Sati in Bengal and the Role of Raja Rammohun Roy*. Calcutta: Naya Prokash, 1987.

Roy, B.K. *The Career and Achievements of Maharaja Nanda Kumar Dewan of Bengal (1705–1775)*. Calcutta: Punthi Pustak, 1969.

Roy, Rammohun. *The Correspondence of Raja Rammohun Roy, Compiled and Edited with Notes and Comments*, Volumes 1–2. Edited by Dilip Kumar Biswas. Calcutta: Saraswat Library, 1997.

———. *Dialogue between a Theist and an Idolater: An 1820 Tract Probably by Rammohun Roy*. Translated by Stephen N. Hay. Calcutta: Firma K. L. Mukhopadhyay, 1963.

———. *The English Works of Raja Rammohun Roy*, Parts 1–7. Edited by Kalidas Nag and Debajyoti Burman. Calcutta: Sadharan Brahmo Samaj, 1958.

———. *The English Works of Rammohun Roy*, Volumes 1–6. Edited by J.C. Ghosh, Calcutta: Srikanta Roy, 1983.

———. *Exposition of the Practical Operation of the Judicial and Revenue Systems of India: And of the General Character and Condition of Its Native Inhabitants, as Submitted in Evidence to the Authorities in England. With Notes and Illustrations*. London: Smith, Elder and Co., 1832.

————.*Rammohun Rachanabali*. Edited by Ajitkumar Ghosh. Calcutta: Haraf Prakashani, 1973.

————. *Selections from Official Letters and Documents Relating to the Life of Raja Rammohun Roy, 1791–1830*, Volume 1. Edited by J.K. Majumdar and Ramprasad Chanda. Calcutta: Calcutta Oriental Book Agency, 1938

————.'Tuhfatul Muwahhiddin'. Translated by Maulvi Obaidullah El Obaide. In *Rammohun Roy*. Edited by Kishori Chand Mitter. Calcutta: K.P. Bagchi, 1975.

Sagari K., and S. Vaid.'Sati in Modern India A Report'. *Economic and Political Weekly* 16, no. 31 (August 1981): 1244–88.

Sarkar, Susobhan. *Notes on the Bengal Renaissance*. Calcutta: People's Publishing House, 1946.

Sarkar, Tanika. *Hindu Wife, Hindu Nation: Community, Religion and Cultural Nationalism*. New Delhi: Permanent Black, 2001.

Sartori, Andrew. *Bengal in Global Concept History*. London: Chicago University Press, 2008.

Sastri, Sivanath.'Rammohun Roy: The Story of His Life with Supplementary Notes by the Editor'. In *Rammohun Roy: The Man and His Work*, edited by Amal Home, 7–68. Calcutta: Rammohun Centenary Committee, 1933.

Sen, Amartya. *The Argumentative Indian: Writings on Indian Culture, History and Identity*. Delhi: Allen Lane, 2005.

Sen, Amiya P. *Chaitanya: Life and Legacy*. Delhi: Oxford University Press, 2019.

————. *Explorations in Modern Bengal, c.1800–1900: Essays on Religion, History and Culture*. New Delhi: Primus Books, 2010.

————. *Rammohun Roy: A Critical Biography*. Delhi: Penguin Viking, 2012.

Sen, Ashok. *The Popular Uprising and the Intelligentsia: Bengal between 1855–1873*. Calcutta: Firma K.L. Mukhopadhyay, 1992.

Sen, Sudipta. *Distant Sovereignty: National Imperialism and the Origins of British India*. London: Routledge, 2002.

Sharma, Arvind. *Modern Hindu Thought: An Introduction*. New Delhi: Oxford University Press, 2005.

————. 'The *Gītā*, Suttee and Rammohun Roy'. *Indian Economic and Social History Review* 20, no. 3 (September 1983): 341–47.

Sharp, Granville.'*The System of Colonial Law' Compared with the Eternal Laws of God: and with the Indispensable Principles of the English Constitution*. London: Richard Edwards, 1807.

Sharpe, Jenny.'Figures of Colonial Resistance'. *Modern Fiction Studies* 35, no. 1 (1989): 137–55.

Shore, F.J. *Life of Lord Teignmouth*. London: Hatchard, 1843.

Singh, Iqbal. *Rammohun Roy: A Biographical Inquiry into the Making of Modern India*, Volumes 1–3. Bombay: Asia Publishing House, 1958.

Singh, Upinder. 'Politics, Violence and War in *Kāmandaka's Nitisāra*'. *Indian Economic and Social History Review* 47, no. 1 (January 2010): 29–62.

———. *Political Violence in Ancient India*. London: Harvard University Press, 2017.

Sinha, J.C. *Economic Annals of Bengal*. London: Macmillan, 1927.

Stevenson, John. *Dialogue between Certain Brahmans, Marattas, and Others and a Christian on the Hindoe and Christian Religions*. London: James Nisbet, 1829.

Sugirtharajah, R.S. *The Bible and Asia: From the Pre-Christian Era to the Postcolonial Age*. Cambridge, MA: Harvard University Press, 2013.

Tagore, Rabindranath. 'Rammohun Roy'. *Modern Review* 28 (1928): 337–39.

Taylor, Miles. 'Joseph Hume and the Reformation of India, 1819–33'. In *English Radicalism 1550–1850*, edited by Burgess Glen and Mathew Festenstein, 285–308. Cambridge: Cambridge University Press, 2007.

Teignmouth, Charles John Shore. *Memoir of the Life and Correspondence of Lord Teignmouth*, Volumes 1–2. London: Hatchard and Son, 1843.

Teissier, Beatrice. 'Texts from India in the Late-Eighteenth Century India and Britain, Culture or Contruct?' *Iran* 47, no. 1 (2009): 133–47.

Thiessen, Jacob. 'Anglo Indian Vested Interests and Civil Service Education, 1800–1858: Indications of an East India Company Line'. *Journal of World History* 5, no. 1 (Spring 1994): 23–46.

Tinker, Hugh. *South Asia: A Short History*. London: University of Hawaii Press, 1966.

Travers, Robert. *Ideology and Empire in Eighteenth Century India*. Cambridge: Cambridge University Press, 2007.

Urban, Hugh. *Tantra: Sex, Secrecy, Politics and Power in the Study of Religion*. London: University of California Press, 2003.

Valentia, Viscount George. *Voyages and Travels to India, Ceylon, Abyssinia and Egypt*, Volumes 1–3. London: William Miller, 1803.

Vansittart, Henry. *A Narrative of the Transactions of Bengal from the year 1760 to the year 1764, during the Government of Mr. Henry Vannistart*. London: Published by the author, 1766.

Verelst, Henry. *A View of the Rise and Progress of the English Government in Bengal, Including a Reply to the Misrepresenatations of Mr. Bolt, and Other Writers*. London: J. Nourse, 1772.

Vishwanathan, Gauri. *Masks of Conquest: Literary Study and British Rule in India*. New York: Columbia University Press, 1989.

Wasson, Ellis. 'The Spirit of Reform, 1832 and 1867', *Albion: A Quarterly Journal Concerned with British Studies* 12, no. 2 (Summer 1980): 164–74.

Wickshire, Franklin, and Mary Wickshire. *Cornwallis: The Imperial Years*, Volume 2. Chapel Hill: University of North Carolina Press, 1980.

Williams, Mukesh, and Rohit Wanchoo. *Representing India: Literatures, Politics and Identity*. Delhi: Oxford University Press, 2008.

Wilson, H.H. *Vishnu Purana*. Calcutta: John Murray, 1864.

Wilson, Jon. "'A Thousand Countries To Go": Peasants and Rulers in Late-Eighteenth Century Bengal'. *Past and Present* 189, no. 1 (November 2005): 81–109.

———. *The Domination of Strangers: Modern Governance in Eastern India (1780–1835)*. London: Palgrave Macmillan, 2008.

———. *India Conquered: Britain's Raj and the Chaos of the Empire*. London: Simon & Schuster, 2016.

Winch, Donald. *James Mill's Selected Economic Writings*. Chicago: Chicago University Press, 1966.

Wittgenstein, Ludwig. *Culture and Value*. Translated by Peter Winch. Oxford: Basil Blackwell, 1980.

Yang, Anand. 1989. 'Who's Sati? Widow Burning in Early Nineteenth Century India'. *Journal of Women's History* 1, no. 2 (Fall 1988): 8–33.

Zastoupil, Lynn. 'Defining Christians, Making Britons: Rammohun Roy and the Unitarians'. *Victorian Studies* 44, no. 2 (Winter 2002): 215–43.

———. 'Notorious and Convicted Mutilators: Rammohun Roy, Thomas Jefferson and the Bible'. *Journal of World History* 20, no. 3 (September 2009): 399–434.

———. *Rammohun Roy and the Making of Victorian Britain*. New York: Palgrave Macmillan, 2010.

Index

About the Author

Shomik Dasgupta has been trained in medieval and modern Indian History. His research interests include the intellectual history of the 18th and 19th centuries, 18th-century social history, and the everyday histories of work in early-colonial government and administration. At a broader level, he is interested in native responses to colonialism from the point of view of the role of language in the creation of social facts, intentionalities, collectivities, and institutions. He completed his B.A. from St. Stephen's College, University of Delhi, in History (hons.), his M.A. from Jawaharlal Nehru University, Delhi, and PhD from King's College, University of London. He is currently an Assistant Professor of History, School of Humanities and Social Sciences at IIT Indore.